Moral Cultivation

Moral Cultivation

Essays on the Development of Character and Virtue

Edited by
Brad K. Wilburn

LEXINGTON BOOKS

A division of
ROWMAN & LITTLEFIELD PUBLISHERS, INC.
Lanham • Boulder • New York • Toronto • Plymouth, UK

Published by Lexington Books
A division of Rowman & Littlefield Publishers, Inc.
A wholly owned subsidiary of The Rowman & Littlefield Publishing Group, Inc.
4501 Forbes Boulevard, Suite 200, Lanham, Maryland 20706
http://www.lexingtonbooks.com

Estover Road, Plymouth PL6 7PY, United Kingdom

British Library Cataloguing in Publication Information Available

The hardback edition of this book was previously cataloged by the Library of Congress as follows:

Library of Congress Cataloging-in-Publication Data
Moral cultivation : essays on the development of character and virtue / edited by Brad K. Wilburn.
    p. cm.
  Includes bibliographical references and index.
1. Ethics, Comparative. 2. Character. 3. Virtue. I. Wilburn, Brad K., 1959–
BJ69.M665 2007
170'.44—dc22   2007009778

ISBN-13: 978-0-7391-1220-5 (cloth : alk. paper)
ISBN-10: 978-0-7391-4668-2 (pbk. : alk. paper)

Contents

Acknowledgments   vii

Introduction   1

1   The Ethics of Style and Attitude   13
      Joel J. Kupperman

2   Literature and Ethics in the Chinese Confucian Tradition   29
      Philip J. Ivanhoe

3   Moral Philosophy and Moral Cultivation   49
      William J. Prior

4   Moral Self-Improvement   69
      Brad K. Wilburn

5   Self-Cultivation and Relations with Others in Classical Rabbinic Thought   85
      Jonathan W. Schofer

6   Moral Naturalism and the Possibility of Making Ourselves Better   101
      Elizabeth S. Radcliffe

7   Self-Development as an Imperfect Duty   125
      Robert N. Johnson

Bibliography   147

Index   157

About the Contributors   161

Acknowledgments

First and foremost, I would like to thank Rachel Cohon, who, as my dissertation advisor over a dozen years ago, played a formative role in my thinking about the issues covered in this volume. In addition, I would like to thank P. J. Ivanhoe, William Prior, and Elizabeth Radcliffe, with whom, along with Rachel, I have engaged in many hours of fruitful conversation on these topics. I would like to thank the participants of an NEH Summer Seminar for College Teachers, "Virtues and Their Vicissitudes," masterfully organized by Amélie Rorty in 1992, and the presenters and attendees of the 23rd Annual Austin J. Fagothey, S.J., Philosophy Conference on "Moral Cultivation" that took place at Santa Clara University in 2001 for much excellent discussion. Finally, I would like to thank the National Endowment for the Humanities and Santa Clara University for funding these two events. I would also like to thank Santa Clara University, Washington University in St. Louis, and Chadron State College for providing institutional support for me while I was working on this project.

Introduction

Brad K. Wilburn

Normative language is intimately connected with improvement. We use talk of what we *should* do, whether as a matter of rationality, etiquette, or morality, because we do not always do what we should and because we can do better. Normative language would lose much of its point if we were already perfect or if we were incapable of doing better. Thus, our need for improvement and our capacity for improvement within a particular domain make normative language appropriate within that domain. It is plausible to suppose that one of the roles played by normative language is to facilitate our projects of improvement. When trying to understand normative concepts, therefore, it can be helpful to consider how our use of these concepts is connected with our attempts to do better within a particular realm.

Moral concepts are normative concepts, and so this general point about normative concepts applies in the moral realm. We use moral concepts because we are in need of moral improvement and because we are capable of moral improvement.[1] Thus, we can expect that one crucial purpose for moral concepts is to help us get a handle on these projects of becoming morally better people. When we engage in moral philosophy then, when we attempt to make sense of these moral concepts and the moral aspect of our experience, we should keep in mind our efforts to improve morally. This is the purpose of this volume. The essays in this volume explore these projects of moral cultivation and connect these explorations to our moral philosophizing.

In doing so, a variety of different perspectives are brought to bear. Joel Kupperman uses Confucius to bolster his claim that style is an important component of morality, and by extension, an important focus of moral cultivation. Philip Ivanhoe makes extensive use of ideas from throughout the Confucian tradition in his discussion of the role that literature can play in moral cultivation. William Prior appeals to ancient Greek discussions in his examination of the role of moral philosophy in moral cultivation. Brad Wilburn develops an Aristotelian account of moral self-improvement. Jonathan Schofer examines some issues concerning moral cultivation and our relations with others that arise within the Rabbinic tradition. Elizabeth Radcliffe argues that an account of moral self-improvement can be constructed within the framework of a Humean naturalism. Robert Johnson uses Kantian ideas to describe and argue for a moral duty to develop ourselves, even in non-moral ways. There are at least two benefits that this breadth of perspectives provides. First of all, it brings out the widespread nature of the concern with moral cultivation. Secondly, it brings a variety of intellectual resources to bear on our discussion of these matters.

These essays discuss questions about moral cultivation that can be grouped into two categories. First of all, we can ask what projects of moral cultivation look like. What are the various features of ourselves that we might need to cultivate? How do these projects of cultivation get carried out? How can we engage in these projects successfully? What methods of cultivation can we apply? Secondly, we can ask about the connections between moral cultivation and various approaches to thinking about morality. How will moral cultivation be accommodated within a given moral theory or moral tradition? How does the given approach to morality illuminate our thinking about moral cultivation? In what ways does thinking about moral cultivation helps us evaluate, either positively or negatively, various ways of thinking about morality? By way of introduction, I would like to indicate some of the various ways in which the essays in this volume speak to these questions.

Describing Moral Cultivation

There is a wealth of material throughout these essays that, taken together, provides a rich and nuanced picture of projects of moral improvement. For one thing, there is material that describes the various parts of us that we can try to improve. The essays by Wilburn and Kupperman focus on this issue, and other essays contribute insights. In addition, there is material that describes the various methods we might use when attempting to cultivate ourselves, discussing the potential, limitations, and challenges involved in using these methods. The essays by Ivanhoe, Prior, and Schofer focus on these issues, and, once again, other essays in the collection have much to add.

What to Cultivate

Working within an Aristotelian framework, Wilburn describes moral improvement as having three aspects: a cognitive aspect, a practical aspect, and an affective aspect. That is, we can aim at developing our moral understanding, our actions, and our feelings. To motivate this account, Wilburn takes on various tasks. One motivation for this account, and a theme that winds its way throughout various essays in this volume, concerns what Wilburn labels the cognitive aspect of improvement. Because moral experience is rich, complex, and highly nuanced, moral understanding must reflect this richness. By extension, our concern with cultivating this understanding must attend to this nuance and complexity. Developing moral understanding goes beyond simply the identification of correct principles of action. Prior makes this point in his essay. He identifies the knowledge of the sage as knowledge of the relative value of things, but he distinguishes between a theoretical and a practical comprehension of value. Knowing that family is more important than money is one thing. Knowing when to come home from work to spend time with my family is quite another, especially given that part of the value of money is that it can be used to support family life. Making these sorts of decisions well is a crucial part of moral understanding, but cannot be reduced to a mechanical application of principle.

Further, developing one's moral character goes beyond simply developing one's moral understanding. Wilburn's discussion of the practical and affective aspects of moral improvement supports this claim as a way of further motivating his account. He argues that practical improvement is a category of improvement separate from attempts to improve our desires and beliefs, even if we conceive of actions as flowing from desires and beliefs. He argues that affective improvement is possible by describing various ways in which we can reshape our emotions and emotional tendencies.

Kupperman, as well, sets out to defend a rich focus for our projects of moral cultivation, a focus that should incorporate the ways in which style and attitude are morally significant. He argues that style and attitude play a causal role in ethical reflection and also that style and attitude are constitutive elements of good choices.

One of the causal roles that he points to is the way in which attitude is connected with the perception of moral salience. "Reflection requires a sense of what is salient," he writes, "And typically there will be an immediate awareness that some things are salient and others are not." (Kupperman, 18) Further, for instance, someone with a sympathetic attitude is more likely to notice the distress of others in various situations. Thus, such a person will be more likely to engage in reflection about what to do in light of that distress. Prior also discusses perception of moral salience, as part of the defense of his claim that the wisdom of a sage goes beyond merely having the right principles. He considers the issue of whether the perception of salience is "a purely cognitive, normatively neutral apprehension of a particular feature of a situation" (Prior, 59) or whether it is normatively laden, providing us with a motivation, a reason for action. Without conclusively settling the issue, Prior suggests that we may be able to separate the pure cognition from the motivation in theory, though in practice, they typically go together. The lesson to be drawn, for our purposes in this volume, is similar to the point made by Kupperman. "Both the virtuous and the vicious or morally weak person may be able to perceive the morally salient facts in a given situation," writes Prior, "Though only the virtuous person sees these facts as a reason for action." (Prior, 60) Thus, if we are concerned with cultivating ourselves, we will want to cultivate the normatively laden apprehension. We will want to go beyond a purely cognitive recognition of some feature of the situation we are faced with. We will want to cultivate our tendency to see certain features as demanding our attention and reflection and possibly our action.

One arena in which style and attitude play a constitutive role in good choice, not just a causal role, according to Kupperman, is the realm of personal relationships. Confucius places a strong emphasis on fulfilling one's obligations to one's parents. But a cultivated person will be concerned, not simply with meeting the obligations, but with doing so in a way that displays the right style and attitude. It is one thing to visit; it is another to visit in a begrudging way. Kupperman points to a passage from Confucius in which Confucius says about such actions that "it is the demeanour that is difficult." (quoted in Kupperman, 21) It might be possible to subsume the style and attitude in this sort of case under Wilburn's categories of practical and affective improvement. The child helping the parent should have the proper feelings, and the performance of the helping action might be described in a precise enough way so as to include the proper demeanor. But the core lesson here still remains: we act to bring about certain results, but also to express our feelings. (Kupperman, 25) This expressive role of action is linked less with our actions as they fit under general categories ("helping one's parents") and more with the more nuanced descriptions of our actions that are connected with style ("helping one's parents graciously"). We can imagine a dutiful son who fulfills his obligations to his parents out of "respect, affection, and concern," (Kupperman, 21) but who does so in such a way that those feelings cannot be read off those dutiful actions. The cultivated person will act properly and will have the appropriate feelings underlying his right actions, but he will also have a manner such that those appropriate feelings are expressed in those right actions.

How to Cultivate

In addition to delineating the different facets of ourselves that we can try to improve, we can describe methods that we might employ in pursuing such improvement. Three such methods that get discussed in various essays in this volume are: habituation, the reading of literature, and the use of role models. Also, several of these essays grapple with the limitations that various methods of improvement bring.

Aristotle famously claims that we acquire virtues of character through a process of habituation. Our tendencies to feel certain emotions and desires tend to shape themselves to the activities in which we engage. Thus, he claims, we develop tendencies of appropriate emotional response, which is how he describes virtues of character, by doing virtuous actions. In her essay, Radcliffe begins by recounting Benjamin Franklin's description of his engagement in just this sort of habituation process. Similarly, in his discussion of the practical aspect of moral improvement, Wilburn describes various ways in which we might try to get ourselves to act properly even though we do not yet have the set of motivations that constitute the virtue in question.

This process, claims Radcliffe, calls for further elucidation: "we need some explanation how we acquire a virtue, which is a motivation, by practicing a behavior without the motivation." (Radcliffe, 113) Radcliffe describes this process as similar to that by which we develop tastes for certain things that might initially be unappealing to us. (Radcliffe, 113) We can develop an appreciation and enjoyment of fine wine by drinking fine wine over time, even given an initial unattractiveness. Greater experience refines our taste, and eventually our motivation for drinking wine is bound up in our own tastes and dispositions. Similarly, by doing virtuous actions, those actions become more familiar to us, more comfortable for us. As a settled disposition develops, that disposition becomes our motivation for doing this action. It makes sense, argues Radcliffe, to identify this disposition with the virtue in question, the particular sort of feeling that generates our approbation.

This process of habituation can fruitfully be compared with engagement in ritual, which is a central part of Confucian accounts of moral cultivation. Kupperman draws this comparison. For Confucians, engaging in ritual should not be a mechanical process. The goal is "harmonizing one's attitudes with the nature of the ritual." (Kupperman, 24) One might start out participating in the ritual in a forced way, but eventually one will become more comfortable in the ritual as the corresponding attitudes develop. One eventually develops expressive command, and "expressive command creates possibilities of style, and also a sense of relaxed ease in the ritual performance." (Kupperman, 25)

Both Radcliffe and Kupperman discuss the example of a small child being expected to express thanks for a gift. We can easily imagine a child that complies with this expectation simply to placate her parents. Radcliffe characterizes this sort of engagement in the ritual as immaturity.[2] As children gain in experience and continue to participate in these rituals they typically develop a fuller understanding of the value of these rituals and a fuller set of motivations prompting their participation in them. We sometimes describe those whose attitudes are harmonized with the nature of these small, but ubiquitous, social rituals as gracious. We talk of the gracious host or the gracious guest. "Gracious" is connected with "grateful." The gracious guest appreciates the trouble the host went to. The gracious host expresses to her guests that the opportunity for fellowship greatly exceeds whatever trouble she went to. But "gracious" is also connected with "graceful." The gracious person engages in these social rituals with a manner and style that reflects her comfort in the ritual and adds to the comfort of others.

In his essay, Ivanhoe provides an illuminating discussion of the ways we can use literature to make ourselves better. He details the different sorts of moral work that the proper attention to literature can accomplish, identifying three benefits of such attention. First of all, studying literature offers "an emotional regimen," allowing us "to experience and come to appreciate certain feelings that play an important role in ethical judgment." (Ivanhoe, 31) Secondly, it allows us to "engage and exercise our distinctively moral imagination." (Ivanhoe, 31) Finally, it can "inculcate what we might call temporal appreciation," allowing us "to see and appreciate how different ethical judgments fit into the span of a full human life." (Ivanhoe, 32) In his essay, Prior joins Ivanhoe in recommending a role for literature to play.[3] (Prior, 64) Two features, in particular, are displayed by literature and allow it to provide these benefits, and both of these features reflect themes that run throughout various essay in this volume.

One such feature is "the detail and richness of the descriptions that literature offers." (Ivanhoe, 31) For instance, Ivanhoe writes, "Only such broad, textured, and nuanced accounts can provide one with the constellation of interconnected feelings, insights, attitudes, and commitments that constitutes a full sense of what is morally wrong with racism." (Ivanhoe, 31) This theme of the importance of attending to the richly complex concrete, in addition to the idealized and abstract, when doing moral thinking winds throughout various essays. Kupperman begins his essay with an extended discussion of the sort of example that often gets used in moral philosophy to pump our intuitions in support of one theory or another. A self-enclosed situation with a clear set of alternatives, each of which has clear repercussions, is set out and we are asked to choose what we would do in such a situation. Though acknowledging that such examples have a role to play in moral philosophizing, Kupperman also argues that they have limitations. One limitation, claims Kupperman, is that, in order to isolate some specific facet of morality, they deal with situations that can be briefly described. What gets left out are "detailed discussions of context-laden life decisions," situations in which "a range of subtly different alternatives [are] available to us." (Kupperman, 14) Prior's appeal to literature is connected with a similar claim about the limitation of these sorts of examples. (Prior, 64) Finally, Schofer points out that in rabbinic literature "the forms of expression are highly concrete rather than abstract," relying on "tropes, narratives, and pedagogical instruction." (Schofer, 87)

Another feature of literature that connects with its educative power is its narrative structure. In literature, we see character displayed over time. This is morally important, as Ivanhoe points out, because the admirable nature of certain characters traits is only revealed over time, just as the destructive nature of other character traits only becomes clear over time. (Ivanhoe, 32) In addition, claims Prior, seeing character traits over time allows us to be aware of the characteristic trade-offs that various commitments might require of us. (Prior, 65)

This theme of the moral significance of a narrative perspective on life is reflected in different ways in the essays by Kupperman and Johnson. Another limitation of philosophical examples giving us self-enclosed decisions to consider, according to Kupperman, is their failure to account for the way in which decisions can rarely be segmented from each other. He points to "the importance of embedding a choice within a pattern of choice." (Kupperman, 20) In his essay, Johnson defends the Kantian claim that the duty to improve ourselves is an imperfect duty. That is, we have some leeway in deciding what to develop and how much attention we will devote to that development. This does not mean, however, that these choices about development are whimsical and arbitrary. Johnson stresses the point throughout his essay that one constraint on these choices is that they should reflect a rational life plan. These choices must fit together in a coherent way.[4] Once again, getting an adequate moral handle on our choices requires taking a narrative perspective on those choices.

Schofer builds his essay around a discussion of "the interplay of self-cultivation and relations with others." (Schofer, 85) One of the aspects of this interplay is that certain relations with others can be an important resource for moving a project of self-cultivation forward.[5] Schofer's focus is on rabbinic communities, which had as an explicit goal the improvement of their members. One crucial resource within such a community was the opportunity to study under the tutelage of a sage.[6] Indeed, the rabbinic tradition is a transmission of material that attempts to pass on the wisdom of sages. Stories are told of these sages trying to engage in moral cultivation. These people face obstacles and overcome them. These challenges and the way they are overcome are then discussed by later thinkers. These stories and the discussion of them provide help for later people engaged in similar projects of moral cultivation.

In his essay, Prior provides an extensive discussion of the value of being able to observe and interact with a sage. (Prior, 63) One benefit is the explicit instruction that the sage provides. This might involve the elucidation of general principles. Typically, however, it will also involve the discussion of specific situation, in particular actual decisions faced by the sage, in order to identify what the sage found to be salient and how the sage balanced various considerations in that circumstance. But, argues Prior, the importance of finding a good role model goes beyond direct teaching: simply observing sages can be tremendously instructive, even when they have no general principle or rational defense of their actions to offer. One example Prior gives is Socrates. Socrates did not transmit an ethical decision procedure. Instead, he insisted that he had no such wisdom to offer. What he did offer, however, was an example of someone "every day conducting philosophical inquiry as if it were the thing that mattered most in life." (Prior, 63) One more potential benefit of surrounding oneself with good people is that doing so can motivate us to improve. Radcliffe builds this point from Hume's observation that we can come to hate ourselves for lacking certain virtuous motives that we see commonly in others, and that this discomfort can motivate us to try to acquire the virtue. Thus, if we surround ourselves with others who are better than us, our falling short will be repeatedly brought to our attention and this motive to improve will repeatedly be activated. (Radcliffe, 112)

These are some of the methods of cultivation that get discussed, but limitations to various methods of improvement get discussed as well. For instance, Prior's main thesis is to oppose what he refers to as "intellectualism": "thinking that the development of moral wisdom is primarily or exclusively a matter of philosophical understanding." (Prior, 50) His opposition to intellectualism springs from his claim, discussed above, that mastery of principle does not by itself provide moral wisdom. Principles need to be put into practice, and understanding how to put principles into practice is not something that can be transmitted solely by principles. It also requires practice, practice supported by things such as the guidance of role models, the reading of literature, and even philosophy

Another example of limitations discussed in these essays is in Schofer's essay. In addition to pointing out ways in which relations with others can provide resources for engaging in cultivation, Schofer also claims that there can be tension between our attempts to get better and our relations with others. First, if we are part of a community devoted to moral improvement, then demands placed on us by those outside of that community, including demands of family and friends, can distract from our participation in that community. A similar issue comes up in Johnson's essay, where he discusses trade-offs between the two obligatory ends posited by Kant: to cultivate ourselves and to promote the happiness of others. (Johnson, 129-30) Second, even within a community devoted to moral cultivation, care must be taken to avoid jealousy and other emotions that can undermine the relationships within the community and can lead the community members to pay more attention to keeping score than to improving themselves.

As a final example, in his discussion of literature as a potential source of moral cultivation, Ivanhoe points to issues raised within the Confucian tradition concerning "the imposing challenges and potential dangers of this aspect of moral cultivation."[7] (Ivanhoe, 32) It can be difficult to figure out what to read. Even if one is reading edifying texts, one must know how to read and interpret them properly. In a related vein, we must have an eye for the right things within the text if they are to contribute to moral cultivation. If we are reading only with an eye for literary style, we may fail to be morally cultivated by the reading.[8] Finally, someone might focus on literature with an eye on the lessons therein, perhaps even on the moral lessons, but the purpose for acquiring this mastery might be "in order to realize more mundane forms of profit." (Ivanhoe, 36) Note that one resource for meeting these challenges, as Ivanhoe points out, is to study under a good teacher, (Ivanhoe, 36-37) once again bringing out the value of having a sage to help one with one's moral cultivation.

Cultivation and Moral Theory

The second set of questions that get wrestled with throughout this collection have to do with the connections between projects of moral improvement and particular ways of thinking about morality, including moral theories and religious traditions. These connections can go in two directions. First of all, unique moral perspectives cast a unique light on our practices of moral cultivation. Secondly, these projects of cultivation also provide moral theories with an interesting set of moral phenomena to account for.

Johnson's thesis reflects this first sort of connection. He raises questions about whether we have a duty to improve ourselves, what grounds this duty, and what shape it has, and he argues that Kant provides the right answers to these questions.[9] In grounding this duty, the central Kantian idea is that this duty is a duty to oneself and that failing to cultivate oneself is failing to respect one's humanity. Johnson provides a compelling account of this core idea. One feature of this account is that this project, this obligatory end, connects us with others in a deep way. "The best way of understanding Kant's position regarding human natural perfection," writes Johnson, "is as a group rather than individual project." (Johnson, 133) By developing our own talents we join with others in the project of developing humanity. We conceive of ourselves as participating in a grand project of exploring and unfolding human potential. We hold ourselves responsible for participating in this project. This requires not just contributing to the project in some support capacity. One of the ways we can fall short, argues Johnson, is to be a self-sacrificer who only works to help others improve. To fail to be concerned with our own improvement is to be disconnected from this part of our humanity, to live a diminished life not worthy of our humanity. (Johnson, 141-42)

In the material describing this duty, giving shape to it, one notion that plays a central role for Johnson is the demand that our projects of improvement fit into a rational life plan. So, for instance, the person who develops randomly, without rhyme or reason, fails to fulfill the duty. (Johnson, 143) To meet this demand, we will take our particular talents into account.[10] (Johnson, 132) We will avoid "embarking on a quixotic project." (Johnson, 133) We will consider how the skills we develop might be of use to others. (Johnson, 138) Though the duty is an imperfect one, giving us leeway as far as how we will pursue it, these decisions still need to be guided by rational reflection in many ways.

Both Ivanhoe and Kupperman claim, in the course of defending their theses about literature and style and attitude respectively, that Confucian thought addresses these issues in a particularly illuminating way.[11] Similarly, claims Schofer, since the rabbinic tradition involves engaging in moral cultivation within the context of a community devoted to such cultivation, this tradition is a particularly rich source of ruminations on the role that community can play in our attempts to become better people.

In addition to looking to various moral perspectives for insight into moral cultivation, we can also use moral cultivation as an interesting test case for various theories. Can a particular theory or tradition accommodate and describe moral cultivation in a satisfying way? Radcliffe's project in her article is to show how someone committed to a Humean naturalism can account for projects of moral self-improvement. The challenge of doing so arises because "his theory of morality is a third-person 'spectator' theory, having no easy account of agency and no obvious account of self-cultivation." (Radcliffe, 107) To regard a character trait as virtuous or vicious, on Hume's account, is to consider how that trait will affect people in general. Through the mechanism of sympathy, and from an impartial point of view, we feel the pleasure and pain that the trait would engender in all the people who might be affected by the trait. When those feelings, transmitted by sympathy, are positive, we regard the trait as a virtue; when negative, a vice. But our actions are caused in a naturalistic way by internal states, which are in turn caused by our experiences. At least two problems crop up when applying this picture to engaging in self-improvement.

First of all, it is hard to see how we would recognize error in ourselves. Seeing a trait as vicious comes down to feeling the negative effects that trait tends to have on others. But *having* a vicious trait seems to involve *not* adequately feelings what others feel. If those feelings are inadequate, how can they motivate a change? Here, Radcliffe appeals to the negative feelings, mentioned in the previous section, that we feel about ourselves when we fail to measure up to those around us. These feelings could then provide us motivation to develop the particular motivations that we lack. (Radcliffe, 112)

Secondly, once we recognize our errors and are motivated to change, what sort of mechanisms of change, consistent with Humean naturalism, can be appealed to? Radcliffe's solution here is to suggest that we can employ tactics on ourselves that parallel tactics that others use on us to affect our behavior, tactics that Hume points to such as exhortation, education, and reward and punishment. Radcliffe explains how such tactics as applied to others might work on a Humean account, and she describes how we can put them to use on ourselves in various ways. (Radcliffe, 111-12)

Other essays also try to show how various theories can accommodate projects of cultivation. Prior suggests that ancient schools of philosophy that seem to buy into the intellectualism that he criticizes, such as Epicureanism, might have been much less intellectualistic in practice than in theory. (Prior, 51) Wilburn argues that the practical aspect of improvement is compatible with a desire-belief model of human action. (Wilburn, 77-78) In the course of recommending Kant's account of a duty to improve ourselves, Johnson does work to show how his presentation of Kant's account squares with other things Kant says.

Conclusion

To conclude, what these essays exemplify and argue for is that moral experience and moral character are rich phenomena. Thus, if we embark on the project of trying to cultivate our characters so as to improve our experiences, we must think about these projects in ways reflect the richness of that which we are trying to understand.

Notes

1. For instance, consider the remarks that Kant makes about imperatives in Chapter 2 of the *Groundwork of the Metaphysic of Morals*, H. J. Paton translation (New York: Harper & Row Publishers, 1964), 80-81. These ought-claims make sense for us because we are creatures with will. Forces outside of our will do not determine our behavior, and so we are capable of acting rightly. Also, these ought-claims make sense for us because our wills are not perfect. For a perfectly good will, "there are no imperatives: 'I ought' is here out of place, because 'I will' is already of itself necessarily in harmony with the law." (p. 81)

2. Compare Radcliffe's claim in this regard to Prior's claim that someone who only has some general principles to follow, ("Say 'thank you' when given a gift") is at "the 'elementary school' portion of moral development." (Prior, 52)

3. Both Ivanhoe and Prior point to fiction and biography as promising sources to study.

4. See, in particular, Johnson's discussion of the Fool on p. 143, which is one of the five sketches of failure to fulfill this duty that Johnson provides.

5. Part of the richness of Schofer's discussion is that he also discusses possible tensions between one's self-cultivation and one's relations with others.

6. Another resource Schofer points to is the companionship of peers who were similarly committed to moral improvement.

7. Though Ivanhoe focuses on concerns of this sort raised within the Confucian tradition, he is careful to argue that similar concerns exist for us.

8. As Ivanhoe's discussion brings out, this was a subject of dispute within the tradition, as some Confucians accused others of being overly focused on literary style to the detriment of moral edification. See, in particular, Zhu Xi's criticisms of Su Shi, discussed by Ivanhoe on pp. 34-35.

9. Johnson limits his focus to non-moral improvement, but the concerns in his piece do nonetheless overlap with the concerns of this volume. First of all, a moral perspective that is centered on figuring out the good human life, such as Aristotle's, will incorporate both moral and non-moral improvement, as understood by Kant. Further, the notion of developing a rational life plan is crucial to Kant's account, as Johnson makes clear. This notion gives shape to the Kantian duty, and involves a concern with one's life as a whole. Finally, as Johnson points out, the claim he is defending that there is a duty to improve is *more* difficult to establish in the case of non-moral improvement, but the conclusion will still hold in the case of moral improvement. He limits his focus in this way to take on what will be the tougher case for the Kantian to make.

10. Johnson argues, however, that the duty does not require us to focus on that at which we are most gifted.

11. For instance, Ivanhoe claims that Confucian thinkers have a much more extensive discussion of the challenges involved in using literature for moral cultivation than we see in modern writers on the subject. (Ivanhoe, 32)

Chapter One

The Ethics of Style and Attitude

Joel J. Kupperman

This chapter will argue for one thesis, and suggest a second. The primary one is that any truly adequate ethics must make it clear that there are many cases within its domain in which the style with which something is done, and the attitude expressed in it, are of great ethical importance. A secondary thesis is that the ethics of Confucius meets this requirement with unparalleled success, and hence that Western ethical philosophers can learn from Confucius.

There need to be some preliminaries though before I can argue effectively for the first thesis and suggest the grounds for the second. The theses will seem so thoroughly counter-intuitive to so many good philosophers, that it is pointless to begin the arguments until the most immediate and obvious objections are disarmed. In a way this amounts to an argument for a third thesis: that there is a sickness in contemporary analytic philosophy that results in many of its practitioners being vision-impaired. The sickness has to do with the power of examples, and a yearning (that set in after Wittgenstein was dead and buried) for broad generalizations.

Examples and Generalizations

Here is an example of an important ethical choice, one with interesting theoretical ramifications. A trolley is out of control, and unless something is done it will kill five (presumably innocent) people. The one thing that can be done is for you to pull a lever that switches the trolley to another track, which will result in its killing a different (again presumably innocent) person; were this person not there, the trolley would loop back and kill the five. (Hence the death of the one innocent person is causally required to save the five.) It may well seem reasonable to pull the lever: after all it is better that only one life be lost than that five be lost. On the other hand, if the five die it is not because of something that you did (i.e., an act that you performed). But if you pull the lever, the blood of the one victim will be, so to speak, on your head.

Cases like this are fascinating, in part because they are so dramatic but also because they appear so disconnected from the rest of life, which makes an adequate brief description of them possible. It is hardly accidental that the trolley problem is a fantasy case, and that the form in which I presented it was developed by a philosopher, Judith Jarvis Thomson.[1] Most of the ethical decisions in our own lives that we find very difficult will be ones, in contrast, in which the options must be considered in the context of commitments and projects we have been involved with; and there may well be a range of subtly different alternatives available to us, the differences having some impact on how our decision will affect friends, family, etc. It is extremely difficult to give an adequate brief description of such cases; anyone who wants to comment on them needs to know the context and also a great deal about how the possible options differ.

It then is hardly an accident that dramatic "one-off" decisions, in which the alternatives look quite discrete, like that of the runaway trolley, are common in the philosophical literature, and that detailed discussions of context-laden life decisions are extremely scarce. David Wiggins has spoken sarcastically of a preoccupation among ethical philosophers with "the casuistry of emergencies."[2] Its roots should be evident.

What can one say about this imbalance in analytic ethical philosophy? It is important not to over-react. One imbalance does not deserve another. It would be wrong to deny that cases like that of the runaway trolley are interesting and important, suggesting reflection on the structure of our theories. More broadly, it would be wrong to deny that there are important choices, many of which occur in the real world and not merely in philosophers' imaginations, which can occur in a way that is radically discontinuous with most of life. (What are sometimes called "existential choices" often have this character.) Further there are major choices which are such that the style with which something is done or is avoided matters far less than the broad nature of what it is that is done or avoided. The vast majority of decisions of whether to kill or to steal are like this.

Imbalance can be avoided if a small number of clever examples do not blind us to the variety that could be offered. We should take care not to let the easy and dramatic kind of case control our vision of what a subject is like, and instead should take the trouble to look at ones that are less easy to present (and less dramatic) but that can be very important in people's lives.

Much of the power of examples can come from our assuming one of two things. If a generalization about ethical judgment has been regarded as plausible, we may assume that one good counter-example will refute it. (When this happens there can be a thrill, rather like one philosopher hitting another in the face with a wet fish.) The working model here is "all or none": the generalization must fit all cases or it is worthless. Alternatively, we may assume that a feature that becomes vivid in the clever example must be true of all cases, and hence that we learn something global rather than merely gaining insight into a single case. It may not occur to us that often part of what makes an example so very clever is precisely that it is atypical, not the sort of thing that most people would think of.

The assumption about method that underlies my remarks here is this. Philosophical claims very often are designed to apply to ranges of cases, and it is not uncommon for variations within a range to be such that the most we can reasonably claim is that "typically" or "often" or "in some cases" such and such holds. There then is no substitute for painstaking examination of the variety of cases within the range.

Even if all of this is granted, it may be felt that it is too strong to speak of a "sickness" within contemporary analytic ethical philosophy. We should reflect though on the kinds of case that tend to get left out. These are the ones that concern major decisions in everyday life, often intimately related to prior projects and commitments, and often also connected with the conduct of close personal relationships. Clearly not all well-known ethical philosophers have ignored this area (Bernard Williams and Alasdair Macintyre come to mind), and for that matter this area of ethics is a major preoccupation of feminist ethical philosophy. Nevertheless anyone who is close to the literature of contemporary analytic ethical philosophy is more likely than not to regard this area of ethics as minor or peripheral. But it is the area in which we all live most of the time, and in which we should be thinking about what we do.

The fact that contemporary Western ethical philosophy has so little to offer on the ethics of private or personal life is over-determined. There is a classic argument, found in works like John Stuart Mill's *On Liberty*, that judgmental pressure should be minimized in relation to decisions that do not involve the prospect of direct harm for anyone but the agent. This is to avoid what Alexis de Tocqueville, and following him John Stuart Mill, termed the "tyranny of the majority." The argument is that by and large people will be happier, because they will feel more free, if in constructing most of their lives they do not have to worry about censorious pressure from moral majorities. Mill does not explain what he means by "direct" as opposed to "indirect" harm. But the context suggests that direct harm will be physical or financial, and that much of the emotional damage that can occur in personal relationships might be viewed as "indirect," in that in such cases much depends on how someone responds to the words or actions of other people.

By itself this does not imply that there cannot be an ethics of private or personal life. Liberalism of Mill's sort merely requires that our judgments of this part of other people's lives not have the same kind of pressure that judgments of directly harmful behavior have: they will express distaste and perhaps an impulse to avoid someone we think little of, rather than the desire that this person be punished. Mill makes it very clear that he sees no reason not to make judgments that someone is foolish or suffers from a "depravation of taste."[3]

Nevertheless a feature of modern Western liberalism is to be reluctant to voice judgments of this sort about the personal or private lives of others. Let me emphasize the word "reluctant" (as opposed to totally unwilling), as well as the fact that there are deep divides in Western societies on these points. Traditionalists who have not been influenced by liberal ideology do remain willing to be highly censorious of features of private or personal life, and there also are many whose response is ambivalent. The recent American political debate on the impeachment of President Clinton illustrates this lack of uniformity.

It remains the case though that for many people there is a natural slide, from reluctance to voice judgments about others' private lives to a tendency not to reflect in any systematic way on such judgments, and hence to banish them from the territory of ethical philosophy. What remains in this territory then is usually judgments that involve the possibility of bodily or financial harm to someone other than the agent. These high-profile cases often involve decisions that readily can be abstracted from the contexts in which they occur, and that can be viewed as susceptible to treatment by highly impersonal sets of rules and principles, so that the context of an agent's character and commitments also can be largely disregarded.

My view is that this is a mistake: both philosophically and also personally for those who come to think this way. There are two reasons. One is that, if ethical reflection is limited to maintaining standards for decisions that involve the possibility of bodily or financial harm to someone other than the agent, then the shortage of ethical reflection outside of this territory can lead to lack of philosophical resources in dealing with most of life. This can contribute to a shoddiness of personal life.

The second is that it makes sense in ethics to ask not only how people should behave, but also what the major values and satisfactions should be that make lives worth living. These issues of what the major values and satisfactions should be are to a large extent personal, and hence they are included in what has been largely ignored in contemporary Western ethical philosophy.[4] We ignore them though at our peril. The risk is that we can create a highly prosperous society in which the character of personal relationships deteriorates, so that many people can turn out to be comfortable but lonely, or virtuous in their decisions that involve possibilities of direct harm to others but sour about their own lives.

Causal Roles of Attitude in Ethical Choice

Ethical reflection and decision can be viewed as a multi-stage process, and it may be helpful to review this in order to isolate possible roles of style and attitude at various stages. The first point to make is that ethical reflection can hardly occur continuously. If one regarded every episode in life as requiring ethical reflection, the result would be paralyzing. At the very least there would be no spontaneity in such a life. The utilitarian philosopher J. J. C. Smart has remarked on this, pointing out that when he plays field hockey he never asks whether something he is about to do contributes to the greatest happiness of the greatest number—and if he were to start to think this way, it would spoil the experience.[5]

It is an interesting question how many occasions per day of ethical reflection a person typically will have. In the preface to his *Five Types of Ethical Theory*, C. D. Broad suggested that the number for him was very low. He had a comfortable life, and one infers there were few or no temptations. On the other hand, it is clear that for Immanuel Kant the number would have been much higher. The requirement that one can will one's maxim to be a universal law is a very demanding one, and even being late for an appointment becomes ethically doubtful. Also, Kant contends that we have an imperfect duty to develop our talents and also one to help others; and there always is room for the reflection that, whatever we are doing, we could do more.

Nevertheless, for reasons already given, even the most moralistic person will have unreflective moments. How do we decide when reflection is called for? We need to bear in mind that reflection has its own costs: it interrupts the flow of our activity, and makes life that much less spontaneous. There has to be something that potentially outweighs these costs. On the other hand, any suggestion that we have to reflect on whether now is a time to reflect would be absurd. It would lead to an infinite regress. Beyond that, it would risk mounting costs in loss of spontaneity.

My suggestion is that most of us have what amounts to a triggering mechanism. There are things that we might notice, or that might come to mind, that can lead to ethical reflection even if there is no intermediate element of articulated justification of reflection.

Noticing that someone is upset or is about to be hurt can have this effect. So can an awareness that something that one is about to do seems to violate the general rules of conduct with which one grew up. The triggering mechanism does not guarantee a conclusion. There can be justifiable choices in which someone is upset or hurt, and the general rules we have been trained to follow might have exceptions (or might not have the authority we used to think they had). The triggering mechanism merely is designed to initiate a reflective process.

No reflective process is guaranteed to go well. People can deliberate badly. But it is also is true that many of the choices in people's lives that we think they have reason to regret are made without any reflection whatsoever. It simply does not occur to them that what they are about to do is morally questionable, or that the quality of their own lives (and perhaps those of family members and friends) will be significantly impaired by their choice. A great many misspent lives and a great deal of bad behavior can be viewed as the results of simple thoughtlessness.

Plainly attitude matters in this process. Someone who cares about other people, and is conscientious, willing to take responsibility for her or his actions, is more likely to notice or think of factors that should trigger ethical reflection. We still have not arrived at the question of how style and attitude can count (constitutively) towards the ethical *quality* of behavior. But the role of attitude in the triggering of ethical reflection strongly suggests that, at the least, attitude often has a causal role in the process that leads to good choices.

Some of this causal role is evident in the stage at which there has been triggering and reflection takes place. Any situation in which reflection is triggered will have innumerable factors that might or might not be ethically relevant. Typically the great majority of them will not, and should not, be considered in a decision of how to behave. Smells, tastes, and distantly glimpsed events usually can be ignored. Facial expressions and words of remonstrance often do turn out to be important.

The first point to make is that reflection usually does not play a part in one's ignoring a factor. Occasionally one thinks "Perhaps this matters?" and then answers "No." But it would be impossible to go through the set of smells, tastes, distantly glimpsed events and other surrounding factors and make such an explicit determination. To put the point simply: reflection requires a sense of what is salient, and typically there will be an immediate awareness that some things are salient and other things are not.[6] It is possible of course to modify this initial picture. Other people may say, for example, "What about such and such?"; and we may realize that something important was being left out of consideration. Nevertheless, typically most of the selection of what is considered in reflection will be immediate, and will be determined by what strikes the agent as salient.

Much of the sense of salience will be contributed by moral codes. One of the functions of these codes, which in most societies are learned by children and are retained through life, is to sharpen a sense of categories of behavior that matter. Even someone who comes to reject elements of a moral code is still very likely to have a strong awareness of elements of potential courses of action that match the categories of the code. In a room in which a huge number of activities are visible, including the fact that John is taking Mary's purse while she is looking elsewhere, that action (and the moral dimension of its being theft) will jump out to someone's attention.

Salience though is not limited to items that match such categories. Someone who is not devoid of human sympathy may notice that someone is suffering or is unhappy in ways that are connected with possible courses of action. Or the thought may occur (based on one's experience of how the world works) that one of the possible courses of action could lead to someone's suffering.

Again, thoughtlessness is a live possibility. People sometimes say, after the fact, "It did not occur to me that so-and-so would be deeply unhappy if I did such-and-such," or "It did not occur to me that so-and-so had been miserable, and that this would be alleviated if I did such-and-such." Thoughtlessness can mingle with obtuseness in such cases. We might notice that so-and-so is in a bad mood, but not connect it with something we are about to do. For that matter, we might notice that John is taking Mary's purse without its "sinking in" that what we are witnessing is theft.

Attitude certainly matters in all of this. Someone who is conscientious is more likely than most people to think twice about actions, like John's taking Mary's purse, that might appear to violate moral norms. A sensitive person will take in factors of unhappiness or dismay that might escape the attention of others. Again, this is a causal (rather than a constitutive) role of attitude in relation to good ethical decisions. But it is an important one.

Attitudes can make a causal contribution to decision making also in the more intellectualized areas of ethical reflection. Often cases to which moral norms are relevant seem, as it were, ready-made for the norms. That is, there will be no room for doubt, as to the rightness or wrongness of an action, in the mind of someone who understands the norm and has taken in the relevant features of the case. This will be true when John takes Mary's purse, unless there are unusual features of the case that were not mentioned.

Some cases though are not ready-made for the norms. Even if we understand the norms and have taken in all relevant features, we might be unsure about rightness or wrongness of an action. Kant's example, in the *Metaphysics of Morals*, of Frederick the Great's taking poison with him into battle (his thought being that if captured he would take the poison rather than being held to ransom in a way that would damage his country) is apt. Kant presents this as a case for casuistical examination.[7] In the *Grounding of the Metaphysics of Morals* he had argued that suicide violates the categorical imperative. Perhaps Frederick the Great's provision of poison represents a readiness to commit suicide, but maybe this would be no ordinary suicide and indeed would manifest a selflessness opposite to the selfishness of a typical suicide? Kant in fact does not supply casuistical examination of this case. Perhaps he was wary of state censorship? Nevertheless I think that we can take at face value his saying that the case calls out for casuistical examination, which in the terms I have been using means that it is not a ready-made case of suicide.

Other cases that are not ready-made include ones (such as that of the runaway trolley) in which a possible action could cause deaths but also prevent deaths, or the one in which John takes Mary's purse but turns out to have what might be a legitimate claim on its contents. Casuistry is not a mechanical activity, and indeed lacks the "programmed" quality that consideration of ready-made cases typically has. Indeed, casuistical argument is akin to legal reasoning, in often involving creative attempts to put a case in a certain light, to emphasize its affinities to cases of certain sorts rather than others.

What occurs to someone engaged in casuistry will be very much a function of her or his attitude, as will the weight given to various factors. Both conscientiousness and sensitivity can play a role in the factors that are taken into account. Bad casuistry will ignore or fail to give due weight to people's misery or suffering, or will ignore features of a course of action that might suggest moral taint to some of us (the suggestion of taint spurring the creative endeavor of articulating why something is bothersome).

What follows reflection (whether or not the reflection involves casuistry) typically is choice. This may be manifested in a single action, or in inaction (which counts as behavior and might be viewed as a sort of negative action), and sometimes in a series of actions or an orientation in life. We shortly will be considering constitutive roles of style and attitude in choice. But let me first point out two pitfalls in regarding choice as the final stage in a sequence that begins with the arousal of reflective processes.

The first (and more obvious) pitfall is that sometimes what amount to ethical choices are made without any thought of alternatives and without any conscious reflective process at all, instead occurring immediately and seemingly reflexively. Someone may simply forego (or embrace) an opportunity, say, to steal or to kill; only later will it sink in that alternatives were open and that a reflective process could have been entered into. Choices without reflective process should not necessarily be scorned. Much of ethical education can be viewed as preparing us, by getting us to view some forms of bad behavior as unthinkable, to make some choices quickly and unreflectively.

The second pitfall is that in many cases it is too easy and tempting to view an action as the culmination and, as it were, closure of the choice. It is plausible, in the case of the runaway trolley, to think that the culmination is that either one shifts the track of the trolley or one does not. But this is over-simple. After pulling (or not pulling) the switch to change the trolley's track, you are not finished. There certainly will be casualties (one person or five people) to be dealt with, explanations to be offered, and almost certainly a sorting out of one's own emotions and structure of judgments. The constancy or stabilizing of choice that Confucius strongly recommends in *Analects* 13.22 is mainly concerned with the importance of embedding a choice within a pattern of choice.[8] But perhaps there is also a suggestion of the ethical importance of following through?

In any event, following through often is important. Whether someone follows through adequately and effectively often will depend on attitude. A kind of conscientiousness that includes a sense of responsibility for foreseeable results is conducive to effective following through. Someone whose conscientiousness amounts to a loyalty to a moral checklist may well regard himself or herself as finished once the basic choice is made.

The persistent temptation to atomize ethical choices, and to isolate them in moments of time, should not blind us to the continuities involved in being a good person, and to the role of people's attitudes in how well these are observed in their lives. Continuities will be important even in the highly artificial case of the runway trolley. In much of the management of real life, their importance will be even greater.[9]

Style and Attitude as Often Constitutive Elements of Good Choices

One area of choice in which style and attitude matter greatly is that which concerns treatment of close connections, such as friends and family. Moral choices that in a way fit traditional broad categories can arise in relation to friends and family: one might have a temptation to steal from them, and then there might be issues of whether promises need to be kept, and so on. It could be tempting to think that the ethics of this part of life, like that of public life, can be codified; and that something like implicit promises could be assigned to close relationships so that much of the ethical work is done by the importance of keeping these promises. Attempts of this sort however have always seemed highly artificial. Indeed the concept of duty, or more modestly of what one is obligated to do, which works reasonably well for normal promise-keeping and honesty looks out of place in this area. The classic story of the nineteenth century English person who, being praised for nursing a sick spouse, murmurs that one was only doing one's duty, makes fulfilling obligations dutifully oddly seem like ethical failure.

Confucius, who took very seriously the obligations of children to parents, at one point (2.8) observes that "it is the demeanour that is difficult." No matter what one does, if one's tone and expression are blank and indifferent-seeming the treatment of parents will be unsatisfactory. Clearly this is because this relationship, especially, should not be thought of as anything like a contractual one: normally respect, affection, and concern are part of any successful playing out of it. Other connections with family, with friends, and perhaps even with colleagues and neighbors will hardly be successful if they are viewed on a contractual model. Again the way one does and says what one does can be as important as the content (described broadly) of the actions and words. A blank, indifferent performance, or one that appears grudging, will be a failure.

Is the kind of failure under discussion an ethical failure? If we were to assume that morality, with its high-pressure insistence on specified, very broadly described standards of behavior, is the whole of ethics, then we might have difficulty in deciding whether the negative comment we want to make on the blank and indifferent child, supposed friend, neighbor, or colleague has anything to do with ethics. Given a broader conception of ethics, in which its concerns include anything that which can be done well or badly that matters significantly to the quality of one's life, or to the quality of interactions with others, it is clear that all of this belongs in ethics. We need not look to Asia for philosophers who would treat this as obvious; Aristotle would, as would Western philosophers as recent as Nietzsche and G. E. Moore.

Suppose that we grant that the attitude and style displayed in our interactions with family members, friends, colleagues, and neighbors matter significantly in whether our behavior is adequate or not. It might be tempting then to respond, "Yes; to the extent that the quality of personal relations matters ethically, style and attitude have to be considered in that domain. But at the core of ethics are a set of impersonal requirements (such as the requirements not to murder, not to steal, etc.) that transcend personal relations, and indeed because of their importance can be viewed as in the public rather than private part of life. These core requirements, like the law, apply irrespective of persons, and require the same thing of everyone."

This response concedes some territory to philosophers, such as Confucians and feminists, who regard the style and attitude of personal relations to be of great ethical importance.[10] But it reserves as it were the heartland of ethics for those who take most seriously impersonal, highly general obligations.

There is no adequate simple reply to this. If a man chooses to kill a hated rival, the attitude and style displayed in the deed will seem insignificant as compared to the bare fact of the murder. Perhaps we will loathe him more if he sneers at his victim than if he acts in a hesitant manner, but this surely is not a major concern of ethics.

On the other hand, when promises are kept or broken, the style and attitude with which this is done can matter a great deal, even to the person to whom the promise was made. It is not merely that we forgive some people more readily than others, or conversely are usually more grateful to the person who keeps a promise in a considerate and graceful way than to one whose fulfilment is clearly grudging. The very quality of the deed is different in these two cases. This is true also of acts that fulfil the "imperfect" duty of helping others. As Mencius remarks (Book VII, Part B, 11) someone who is out to make a reputation for himself can behave very generously; "but reluctance will be written all over his face if he had to give away a basketful of rice and a bowl of soup when no such purpose was served."[11]

Finally, there are issues of what someone might regard as the fundamental purposes and hoped for rewards of her or his life. Since Plato and Aristotle many philosophers in the West have regarded this as part of the heartland of ethics. It is possible, as in the case of morality, to reduce this subject to a checklist: a specification in general terms of greatest goods. The checklist approach cannot be sustained, however, when we consider the phenomena of wonderful lives and how greatly their imitations—even clever imitations—can differ from them in value. As Albert Camus remarks, a sense of vocation is necessary for effective following of a model.[12] Nuance and detail also turn out to matter. Novelists have taken up this theme. The life of a dedicated scholar can be very fine indeed, but then we have George Eliot's withering portrait of Casaubon in *Middlemarch*.

The reply then to the claim that the heartland of ethics is concerned almost exclusively with general, highly impersonal obligations is that there are important moral decisions (e.g., related to promising or to helping others) in which style and attitude do matter significantly (and which hence are not highly impersonal), and also that the axiological investigation of what is most desirable in life is part of the heartland of ethics. It is not true that style and attitude matter greatly in every kind of case. But in a variety of cases they do matter, as they do in the general quality of life.

Style and Attitude as Both Causal and Constitutive Factors

The remainder of this paper will be devoted to two tasks. One is to connect the causal and constitutive roles of style and attitude in what is ethically admirable.

Thus far we have treated these as separate, but often they are intertwined in an important way. The other task is briefly to outline Confucius' account of the ethical importance of style and attitude. As the outline proceeds, the value of the account may become more evident.

Before beginning this, we should disabuse ourselves of an attractively naive assumption about ethical philosophies. This is that their primary role is to provide us with decision procedures, and that in doing this they function as morality software. On the face of it, both Kant's ethics and classical utilitarianism do this. But, as Kant himself points out, "a power of judgment sharpened by experience" is a crucial factor in connecting the categorical imperative with specific cases.[13] What does Kant's ethics yield as a judgment about, say, the acceptability of capital punishment? Kant himself contends that (at least in some cases) capital punishment is morally required.[14] Many of Kant's admirers would argue that here he misapplied his own theory. But how do we decide?

In the case of classical utilitarianism, the philosophy imaginably might be a clear-cut and straightforward decision procedure if we had a clear and precise idea of what counts as pleasure and pain, and if we knew the future. Because neither of these things is true, actual utilitarian decision procedures tend to pick out elements of possible actions that in the past have tended to have what we would roughly consider good or unfortunate consequences. Judgment again turns out to be crucial in this, and variations in judgment are such that it is often impossible to say what "*the* utilitarian" recommendation would be in such-and-such a situation.

Kant's ethics and classical utilitarianism look most like straightforward decision procedures in easy cases, ones in which almost all of us would see the case in much the same way and (even if we had read no philosophy) would gravitate to much the same decision. Where points of view and interpretations are likely to differ, both Kantians and utilitarians are likely to disagree among themselves. Does this mean that these ethical philosophies are valueless? Annette Baier and others have argued that the major interest of ethical philosophies is in increasing our understanding of the form and workings of ethical judgments. Both Kant and the classical utilitarians arguably have important and highly original insights to offer here.

Another concern that is characteristic of many, if not all, ethical philosophies is with the shape of good lives: what is it to be a really good person, and what is it to have a really desirable kind of life? Plato argued that these two questions are really one; Kant and Mill both treat them as at least somewhat separate.

A natural part of this inquiry (or pair of inquiries) is to ask how someone becomes a good person who will have a highly desirable life. This would appear to be an investigation of causal processes. But to think simply this is to overlook the ways in which all of us are compounded by our histories. We may change directions at several points in our lives, but all the same what we have been and done will remain part of who we are. In the realm of personhood, the causal is also (at least to a degree) the constitutive.

Confucius' view of what it is to be a really good person, and to have a life of real value, centers on refinement. The saying of the *Book of Songs*, "As thing cut, as thing filed, As thing chiselled, as thing polished," is held to point to this. (1.15) It seems plausible to think that Confucius, like Aristotle, held a two-phase view of the process of becoming a really good person. Aristotle's Phase One centered on the acquisition of habits, in which the child would be steered using the "rudders of pleasure and pain."[15] Phase Two then would involve both judgment of cases growing out of experience and also philosophical understanding. Confucius says very little about Phase One, but at the least it would have to involve basic orientation within the network of family and community.[16] In contrast the *Analects* have a great deal to say about the advanced stage of ethical development.

The sequence of advanced ethical development, in outline, is "Let a man be first incited by the *Songs*, then given a firm footing by the study of ritual, and finally perfected by music." (8.8) Repeatedly the *Book of Songs* is quoted as containing coded messages that relate to ethical guidance. Its role in 8.8 is to inspire, and to put on the right track, someone on the way to being a really good person. But it is not merely inspiration; there seems to be important knowledge in it, although it also appears that only someone with a prepared mind (which may presuppose a degree of ethical advancement) will be able to discern the knowledge.

If ritual is to provide a firm footing, this suggests that there is at least a little in common between the Confucian emphasis on ritual and the Aristotelian emphasis on habit. In both cases, the concern is with what amounts to a behavioral default position: ways of behaving that gain a hold over a person so that they come naturally, that will be evident in quick responses, and that at the least will provide the starting points for considered responses. However there is an important difference between the two accounts, one that is especially relevant to the theme of this paper. Training in ritual is for Confucius to a very large degree training in style of ritual performance, and especially in harmonizing one's attitudes with the nature of the ritual.

As Master Yu says, "In the usages of ritual it is harmony that is prized." (1.12) I interpret the *he* (harmony) as requiring a harmony between what the ritual does and what the attitudes are of the person performing it. An example would be the various displays of ritual politeness that are directed toward those in superior positions, which require (1.7) an "air of respect." Presumably effective performance will require more than saying appropriate words and holding one's face at an appropriate angle. Actually having an attitude of respect will be crucial.

On the other hand, it would be simplistic and wrong to regard the attitude of respect as something that one, as it were, works up from inside before one is ready to try to learn the ritual. Typically, performance plays a key role in the development of such attitudes. The first performances of a child, or those of an utterly unrefined person, may be (as Xunzi pointed out) crude and unlovely. But through practice one gets the hang of performing various attitudes; and at the same time the attitudes come to seem natural, coming to be very much one's own.

The process of becoming at home in ritual performances has to change the relationship between the person and the ritual. At the start (for the child, or the utterly unrefined person) the ritual is merely a constraint. One is forced (to give a simple example) to say "Thank you" for a favor or a present, perhaps one that was not even wanted. To become at home in the ritual is to find oneself expressing something (such as appreciation for the thought behind the unwanted present) in the ritual. Expressive command creates possibilities of style, and also a sense of relaxed ease in the ritual performance. Hence Confucius' manner is described (7.37) as "affable" and as "polite but easy."

Antonio Cua has observed that paradigmatic individuals often have a central role in ethics.[17] Clearly this applies to the elaborate and extended portrait of Confucius that appears in the *Analects*. Undoubtedly actually being with Confucius would have been far better than merely reading the descriptions, but nevertheless the portrait (like the one of Socrates that emerges in Plato's dialogues) provides valuable indications of what the style and character of an outstanding human being could be. It is important that Confucius is dignified but never haughty; (13.26) it is important that at court, when conversing with the under ministers his manner is friendly and affable while it is restrained and formal with the upper ministers. (10.2)

Finally, the nature of the refined person is supposed to be perfected by music. The *Analects* are full of remarks about the kind of music that is helpful for this purpose, as well as kinds that would be damaging. We know that Confucius played the zithern. There is the amusing incident in which one of Confucius' students is given command of a walled town and then promotes musical performances. Confucius, coming to visit, hears stringed instruments and singing, and teases his student by comparing this to using an ox-cleaver to kill a chicken. (17.4) The incident is interesting in two ways: as indicating the importance that music had been given in Confucius' circle, and also as providing a glimpse of Confucius in an informal and playful role.

There is a huge recent literature on the emotions in music, some of which centers on issues of how music achieves its effects. One theory, associated with the musicologist Leonard Meyer, holds that music is interesting only if it builds up and then in some details violates expectations. This is compatible with the possibility that music that has surprised and delighted us in this way might then, at the end of the sequence, return to something we would recognize as a harmonious norm or resolution. The pattern of going beyond the conventionally expected, but then returning to some kind of resolution, is somewhat similar to the pattern of increasing tension and eventual resolution that Charles Rosen finds in the classical style of Haydn, Mozart, and Beethoven.[18]

There also may be an affinity between these models of good music and Confucius' model of good ethics. It is clear that the Confucian worthy is willing to depart from what is conventionally expected. For Confucius, as for Aristotle, real wisdom may be required to judge what is appropriate to the case at hand; a set of familiar rules may well not be enough. One should not "take things for granted" or be "overpositive or obstinate." (9.4) As Confucius says, in comparing himself to various worthies of old, "I have no 'thou shalt' or 'thou shalt not.'" (18.8) Perhaps the dialectic of going beyond the conventionally expected, followed by harmonious resolution, in music might in some cases have a psychological relation with a similar pattern in ethics?

The emphasis in the *Analects* on the refinement of style and attitude is closely connected with an axiology in which the person one is becomes the source of major values. Without real goodness, Confucius insists, a man "Cannot long endure adversity, Cannot for long enjoy prosperity." (4.2) Someone who is really good can never be unhappy. (9.28) The reason presumably is that what matters most to a person who is really good will be the inner qualities of personhood.

The Western counterpart of this value might in some cases center on the thought "I have done the right thing." In Confucius' model, as in Plato's, it is clear that what is valued goes far beyond a set of chosen actions. It instead is a degree of harmony within a person's emotions and motivations. If neurosis is an incapacitating inner struggle, it is the opposite of neurosis. This will take the form of a degree of satisfaction with the results of self-creation.

The satisfaction can be keen without amounting to complacency. Repeatedly Confucius insists that one should be mindful of personal faults, take other people's points of view seriously, and be open to criticism. In action also the primary focus is on those who can be helped or protected, such as the peasants who should benefit from an official's enlightened policy, rather than on any inner states of one's own. The Confucian worthy, despite the inner sources of satisfaction and the ongoing critical work on self, is not (where it matters) self-absorbed.

This completes a sketch of how Confucius emphasizes the roles of style and attitude, both in making someone a better person and in providing a major satisfaction in such a person's life. Is this unparalleled in Western philosophy? There are some obvious points of comparison between Aristotle's ethics and that of Confucius. But law and philosophical reflection play much of the role for Aristotle that the *Songs*, ritual, and music do for Confucius. Attitude matters for Aristotle, but he supplies much less detail on processes of refinement of attitudes than Confucius does. Plato does talk a great deal about the education of men and women whose systems of attitudes and values will be good. But, in part because of his preoccupation with generalizations, there is hardly anything said about the ethical importance of style and nuance.

The one major Western philosopher who may be closest to Confucius in putting style and attitude at the center of ethics is Nietzsche. Interpretations of Nietzsche notoriously vary; let me merely say what mine is. Nietzsche famously has little or no use for morality, partly because so much in it seems to him closely linked with conformity to local custom, but more fundamentally perhaps because morality can represent societal extreme pressure on independent individuals. Nevertheless it is clear that Nietzsche takes very seriously the part of ethics that concerns estimation of people and of the lives they lead, and that there is nothing "relativistic" about his approach to this part of ethics. Strong, independent, and creative people simply are better and have better lives, in his view, than weak-minded conformists. Style and attitude matter greatly to the quality of a good life.

There are obvious differences, even in this interpretation, between Nietzsche and Confucius. One might begin with Nietzsche's relative lack of concern with social responsibility. But the difference that I want to emphasize concerns the education of style and attitude. This is a major concern in the *Analects*, and Confucius has a great deal to say about the details of the form that such education should take. Nietzsche's extreme individualism precludes anything comparable in his philosophy. Because he does not want to say anything about the directions that someone's strength, independence, and creativity should take, he does not have a great deal to say about the learning tools with which it can be developed, and not a great deal either about the forms which admirable style and attitudes can take.

Conclusion

Style and attitude are not always crucial to the quality of conduct, but they often make a major difference. I have argued also that they can represent major values within a good life. If we want greater insight into the ethical roles of style and attitude, and the ways in which they can be refined, there is no better place to turn than the *Analects* of Confucius.

Notes

1. See "The Trolley Problem," in Judith Jarvis Thomson, *Rights, Restitution, and Risk*, ed. William Parent (Cambridge, MA: Harvard University Press, 1986). For ingenious further discussion see Frances Kamm, "The Doctrine of Triple Effect," *Supplementary Proceedings of the Aristotelian Society* 74 (2000): 41-57.

2. David Wiggins, "Truth, Invention and the Meaning of Life," in *Needs, Values, Truth: Essays in the Philosophy of Value*, 3rd edition (Oxford: Clarendon Press, 1988), 87-137. The phrase quoted is on p. 88.

3. *On Liberty*, ed. Elizabeth Rapaport (Indianapolis: Hackett Books, 1978), 75 (fifth paragraph of Chapter 4). A relevant passage is in the fourteenth paragraph of Chapter 5 of *Utilitarianism*: "We do not call anything wrong unless we mean to imply that a person ought to be punished in some way or other for doing it—if not by law, by the opinion of his fellow creatures; if not by opinion, by the reproaches of his own conscience." Foolishness and depravation of taste are to be disesteemed, in Mill's view, but are not "wrong."

4. This field has been largely but not entirely ignored. See J. N. Findlay, *Axiological Ethics* (London: Macmillan, 1970); James Griffin, *Well-Being* (Oxford: Clarendon Press, 1986); Joel J. Kupperman, *Value . . . And What Follows* (New York: Oxford University Press, 1999).

5. J. J. C. Smart, "Benevolence as an Over-Riding Attitude," *Australasian Journal of Philosophy* 55, no. 2 (1977): 127-35.

6. Much of what follows is I think consonant with the excellent discussion of salience in Nancy Sherman, *Making a Necessity of Virtue* (Cambridge: Cambridge University Press, 1997), 39ff.

7. *The Metaphysics of Morals*, trans. Mary Gregor (Cambridge: Cambridge University Press, 1996), Part II, *Metaphysical First Principles of the Doctrine of Virtue*, 178.

8. "Stabilizing" is Arthur Waley's word. Subsequent quotations in English from the *Analects* will be from Arthur Waley's translation (New York: Vintage Books, 1938).

9. How reliable continuities are, or can be, in real life is a current issue both in philosophy and in psychology. See Gilbert Harman, "Moral Philosophy Meets Social Psychology," *Proceedings of the Aristotelian Society* 99 (1999), 315-31; Joel J. Kupperman, "The Indispensability of Character," *Philosophy* 76 (2001), 239-51; L. Ross and R. Nisbett, *The Person and the Situation: Perspectives of Social Psychology* (New York: McGraw Hill, 1991); David C. Funder, *Personality Judgment: A Realistic Approach to Person Perception* (San Diego: Academic Press, 1999); John Sabini and Maury Silver, "Why Psychologists Haven't Killed Off Character: Disappointing Harman," unpub. ms.

10. For connections between Confucianism and Western feminist philosophy, see Li, Chen-yang, "The Confucian Concept of *Jen* and the Feminist Ethics of Care: A Comparative Study," *Hypatia* 9, no. 1 (1994); Li, Chen-yang, ed., *The Sage and the Second Sex* (La Salle, IL: Open Court, 2000).

11. *Mencius*, trans. D. C. Lau (London: Penguin Books, 1970), 196. Certainly Western philosophers, especially those in the Aristotelian traditions, also have emphasized the importance of appropriate attitudes (and feelings) to the quality of an action. Cf. Rosalind Hursthouse, *On Virtue Ethics* (Oxford: Oxford University Press, 1999), 125.

12. *Myth of Sisyphus*, trans. Justin O'Brien (New York: Vintage Books, 1955), 51.

13. *Grounding for the Metaphysics of Morals*, trans. James W. Ellington (Indianapolis: Hackett Books, 1993), 3.

14. See *The Metaphysics of Morals*, Part I, *Metaphysical Principles of the Doctrine of Right*, 106.

15. Aristotle, *Nicomachean Ethics*, in *The Complete Works of Aristotle* vol. 2, ed. Jonathan Barnes (Princeton, NJ: Princeton University Press, 1984), X, 1, 1852.

16. For extended comparison of Aristotle and Confucius on these topics, see my "Tradition and Community in the Formation of Character and Self," in *Confucian Ethics: A Comparative Study of Self, Autonomy and Community*, ed. David Wong and Kwong-loi Shun (Cambridge: Cambridge University Press, 2004), 103-23.

17. Antonio S. Cua, *Dimensions of Moral Creativity: Paradigms, Principles, and Ideals* (University Park: Pennsylvania State University Press, 1978).

18. Leonard Meyer, *Emotion and Meaning in Music* (Chicago: University of Chicago Press, 1956); Charles Rosen, *The Classical Style* (New York: Norton, 1972).

Chapter Two

Literature and Ethics in the Chinese Confucian Tradition

Philip J. Ivanhoe

Kongzi said, "It is written that, 'Words enable one to completely express one's intentions and style (*wen*) enables one to completely express one's words.'[1] If you do not speak, who will know what you intend? If your words lack style, they will not go far."

> *Zhuozhuan*, Duke Xiang 25th year (tr. 547 B.C.E.)

Style (*wen*) is the vehicle of the Way. If the wheels and shafts [of a cart] are decorated but no one ever uses [the cart], then the decorations are pointless. How much more pointless is a cart that carries nothing! Form and style are matters of art while the Way and Virtue are matters of substance. When one devoted to substance and skilled in art writes about the Way and Virtue, what they write will be beautiful and loved. Since it is loved, it will be passed on. The worthy then can study it and achieve its object. This is what it is to teach. This is why [Kongzi] said, "If your words lack style, they will not go far."

> Zhou Dunyi (1017-1073 C.E.), *Tongshu*, section 28

It should be uncontroversial to claim that reading literature can contribute in a variety of ways to enhance the quality of human life. It can expand our understanding of the world by providing us with new information, and it offers an opportunity to exercise faculties such as imagination, a basic human capacity that is critical for leading a full and flourishing life.[2] A number of contemporary philosophers have argued that the reading of literature can and should play a central role in the development of certain sensibilities that are crucial constituents of distinctively moral understanding and the good life of which it is a vital part.[3] In addition, literature is said to achieve this effect in an indirect and non-codifiable manner. It helps to inculcate certain sensibilities by way of a subtle, therapeutic effect upon the reader, rather than by offering an explicit formal procedure or specific information. Arthur Danto describes how certain texts are aimed at more than reporting or informing, "something is intended to happen to the reader other than or in addition to being informed . . . [to get at certain kinds of truth] . . . involves some kind of transformation of the audience, and the acquiescence in a certain form of initiation and life."[4]

These kinds of claims will be the focus of the present essay and the common theme among its different parts. In section one, I describe three ethical benefits that contemporary philosophers claim can come from the reading of literature. In the latter parts of this section, I draw upon certain features of traditional Confucian thought to question, amend, and extend aspects of these claims.[5] In section two, I go on to describe some of the distinctive characteristics of traditional Confucian teachings regarding the role of literature and ethics, noting some of the similarities and differences between these views and those described in section one. In conclusion, I review and further consider the lessons that a careful study of Chinese Confucian views on the relationship between literature and ethics can provide to contemporary philosophy.

The Virtues of Literature

I will focus on three benefits that literature is said to offer to the development of moral understanding. First there is what I shall call reading as an emotional regimen. Second is reading as an imaginative exercise. Third is reading as a form of temporal appreciation.[6] The names that I have chosen to identify each of these different purported benefits may remind some readers more of physical fitness than ethical understanding. Such a comparison is intended in order to highlight the ways in which reading literature with the aim of moral improvement is like training oneself to be physically fit. For example, the therapeutic manner in which the practice of reading is supposed to inculcate certain sensibilities and tendencies is not unlike the way in which physical exercises can develop strength, flexibility, reaction, speed, and endurance. In both cases, these excellences come out of the regimen in the sense that they arise primarily through the practice and are not simply a matter of gaining new information or understanding some proposition or theory. One is led to acquire abilities that one possessed only *in potentia* or at most in nascent form by pursuing a course of study and practice. Another similarity is that, in reading, as in physical training, the level of trust that one has in one's trainer (teacher) or program of training (education) can play a decisive role in how effective it will be. An additional similarity is that both physical fitness and the ethical benefits of reading literature are aimed at some general but still clear conception of health or excellence. Whether one is training oneself to be physically or ethically fit, the goal is a state of being that is regarded as desirable in itself and as a constituent of a larger conception of what it is to have a good life. In these respects, physical exercise and the reading of literature are like one another and both bear significant similarities to what Pierre Hadot calls "spiritual exercises."[7]

Returning now to the three purported benefits noted in the opening part of this section, reading literature is said to offer an emotional regimen that can have a salubrious effect upon our moral sensibilities. The detail and richness of the descriptions that literature offers present rare opportunities to experience and come to appreciate certain feelings that play an important role in ethical judgment. For example, every decent human being knows that racism is wrong, but unless one has suffered from or witnessed racist acts, it is only by reading or listening to particularly vivid and well-drawn accounts of people who have suffered racism, that one can gain a deep and full appreciation of the ways in which it is wrong, the ways in which it tends to seep into and infect every corner of society and so many aspects of experience. Even those who have directly experienced or witnessed racism may not possess as complete and careful an understanding as one can find in well-turned accounts. As a result, they may not be particularly adept at helping others to appreciate the true nature of racism. Sensitive and well-turned accounts may even help those who have personally endured racist behavior understand many of their own past experiences, feelings, and thoughts in deep and more powerful ways.[8] Only such broad, textured, and nuanced accounts can provide one with the constellation of interconnected feelings, insights, attitudes, and commitments that constitutes a full sense of what is morally wrong with racism. Martha Nussbaum has discussed this aspect of literature in revealing ways and illustrates it with a line from Henry James who described how literature can make one "finely aware and richly responsible" to the ethical dimensions of life.[9] The fact that such sensibilities take time, considerable effort, and personal commitment to cultivate offer other reasons for thinking of them on the analogy of physical fitness and in favor of calling this aspect of ethical education an emotional *regimen*.

The second benefit claimed for the reading of literature is that it can engage and exercise our distinctively moral imagination. When we read *A Christmas Carol* we not only feel certain emotions, we feel these emotions toward and often for the sake of the characters. Imagination takes us out of ourselves and in various ways projects us into the lives of others. We experience contempt and pity for Scrooge throughout the early parts of *A Christmas Carol*. We approve of and feel joy for and about him as he is transformed in the course of the story. We feel concern for Tiny Tim and respect and admiration for Bob Cratchit. Literature invites and often seduces us into taking up the exercise of our moral imagination, and this can strengthen and refine our ability to sympathize with and understand others.[10] The literary exercise of our moral imagination can teach us a great deal about the complexity and difficulty of living actual ethical lives. Sometimes it leaves us with feelings of ambiguity and unease, as one might feel about the character Captain Vere in *Billy Budd: Sailor*.[11] In any event, imaginatively experiencing such emotions cultivates in us a richer repertoire of feelings, attitudes, and ideas concerning what it is to live a moral life and a greater capacity for how to go about understanding other people and the challenges they face.

A third moral benefit claimed for the reading of literature is its ability to inculcate what we might call temporal appreciation. Literature, and some have claimed novels in particular, often present human life as a narrative, which allows us to see and appreciate how different ethical judgments fit into the span of a full human life.[12] By allowing us to see over the horizon of the moment and beyond the pull of immediate desires and needs, such narratives can alter our assessment of many of the things we do. Without such a perspective, we tend to misjudge the value of certain actions, events, and states of affairs, for we see them only in the constricted light of the moment. We lose sight of how they relate to what we have already done, what they may lead us to become, and what this will do to the overall trajectory and shape of our lives.[13] This longer range and more holistic perspective on human life is precisely what the character Scrooge comes to see in the course of *A Christmas Carol*.

As is true of the earlier two benefits claimed for the reading of literature, temporal appreciation is not so much an idea about or principle governing what is valuable but rather a sensibility or attitude one cultivates in regard to one's actions and how they fit into one's life. By taking up a characteristically human perspective on the course of a person's life and imaginatively experiencing a variety of different life scenarios, one comes to endorse some as preferable to others. The only way to develop such a sense is by vicariously "living" different lives through imagination, and literature offers one the possibility of doing this with the vividness, detail, and texture needed to get a proper sense of what different lives have to offer.

Most traditional Confucian thinkers would endorse all three of the benefits of reading literature described above.[14] As we shall see in the following section, in addition to reading, *writing* and other forms of art also played a central role in traditional Confucian conceptions of moral education. Nevertheless, most Confucians expressed considerably more concern than contemporary advocates of the ethical value of literature do about the imposing challenges and potential dangers of this aspect of moral cultivation. Confucian writings on this topic are extensive and complex, and so I can present only a selective and somewhat simplified account of what the tradition has to offer. I will describe four representative Confucian concerns and say a bit about how, in one form or another, these remain legitimate challenges for us today.

The first potential problem is perhaps the most familiar, for people can be given or simply choose to read the wrong things. If one's goal is moral edification, one cannot simply encourage people to read just anything. A great deal of literature will prove to be of little help in such an effort and much that is out there might prove counter-productive simply in virtue of its inherent banality.[15] There is also the harm that can be done by writing that casts wicked ideals in an engaging and seductive manner. If good literature can lead one toward higher goals, bad literature can lead one to spiral down as well.[16] Such concerns led traditional Confucian thinkers to endorse the prohibition of certain works, to insist on an explicit curriculum, a specific course or progression of texts, and the need for the guidance of a proper teacher.

Even if one is reading a text that all would agree offers the promise of considerable enhancement of one's moral sensibility, it is not an easy matter to reap such benefits, and there remains the potential for damage as well as gain. One may not read even the right things in the right ways. There are challenges right from the start, for most Confucians believed that the best texts are not easy to read. The inherent difficulty of classical texts could lead one to fail to grasp their message or even to misread them in ways that lead one to turn away from an ethical life. Such concerns were expressed by early Confucians like Xunzi (310-219 B.C.E.) who warned, "The *Odes* and *History* contain ancient stories but no explanation of their present application. The *Spring and Autumn Annals* is terse and cannot be quickly understood."[17]

Another, related way to go wrong is to read the right texts but with an eye for the wrong things within them. We find examples of this kind of concern throughout the early writings of the tradition, often expressed as the general worry that students are pursuing their studies for material profit rather than for moral understanding.[18] This issue was a central concern for the later Confucian, Zhu Xi (1130-1200), and in his writings it took on a specific and distinctive form. Zhu Xi gave a great deal of thought to issues of pedagogy. Among his many proposals, was a well-defined curriculum that consisted of an ordered series of different kinds of texts and explicit instructions about how to read them—what he called a "reading method" (*dufa*). Zhu Xi insisted that certain classical texts be mastered first, as these contained the most clear and concise explanations of basic moral principles. Even among the classics, a particular order was to be observed.[19] After one had absorbed and embodied the teachings in these texts, Zhu Xi insisted that students embark on a thorough study of history, for historical examples help one to appreciate the many ways in which the moral principles contained in the classics could be played out under various circumstances and conditions. Throughout this process though, one had to be looking for the right things. From start to finish, one was to be searching for an ever richer and enhanced understanding of moral principle. This proper guiding focus was critical, for some people, even those who read the right things, did so with the wrong inspiration, intention, or goal and this could thoroughly corrupt one's understanding. Zhu Xi criticized two people in particular for different versions of this general form of failure: Wang Anshi (1021-1086) and Su Shi (1036-1101).[20]

According to Zhu, Wang went wrong by looking at the classics as a repository of different approaches to organizing society, records of various social and political techniques and methods that had been employed in the past. Wang maintained that if one grasped the various techniques and methods described and illustrated in the classics and understood how and why they were deployed in different times and circumstances, one could gain a sense for how the ancients had established institutions and administered their governments. Such insight into earlier regimes could be used to ensure that one's own policies and practices always led to order and flourishing and avoided chaos and decay.

What one found in the course of such study was not so much the blueprint for how to organize and administer one's own social and political situation but rather the skill that would allow one to forge such a plan in one's own age. The knowledge and know-how that one sought was practical; it concerned the structure and nature of social and political institutions and how to implement them in the administration of a state. But according to Zhu Xi, Wang Anshi's approach to the classics was terribly mistaken. It manifested a gross misunderstanding of what the classics are and what study of them was to produce. Zhu Xi insisted that the classics are records of the "Way" (*dao*). Their central lessons concern not administrative and managerial techniques but moral principles, and the aim of grasping these principles must guide one's reading of them.

Su Shi represented another form of this general error. He did not read the classics in order to gain a mastery of social and political institutions and techniques but in order to appreciate their literary style. This was part of a larger and very subtle view about how moral self-cultivation should be carried out.[21] Su Shi and certain other Chinese thinkers, both earlier and later, saw literary style as playing a central role in moral development. For these thinkers, style reflected character and especially those subtle and elusive attitudes and sensibilities that were constitutive of the highest levels of ethical and spiritual attainment. Rather than *what* someone did or even *why* they did it, the *style* or *way* in which they did what they did, when and where they did it, was seen as the key to understanding those who had mastered the way, and through such knowledge, to becoming morally accomplished oneself.[22] Zhu Xi and other more conservative Confucians found such views dangerous and intolerable. While they too believed that moral knowledge was not simply a technique or some simple list of principles or rules, they insisted that it had a clear and well-defined content and could only be attained through sincere and sustained commitment to a specific, systematic course of study.

These aspects of Su Shi's thought bear significant similarities to characteristic features of important strains of Daoist and Buddhist thought. Indeed Zhu Xi and others often criticized Su Shi and like-minded thinkers for being "Daoists" and "Buddhists" in Confucian garb. I take such accusations as expressing a criticism more about the way such thinkers conceived of learning than about the specific content of their beliefs. Zhu Xi was well aware that Su Shi and likeminded thinkers did not believe in the Buddha, the Dharma, and the Sangha etc. What was less clear to him was how many of their views on learning could be distinguished from those advocated by Daoists and Buddhists. What Zhu and others were sensing and reacting to was that for thinkers like Su Shi, *style* was much more important than content. According to Su Shi, the most important aspects of the Way can *only* be found in the style of one's thoughts and actions and by extension in the style of an author's writing.[23] A properly sensitive person could discern the Way in a wide variety of expressive mediums, and the goal of self cultivation was to develop precisely this kind of sensitivity. One quite radical implication of this approach to learning was that the Way is not exclusively or even primarily lodged in the classics.

Such ideas resemble characteristic aspects of Daoism and Buddhism. Most Daoists believed that the Way could be found everywhere and in every thing. What one needed was the ability to see and appreciate each thing in its proper role as a part of the great *dao*, which, among other things, required one to abandon inflated notions of one's own importance. Many Buddhists saw emptiness as the true nature of all existence, so for them, and especially for those in the Chan tradition, what one needed is to see the world *as* empty. What you looked at or thought about did not matter as much as how you looked at and thought about it. Looking at even the right things in the wrong way could only do one harm. For example, looking at a *sutra* as if it held the ultimate truth or at one's teacher or oneself as a locus of enduring value would lead one to fail to appreciate that these things too are empty. Such mistaken beliefs in turn generate the kinds of debilitating attachments that keep one from achieving the highest ethical and spiritual states. These aspects of Daoism and Buddhism tended to undermine any codifiable or systematic approach to learning or practice. What they looked for and sought to develop is a certain style and sensibility.

These Daoist and Buddhist ideas deeply influenced Su Shi. For him, the *how* was much more important than the *what* or the *why*. Style and form ruled over content, structure, or reason. But for Zhu Xi, true literary style (*wen*) could never exist apart from the moral wisdom of the Way. Su Shi was not only wrong to claim that one could cultivate style apart from the "substance" of the Way, this mistaken belief corrupted his writing in subtle yet critical respects. Zhu Xi explains: "Now Su Dongpo (Su Shi) says, 'What I call style must be joined with the Way.' This is to say that style comes from [working at] style and the Way comes from [working at] the Way. One waits until one finishes one's composition and then turns to find some Way to put into it. This is where he goes greatly awry."[24]

For Zhu Xi, style was something that properly arose out of practice of and reflection upon the substantial moral lessons of the Way. Style was important as it added flavor or spice to the moral teachings of the Way, but it was clearly of secondary importance: "How could style ever comprehend the principles of the Way? Style is style while the Way is the Way. Style (*wen*) is nothing more than something one eats to help the rice go down!"[25]

Despite Zhu Xi's best efforts, this issue remained unsettled and continued to resurface in different guises throughout the later Confucian tradition. One notable exponent of the "style over content" view was the Ming dynasty thinker Li

Zhi (1527-1602). Li Zhi held a cluster of views that marked him as an "icono-
clast." He was generally anti-authoritarian and to some extent antinomian. He
wrote remarkable essays arguing for the intellectual, moral, and spiritual equal-
ity of women, and became infamous for extolling popular literature as equal in
value to the classics as a source for moral and spiritual knowledge. These various ideas have given rise to a wide range of mistaken views about Li Zhi. For
example, he has been held up as an exemplary defender of proletarian values, as
a humanistic advocate of tolerance, and as an exponent of "relativism."[26] But
none of these interpretations provide or incorporate an adequate account of Li
Zhi's distinctive and important teachings regarding what he called the "child's
mind" (*tongxin*). As a whole, his writings make sense but only when understood
in light of his views concerning this innate and uncorrupted moral mind, which
he believed all human beings possess.

For Li Zhi, the child's mind was the source of all true moral insight. As
long as it was preserved from the hypocrisy of conventional society, it would
express itself sincerely, insightfully, and always morally correctly in whatever
one thought, said, or did. One did not need to be an elite member of society in
order to possess, preserve, and give expression to one's child mind. One did not
need to be highly "educated"—a process that Li Zhi thought usually resulted in
twisting people into money and prestige-grubbing phonies and hypocrites. Since
women as well as men possessed this innate endowment, they were full equals
in intellectual, moral, and spiritual abilities. Since the child's mind was not bur-
dened with prejudice or preconception, it expressed itself and could be found in
writings of every kind. What mattered was not the content of the writing or the
pedigree or gender of the author but whether or not it was a sincere expression
of the child's mind. In other words, it was more a matter of "style"—the way in
which one acted—rather than "substance"—the particular things one did.

Returning to our central theme, another way in which the reading of literature can prove to be misdirected and counterproductive is when one pursues
such studies in order to realize more mundane forms of profit. In the case of
Neo-Confucians, this criticism often was linked to success in the Imperial Ex-
aminations and the acquisition of highly coveted official appointments. But we
need not look to traditional Chinese culture to find examples of this kind of misdirected learning. The problem is familiar to contemporary teachers who are
faced with students who read a work or pursue their studies in general only with
an eye for doing well on an exam or getting a good grade in order to get into the
professional school of their choice. Confucians also note that being "well read"
can be a source of moral failure when it is undertaken only for self-
aggrandizement or one's learning is deployed only in order to put down others.
Such intellectual snobbery and bullying is not unknown in our own age.

In an effort to avoid these and other mistaken types of learning, Confucians
argued that most people not only need the right curriculum but the right kind of
teacher as well.[27] Since the most important texts and practices of moral education are difficult to understand and apply, in order to have any chance of avoid-

ing error and grasping the true lessons the classics had to teach, one's reading and practice needed to be guided by a kind of ethical coach. As we saw in the case of Li Zhi, certain Confucian thinkers defended a very broad conception of what kinds of texts could prove morally beneficial to their readers. Nevertheless, no Confucian thought that all texts were equal. And regardless of their view on the range of admissible texts—most often cast in terms we recognize as a debate about the breadth of the canon—most thought that students needed to be carefully guided in how to read.

Confucian Views About Literature and Ethics

One important difference between Western and Confucian views on the role of literature is that for the former, literature often seems to be something added to a more fundamental "core" of ethics. The point here is not unlike Kant's view that the right kinds of social practices and sensibilities offer "a garment that dresses virtue to advantage" and make it more appealing.[28] Even in the case of virtue ethicists, whose ethical theory seems most amendable to according such sensibilities an important role in the moral life—the advocacy of literature as an important part of moral learning is something quite new. Neither Plato nor Aristotle saw the reading of literature as playing a central and substantial role in moral cultivation.[29] In fact, both expressed a great deal of concern about literature's capacity to incite emotions that disrupt the proper exercise of reason, which was necessary for the moral life. In contrast, for Confucians, an appreciation of literature and other arts has always played a central role in developing the humane sensibilities thought to be characteristic of the sage.[30]

A further respect in which traditional Confucian ideas about the role of literature and other arts contribute to moral understanding is that Confucians tended to insist that an ability to perform such arts—as well as to appreciate them—was critically important. The practice of writing, calligraphy, and painting were seen as essential elements of a proper education.[31] These pursuits were justified in a number of ways, but the most basic line of argument is that, in one way or another, such practices allow one to develop a deeper understanding of the Way. For example, in the case of writing well, the idea is that someone who can express moral truths in moving and compelling ways possesses an important type of moral knowledge. Since one's learning is valued for the good it can do for society as well as self, the ability to move others toward the way was seen as a critical measure of one's moral achievement.

A number of Confucian thinkers have noted that in several respects cultivating the ability to write well mirrors the process of moral development. In both cases, one begins by understanding and gaining a sense of the proper standard by reading the classics. One then learns to express this same sensibility in one's own life by writing about or acting in one's own age in light of one's own situation and circumstances. Zhang Xuecheng (1738-1801) argued for further similarities. He insisted that the most morally developed individuals would—for the reasons noted in the previous paragraph—also be culturally accomplished.[32] He further noted that in the case of both moral or literary achievement, one must avoid thinking that one's insights and accomplishments are uniquely and wholly one's own.[33] Such a possessive and prideful attitude displays a lack of understanding concerning the nature of any truth. For the very nature of truth requires it to be universal and public—not the possession of any one person.[34]

Another distinctively Confucian concern about the role of literature in the cultivation of moral sensibility centered around the relative value of fiction versus non-fiction writings. Contemporary advocates of the value of literature in the moral life focus exclusively on fiction and, as discussed in section one of this essay, they tend to see special importance in the genre of the novel because such works often present life in terms of a temporarily extended narrative. Earlier, we noted that Zhu Xi advocated the reading of history as an essential part of his curriculum. He thought that historical writings offered students the chance to see how moral principles are applied—successfully or not—by real people in actual situations. In assessing his view and this general point, it is important to keep in mind that in presenting past actions and events Chinese historians relied extensively on the genre of historical biography.[35] Such works were written in a lively and engaging style and were always quite popular among Chinese readers. They offered an opportunity to enjoy all three of the primary virtues of reading literature that were discussed in section one.

The genre of historical biography might in fact offer certain distinctive advantages over works of fiction. It may be a simple fact of human psychology that a paradigm based on the life of an actual person possesses more persuasive power than one based on a fictional character. A paradigm based on the life of someone who is thought to be in some sense *one of us* may be more effective still. In the case of Chinese appeals to historical precedents and paradigms, the belief that these figures were regarded as ancestors added to the sense of identity and the inspirational power they could command. Another reason that historical biography might be preferable to fiction is that the former, at least when accurately written, avoids the potential problem of proffering unrealistic and potentially counter-productive ethical ideals. One of the virtues people attribute to great works of fiction is that they present "life-like" characters and capture "what it's really like" to live through certain experiences. Good historical works don't need to strive as hard to realize such qualities, as they are about real people and events.[36]

This last point should not be misunderstood or overstated. It establishes that good historical writing and especially good historical biography possesses an important virtue that not all fiction can claim. On the other hand, it is clearly possible for works of fiction to possess such virtue. Provided that they are careful about not overstepping the constraints of reality and avoid offering implausible ideals, works of fiction can offer the further advantage of being able to explore certain ethical ideas in novel ways and across unprecedented contexts. No one may ever have gone to the guillotine to a *far greater peace than he has ever known* and yet Sydney Carton offers a stirring and plausible ideal of self-sacrificing love. Odysseus and his world are obviously unreal, and yet his choice to leave Calypso's island and return to wife, children, father, and friends and his mortal life, back home in Ithaca, offers us a profound lesson concerning what it is to pursue a good human life.[37] Iris Murdoch perceptively notes that even the explicitly unreal genre of science fiction can offer us important moral lessons, but that it does so only when it describes creatures and lives that share enough of our own real concerns to make them effective objects of sympathy and concern.[38] If the characters in a work of fiction become too "alien," we simply don't care what happens to them, and this makes such works of little value to the cultivation of moral sensibilities.

Conclusion

Our examination of Confucian views about the relationship between reading literature, writing, and the practice of other arts has shown that reflective members of a very different ethical tradition shared a concern that has become an important theme among contemporary ethicists. The reasons for this are complex but at their heart is a common interest in human excellence and the shared capacities, needs, and concerns of literate and reflective human beings. For traditional Confucians, an appreciation of and facility in a range of arts played a central role in the cultivation of various dispositions that were regarded as important constituents of the ethically good human life. Rather than focusing on abstract theoretical accounts of what morality is, Confucian thinkers showed much greater concern with discovering and practicing the right ethical or spiritual "Way," one that would enable them to cultivate moral sensibilities. The ideal Confucian was more a cultured connoisseur than an accomplished theoretician.

In exploring some traditional Confucian debates about the proper role of literature in the ethical life, we came to appreciate some of the ways in which their responses to this commonly held concern differed and could augment contemporary explorations of this topic. For example, we came to see that like their Confucian colleagues, contemporary philosophers who defend the importance that literature holds for ethical development note that certain kinds of texts are much more effective than others. But rather than defending a definitive list or explicit cannon, contemporary thinkers tend to offer more general standards for what kinds of texts are best. For example, Martha Nussbaum argues that works that incline one to be more "finely aware and richly responsible" are favored over those that don't. This more general and open-ended way of describing what kinds of texts can contribute to the development of ethical sensibilities is appealing for a number of obvious reasons and yet it is not altogether different in spirit from the Confucian ideal. For both traditional Confucians and contemporary ethicists, *what* one reads is an important and fundamental issue.

While some contemporary ethicists offer reasons for why some kinds of literature are better suited for moral development than others, most tend to ignore
the related issues of whether and why certain kinds of literature might pose a
positive harm to one's moral development. Our discussion of the views of Confucian thinkers showed that this is an important aspect of the role that literature
might play in ethical development. As we saw, this is a difficult and complex
topic. A piece of writing need not be recommending or encouraging morally bad
ideals and yet may still prove to be morally bad for one.[39] One may be ill-
prepared for the lessons of a given text and misinterpret it in ways that harm
one's character. Writing in general and certain kinds of fiction in particular can
endorse and advocate morally excellent ideals but present them in ways that encourage overly optimistic or wholly implausible ethical lives. Finally, one can
read texts that offer laudable ideals but still fail to read them *in the right ways*.[40]
Confucian thinkers showed great concern and developed interesting views about
such topics. They offered and defended various ideas about *how* to read texts
and engaged in extended and revealing debates about the role that fiction can or
should play in the task of moral development. In all these respects, their views
can enrich contemporary discussions.

In conclusion, I would like to describe two cases where a consideration of
explicit and well-developed Confucian views helps us to think more clearly and
see more deeply into contemporary approaches to the ways that the reading of
literature can contribute to ethical development. We have seen that traditional
Confucians were concerned with what I have described as the *what* and the *how*
of literature. They had different but firm views on what kinds of literature
should be read and how such works should be studied. In regard to the former
topic, they argued that certain texts are necessary or at least strongly recommended for proper ethical cultivation, while others must be avoided or at least
handled with great care. In regard to the latter issue, they insisted that most people needed to be guided through the right texts and they offered explicit instructions about how to approach the study of such works.

An awareness and proper appreciation of these two Confucian concerns
helps us to see that the best contemporary philosophers writing on the role of literature in ethical development also offer views on the *what* and the *how* of reading. For example, throughout her impressive and revealing collection of essays
on the role of literature in the moral life, *Love's Knowledge*, Martha Nussbaum
advocates the reading of certain works, the writings of authors such as Henry
James and Charles Dickens. While she does argue, often persuasively and eloquently, that certain features of such recommended texts make them more conducive to the goal of moral development, the general topic of what texts to read
and why is less explicit. There is no discussion of the ways in which bad literature might damage one's character or how one might read good works in the
wrong way and to ill effect.[41] The point is that the topic of *what* literature to read
is an important part of what Nussbaum teaches us but much more can be said
and perhaps would have been said had this been an explicit and well-developed
theoretical concern.

The case of *how* to read literature is even more clear. For many if not all of the essays in *Love's Knowledge* are best understood as examples of what in the Confucian tradition is called a "reading method" (*dufa*). Nussbaum's elegant explorations of certain great works of literature guide our reading of these classics in ways that facilitate their salubrious effect upon us. In the absence of such guidance, the uninitiated reader might well founder and fail to benefit from her encounter with these great works. Some may fail because of the inherent complexity of these works, others because they are too young and inexperienced to appreciate what these texts have to teach. Others may fail because they read such works with the wrong aims in mind. As we have seen, these were among several explicit concerns that traditional Confucians identified and explored in their philosophical reflections on the role of literature in the ethical life.

In addressing these kinds of concerns about how to read, Confucians have paid much more attention to the role that teachers are to play as ethical guides. A proper teacher is able to direct a student's attention to the ethically salient features of great works and lead the novice to appreciate their significance. Such an ability is a critical part of what it is to be a good teacher.[42] As is true in the case of *what* to read, a careful consideration of Confucian reflections on *how* to read can directly enhance and deepen the impressive work that is currently being done on the topic of how literature can contribute to moral development. A well-conceived contemporary "reading method" (*dufa*) might offer the most effective way to deploy and benefit from the theoretical advances that have been made in ethical theory. This would enable us to harmonize and integrate the best that ethical theory has to offer with the particular and practical lives that we all must live.[43]

In section two of this essay, we noted that writing as well as reading was a core part of Confucian moral cultivation. The ethically developed person will express the Way in an elegant and powerful manner. According to thinkers like Zhu Xi this is because such a person cares for others and will endeavor to cultivate literary style as an effective vehicle for the Way. Other Confucians though argued more explicitly that the style itself is an aspect of one's understanding of the Way (and Zhu Xi makes similar claims at various places in his own writings). In any event, Confucian discussions of how the *writing* of literature and the practice as well the appreciation of other forms of art play a critical role in the development of ethical sensibilities offer further remarkably rich resources for comparison, reflection, and mutual edification.

Notes

Thanks to Karen L. Carr, Mark Csikszentmihalyi, Eric L. Hutton, De-nin Lee, Pauline Chen Lee, Paul Kjellberg, T. C. Kline III, Joel Kupperman, and Justin Tiwald for corrections and helpful suggestions on earlier drafts of this essay.

1. The word *wen* translated here as "style" had a range of meanings in classical Chi-

nese. In some cases, it referred to inherent "patterns" in the natural world that often were regarded as in some way normative for human beings. It also referred to any form of decoration or embellishment, anything purposively added to the basic substance of a thing or person. *Wen* could also be used to refer to a specific written character or writing in general and is seen in the modern word for literature, *wenxue* (literally, "writing study"). This extension of meaning was facilitated by the fact that in their earliest form, a number of written characters where pictographs or contained pictographic elements. The idea that *wen* is a contrived but intentional embellishment added to unrefined native substance helps to capture the general sense of it as "culture." The modern word for culture *wenhua* (literally, "embellishment transformation") connotes the idea that through embellishment (of the right sort) one's original nature is transformed. It also implies the related belief that one with culture possesses an ability to influence and ultimately transform others. In this last respect, what is *wen* is contrasted with what is *wu* "martial." While what is martial has the ability to frighten, intimidate, and conquer others, true culture it thought to please, satisfy, and attract them. In this essay, *wen* is used in reference to literature but in the broad sense that includes poetry and song.

2. Such benefits are recognized by early members of the Chinese Confucian tradition as well. For example, in *Analects* 17.8, Kongzi tells his disciples that one among many reasons for studying the *Book of Odes*, is that it "teaches one the names of many birds, beasts, plants, and trees." In *Analects* 8.8 he encourages them to "Be inspired by the *Odes*," and throughout the text he illustrates ethical points by drawing appropriate analogies to passages from this classic.

3. The most sophisticated and sustained case for the importance of literature in ethics is the anthology by Martha C. Nussbaum. See *Love's Knowledge: Essays on Philosophy and Literature* (New York: Oxford University Press, 1990). The importance of literature for both ethical practice and ethical theory has been more clearly recognized and more thoroughly explored in the field of philosophy of religion. In regard to practice, works such as John Bunyan's *Pilgrim's Progress* proved to be extremely popular and influential, especially in the centuries immediately following its publication. One modern scholar claims that in terms of popularity and influence it was, "second only . . . to the English Bible." See Kathleen M. Swain, *Pilgrim's Progress, Puritan Progress: Discourses and Contexts* (Chicago: University of Chicago Press, 1993), 1-2. In regard to theory, literature plays a prominent role in certain contemporary defenses of religious beliefs. For example, R. B. Braithwaite argues that religious claims express intentions to act in particular ways (moral beliefs) taken together with and informed by the "stories" characteristic of a given tradition. Much the same can be said for ethical claims. See his "An Empiricist Looks at Religious Beliefs," in *The Philosophy of Religion*, ed. Basil Mitchell (London: Oxford University Press, 1971), 72-91. Thanks to Karen L. Carr for pointing out the importance of this work for my project. For a cross-cultural comparative study of literary style as a form of philosophy, see Karen L. Carr and Philip J. Ivanhoe, *The Sense of Antirationalism: The Religious Thought of Zhuangzi and Kierkegaard* (New York: Seven Bridges Press, 2000), especially chapter 4, "Philosophical Style," 90-116.

4. Presidential Address to the Eightieth Annual Eastern Division Meeting, "Philosophy as/and/of Literature," *Proceedings and Addresses of the American Philosophical Society* 58 (1984): 8.

5. Chinese conceptions of "reading literature" in general are broader than our contemporary idea of reading a book. They include the chanting of and listening to poetry and song as well as the silent reading of texts. While these distinctive features of the Chinese case are not the focus of the present study, they offer additional ways in which such

comparative studies might enrich contemporary work. Thanks to Eric Hutton for pointing this out to me.

6. Martha Nussbaum describes forms of each of these in *Love's Knowledge,* though she does not employ my particular terms to mark them. Iris Murdoch also offers revealing discussions of how both literature and art can affect us and help to shape us morally. See her *Metaphysics as a Guide to Morals* (New York: Penguin Press, 1992). See especially chapters 5 and 11.

7. Pierre Hadot, *Philosophy as a Way of Life,* Reprint (Oxford: Blackwell Publishers, 1998). These similarities should not be taken as an attempt to obscure the important differences between being morally and physically fit. For example, at least at more advanced levels, the former requires a degree of theoretical reflection that is not a critical part of the latter. Athletes can improve the results of their training by possessing more theoretical knowledge about nutrition, physiology, etc. However, unlike the case of the morally fit, they can enjoy most of these benefits simply by having such knowledge as part of their training regimen. They need not possess it themselves.

8. Ralph Ellison's *Invisible Man* is a brilliant example of a work that can teach a wide range of people about the evils of racism. In a similar way, the best accounts of war can offer insights into this aspect of human experience to civilian and veteran alike. Very few combat veterans are capable of conveying the horrors of war and more than a few appreciate and learn from their more perceptive and literally more gifted comrades.

9. This theme appears in a number of places in *Love's Knowledge,* but for the most focused discussion of this aspect of literature and ethics, see "Finely Aware and Richly Responsible: Literature and the Moral Imagination," in Nussbaum, *Love's Knowledge,* 148-63. Among the things that one can acquire in the course of pursuing such an emotional regimen are new understandings of familiar, raw emotional states and a richer and more nuanced palette or repertoire of emotional resources. An example of the former is the very different senses of "jealousy" that one can feel in light of critical reflection on the raw emotion. For a helpful discussion of this point, see Stuart Hampshire, *Morality and Conflict* (Cambridge, MA: Harvard University Press, 1983), 49-50. An example of the latter is the growth from raw feelings of anger to a refined sense of the difference between righteous indignation, vengeful spite, festering frustration, etc. Thanks to T. C. Kline for suggesting this point and helping me to develop it.

10. There are many ways in which we can "feel things with and for others." Sympathy can include celebration and joy in regard to another's good fortune as well as distress and concern about people in difficult straights. Sometimes we even experience morally reprehensible thoughts and feelings vicariously and these may teach us important lessons about our own moral frailty. For a penetrating exploration of this topic, though one which tends to focus on feelings of distress rather than joy, see Stephen Darwall, "Empathy, Sympathy, Care," *Philosophical Studies* 89 (1998): 261-82.

11. This is a different feeling than the paradox one might feel when faced with clashing and irreconcilable imperatives. In the latter case, one is not sure of what to do in a given moment while in the former one is sure that over the course of events, the character acted well, but one still feels regret and some level of dissatisfaction with the result. Nussbaum argues that one of the special ethical values of literature is its ability to convey a sense of the pervasiveness of temporally extended moral conflicts. See "Flawed Crystals: James's *The Golden Bowl* and Literature as Moral Philosophy," in Nussbaum, *Love's Knowledge,* 125-47.

12. A number of philosophers have argued for the general importance of such a narrative perspective in the evaluation of human lives. For example, see Alasdair MacIntyre,

After Virtue (Notre Dame, IN: University of Notre Dame Press, 1984) and Charles Taylor, *Sources of the Self: The Making of the Modern Identity* (Cambridge, MA: Harvard University Press, 1989). For a revealing discussion of how narratives and other works of art provide ways for focusing and shaping emotions, see "Art, Narrative, and Emotion," "Art, Narrative, and Moral Understanding," and "Simulation, Emotion, and Morality," in Noël Carroll, *Beyond Aesthetics: Philosophical Essays* (Cambridge: Cambridge University Press, 2001), 215-35, 270-93, and 306-16. Thanks to T. C. Kline for pointing out the importance of Carroll's work for my project.

13. J. David Velleman argues for a similar conclusion in "Well-being and Time," *Pacific Philosophical Quarterly* 72 (1991): 48-77.

14. There would though be some important qualifications. For example, many Confucians would insist that such benefits could only be gained by reading a select group of classic texts. As we shall see in the following section, Confucian thinkers expressed a wide range of views on what texts could prove morally edifying. Some argued for an expansive and open-ended canon, including contemporary works of popular fiction. However, others argued that fiction in general and popular fiction in particular not only did not aid but actually hindered moral development. A number of contemporary thinkers who advocate the reading of literature single out certain texts and genres as better than others, but, as I argue below, in general there is less explicit and thorough discussion of this issue among philosophers today.

15. I believe there is a considerable and underappreciated threat to our moral well-being from what we might refer to as "the evil of banality." If one is regularly engaged with works that pose no challenge to one's present state of being and offer no inspirational ideal, there is a real danger that one will become an ethical as well as a physical and intellectual couch potato.

16. Of course, one might argue, as some Confucian thinkers did, that bad examples can help one to be good too. However, such examples must be seen as bad and are probably best considered by more mature moral agents. Such points receive additional treatment below.

17. From the chapter "An Exhortation to Learning," tr. Eric L. Hutton, in *Readings in Classical Chinese Philosophy*, ed. Philip J. Ivanhoe and Bryan Van Norden (New York: Seven Bridges Press, 2001): 251.

18. See for example *Analects* 14.24, *Mengzi* 4B14, and *Xunzi*, "An Exhortation to Learning," in Ivanhoe and Van Norden, *Readings*, 250-51.

19. For a study of these aspects of Zhu Xi's philosophy see the following three works by Daniel K. Gardner, "Principle and Pedagogy: Chu Hsi and the Four Books," *Harvard Journal of Asiatic Studies* 44.1 (June, 1984): 57-81; "Transmitting the Way: Chu Hsi and His Program of Learning," *Harvard Journal of Asiatic Studies* 49.2 (June, 1989): 141-72; and *Learning to Be a Sage: Selections from the Conversations of Master Chu, Arranged Topically* (Berkeley: University of California Press, 1990). Other important studies of Zhu Xi's approach to reading and moral cultivation are, Yü Ying-shih, "Morality and Knowledge in Chu Hsi's Philosophical System," and Richard John Lynn, "Chu Hsi as a Literary Theorist and Critic," both in *Chu Hsi and Neo-Confucianism*, ed. Wing-tsit Chan (Honolulu: University of Hawai'i Press, 1986), 228-54, 337-54.

20. Wang Anshi was a powerful political reformer while Su Shi was one of the most accomplished and renowned writers of his time. Both of them were roundly criticized by Cheng Yi (1033-1107) an earlier Song thinker whose thought influenced Zhu Xi greatly. For more on Cheng Yi, see Angus C. Graham *Two Chinese Philosophers*, Reprint (La Salle, IL: Open Court Press, 1992). For Wang Anshi and Su Shi, see Peter K. Bol, *This*

Culture of Ours (Stanford, CA: Stanford University Press, 1992), 212-99.

21. In general, I understand Su Shi as disagreeing with people like Cheng Yi less about the content or nature of moral knowledge and more about how one can gain such knowledge. Su Shi thought of moral knowledge as a kind of skill or know-how that is best seen and learned in the creative moment. The aim was to engage and express one's nature in the particular circumstances of one's place and time or understand another as doing so in his or her place and time. As a result of such views, Su Shi insisted that moral knowledge could never be codified and always remains highly particularistic. Richard John Lynn seems to have a similar view of Su Shi's thought and helpfully describes him as a "fox" in contrast to Zhu Xi's "hedgehog." See "Chu Hsi as a Literary Theorist and Critic," in Chan, 339-40.

22. Myles Burnyeat argues that Aristotle advocated a two-stage course of ethical education. At the first stage one gained an appreciation for what things were good and admirable by practicing them and experiencing such actions for oneself. The second stage entailed learning the *why* of such activities, what makes them excellent. See Myles Burnyeat, "Aristotle on Learning to Be Good," in *Essays on Aristotle's Ethics*, ed. Amélie Oksenberg Rorty (Berkeley: University of California Press, 1980), 69-92. Su Shi and thinkers like him offered a more aesthetic conception of what one gains in the process of moral knowledge. For a view that bears some similarity to that of Su Shi, see Joel Kupperman's contribution to this volume.

23. Su Shi and like-minded thinkers also believed that the appreciation and practice of calligraphy and painting as well as writing, should play a central role in moral education. For a revealing article on Confucian views on painting, see James F. Cahill, "Confucian Elements in the Theory of Painting," in *The Confucian Persuasion*, ed. Arthur F. Wright (Stanford, CA: Stanford University Press, 1960), 115-40. See also, Andrew March, "Self and Landscape in Su Shih," *Journal of the American Oriental Society* 86.4 (October-December 1966): 377-96. For Su Shi and calligraphy, see chapter 4 of Amy McNair, *The Upright Brush: Yan Zhenqing's Calligraphy and Song Literati Politics* (Honolulu: University of Hawai'i Press, 1998), 60-82. Thanks to De-nin Lee for this citation.

24. *Zhuzi yülei*, Volume 8, (Beijing: Zhonghua shu ju, 1986): 3319 (*juan* 139).

25. *Zhuzi yülei*, Volume 8, (*juan* 139): 3305. In this respect, Confucian debates about the nature and role of style are not wholly unlike some Western debates about the nature and function of metaphor.

26. For a characteristic Marxist interpretation of Li Zhi, see the introduction in *Chu-tan Ji*, "Writings from Chutan" (Beijing: Zhonghua shuju, 1974), 1-8 and *Zhongguo sixiang tongshi*, "A Comprehensive History of Chinese Thought," Volume 4, ed. Hou Wailu (Beijing: Renmin chubanshe, 1960). For studies on the reception of Li Zhi in contemporary China, see Pei-kai Cheng, "Continuities in Chinese Political Culture: Interpretations of Li Zhi, Past and Present," *Chinese Studies in History* 17:2 (1983-84), and Hoklam Chan, *Li Chih (1527-1602) in Contemporary Historiography* (New York: M. E. Sharpe, 1980). For Li Zhi as a humanistic individualist, see William Theodore de Bary, "Individualism and Humanitarianism in Late Ming Thought," in his *Self and Society in Ming Thought* (New York: Columbia University Press, 1970). Willard Peterson describes Li Zhi as a "relativist" throughout his recent contribution to the *Cambridge History of China*. See Dennis C. Twitchett and Frederick W. Mote, eds., *Cambridge History of China*, Volume 8 (Cambridge: Cambridge University Press, 1998), 745-54. For a thorough and incisive criticism of such interpretations and an accurate and revealing account of Li Zhi's philosophy, see Pauline Chen Lee, *Li Zhi (1527-1602): A Feminist Literatus*

in Late Ming China, PhD dissertation, Stanford University, 2002. See also the revealing study of Li Zhi's persecution and eventual suicide by Jiang Jin, "Heresy and Persecution in Late Ming Society—Reinterpreting the Case of Li Zhi," *Late Imperial China* 22.2 (December, 2001): 1-34.

27. There was a rich and fascinating discussion throughout the Chinese tradition on the nature and proper role of the true teacher. This concern was expressed by several early Confucians. For example, see *Xunzi*, "An Exhortation to Learning," in Ivanhoe and Van Norden, *Readings*, 251, 266.

28. Immanuel Kant, *Anthropology from a Pragmatic Point of View*, tr. Mary J. Gregor (The Hague: Nijoff, 1974), 147. Nancy Sherman argues valiantly that Kant in fact sees more than instrumental value in such practices. See chapter 4 of her *Making a Necessity of Virtue: Aristotle and Kant on Virtue* (New York: Cambridge University Press, 1997).

29. In both the *Republic* and the *Laws*, Plato does allow a place for poetry, and in his *Poetics*, Aristotle notes that the catharsis one experiences in the course of watching dramatic productions plays an important part in the development of one's character. Nevertheless, in neither case does literature play a substantial role in moral knowledge or the shaping of character, as it does in the Confucian tradition. Thanks to Eric Hutton for helping me on this point.

30. For example, see *Analects*, 6.27, 9.11, and 12.15.

31. The earliest expression of this idea is the so-called six arts: ritual, music, archery, charioteering, writing, and mathematics.

32. Less plausibly, though characteristically, he also argued for the converse: that the culturally accomplished individual would also be morally good.

33. Zhang Xuecheng expresses all of the ideas mentioned above. The last is developed by him in a distinctive and fascinating way in his essay, "Words for Everyone" (*Yan gong*). For a discussion of this idea, see David S. Nivison, *The Life and Thought of Chang Hsüeh-ch'eng (1738-1801)* (Stanford, CA: Stanford University Press, 1966), 127-33.

34. I have argued that such ideas played an important role in creating an environment in pre-modern China that was not only not conducive to but in certain ways hostile toward a robust conception of intellectual property. See my "Intellectual Property and Traditional Chinese Culture," in *Topics in Contemporary Philosophy, Volume 3, Law and Social Justice*, ed. Joseph Keim Campbell, Michael O'Rourke, and David Shier (Cambridge, MA: MIT Press, 2004), 125-42.

35. In addition, many historians subscribed to the general principle that written histories should judge the past and serve as ethical guides for the future. For an overview of Chinese views about the nature and character of history, see my "History: Chinese Theories of" in *The Routledge Encyclopedia of Philosophy*, Vol. 4, ed. Edward Craig (London: Routledge, 1998), 446-52. In his study of China's first historian, Burton Watson offers an insightful discussion of Sima Qian's (145-90? B.C.E.) approach to history and in particular his use of historical biography. Watson offers a revealing illustration of Sima Qian's approach to historical writing by presenting American history as it might have been seen by him. See *Ssu-ma Ch'ien: Grand Historian of China*, tr. Burton Watson (New York: Columbia University Press, 1958), 104-7. The Chinese preference for historical biography was shared by many intellectuals during the founding period of the United States as witnessed by the popularity of Plutarch's *Lives*. For example, *The Federalist* contains several quotes from the *Life of Pericles*. Thanks to Joel Kupperman for pointing this out to me.

36. In his insightful discussion of the ways in which the practice of rituals can achieve many of the aims that contemporary proponents of literature claim for reading, Eric Hutton notes that the authors of fictional works often try to understand the phenomena they write about either through extensive research or simulation. This shows that they too recognize the need to be constrained by a kind of reality principle. Hutton's discussion of how rituals like fasting can be much more effective than reading about fasting opens up another productive line for comparative inquiry. See Eric L. Hutton, *Virtue and Reason in Xunzi*, PhD Dissertation, Stanford University, (June 2001), 411-36

37. Martha Nussbaum offers a remarkably insightful and moving account of this aspect of the *Odyssey*. See "Transcending Humanity" in Nussbaum, *Love's Knowledge*, 365-91.

38. See Iris Murdoch, "Derrida and Structuralism," in *Metaphysics as a Guide to Morals* (New York: Penguin Press, 1992), 208-9. Murdoch's point is cast more in terms of how human interests constrain the imagination even in the case of the most creative genre, science fiction. See also her remark in "The Ontological Proof," that, "If space visitors tell us that there is no value on their planet, this is not like saying there are no material objects. We would ceaselessly *look* for value in their society, wondering if they were lying, had different values, had misunderstood." (Murdoch, *Metaphysics*, 427)

39. One need not agree with the general Confucian tendency to advocate the banning of wicked books or music in order to engage in their denunciation. Of course in our own society we do in fact ban certain kinds of publications, for example, child pornography and restrict the access of other forms of literature, particularly to the young.

40. The kinds of errors that I have discussed do not exhaust the range of possibilities. For example, one can go wrong reading even good works if one reads selectively and ignores the overall message of a work. Indeed the early Confucian Mengzi noted this as one way one could go wrong in one's study of the classics. See *Mengzi* 5A4, "Those who explicate the *Odes* should not use one word to violate the meaning of a line, nor one line to violate the overall intention [of a poem]." Thanks to Justin Tiwald for help in exploring this possibility.

41. In other published work, Nussbaum does pursue something like the former issue in the specific case of pornography. For example, see *Sex and Social Justice* (New York: Oxford University Press, 1999). In particular, see chapters eight, "Objectivity," and nine, "Rage and Reason," 213-52. Thanks to Justin Tiwald for pointing out the importance of these essays.

42. The capacity of a good teacher to guide one in the proper reading of a text reflects the greater sensitivity and perceptiveness of cultivated individuals. In addition to the case of literature, a good teacher serves as the model and guide for students in their "reading" of music, art, history, and all human actions, and events. A teacher enhances a student's ability to understand what she is looking at and can lead a student to see things in a new light, for example, that a certain act is benevolent or cruel. For example, in *Mengzi* 1A7, one can see Mengzi guiding King Xuan of Qi in the proper "reading" of his action of sparing an ox that was being led to ritual slaughter. He brings the king to see this act as a spontaneous manifestation of compassion. This connects with the point noted earlier about how ethical connoisseurs can help people understand their own experiences as well as the experiences of others. Thanks to Eric Hutton for pointing out the significance of *Mengzi* 1A7 for this set of issues and to T. C. Kline for help in developing this point. For an insightful discussion of the ways in which a good teacher can lead a student to see the world differently—for example in distinctively moral terms—see chapters 3 and 4 of T. C. Kline, *Ethics and Tradition in the Xunzi*, PhD Dissertation, Stanford Uni-

versity (August, 1998), 74-204.

43. The right kind of *dufa* "reading method" might also explore the issue of what general goals and overall effects one should be seeking in terms of how wise people in the past read the texts of their tradition. So the point might be not so much "read the *Book of Odes*" or even "read it with and eye for certain themes and ideas," but rather "consider how Confucius read the *Book of Odes*." What attitudes and expectations did he bring to his reading of the text and how did it affect him? This might help to ameliorate the problems associated with reading certain classical texts, which while extremely valuable in some respects also present beliefs and ideals that are now recognized as narrow and prejudiced. I am indebted to Mark Csikszentmihalyi for raising and helping me to think about this issue.

Chapter Three

Moral Philosophy and Moral Cultivation

William J. Prior

The Insufficiency of Moral Philosophy for Moral Cultivation

Moral cultivation is a practice, any practice, by which one attempts to direct the course of moral development either of oneself or others. The aim of this practice is the attainment of moral wisdom, or the closest approximation to that ideal that human beings can attain. In the ancient Greek tradition of philosophy, as well as in the Chinese tradition, the name often given to one who has attained moral wisdom is "the sage." Writers in the ancient Greek tradition, with which I shall be concerned here, attempt to show that the life of the sage is one that we all have reason to strive to attain, because that life is, of all lives possible for human beings, uniquely, or especially, or most nearly happy. The cultivation of moral wisdom is thus part and parcel of the pursuit of happiness (*eudaimonia*).

The question I wish to discuss in this essay is whether the study of moral philosophy is sufficient for the attainment of moral wisdom. I shall argue that it is not. This may seem an unsurprising conclusion, hardly worth arguing for. Yet in contemporary higher education we approach the teaching of ethics as if the study of moral philosophy were, if not sufficient for the acquisition of moral wisdom, at least the only tool available to us. Even some of the ancient Greek moral philosophers, who I shall argue showed both by their theory and practice that they knew better than this, made very strong claims on behalf of the study of moral philosophy. Socrates, at least as Plato portrays him, seems to regard the acquisition of theoretical knowledge of the nature of the virtues as both necessary and sufficient for the possession of virtue.

The main argument of this paper will be that this view is incorrect. Even the specifically cognitive aspect of moral development requires more than the acquisition of theoretical principles of moral philosophy. It requires as well the development of the ability to discern the moral features of specific situations and the related ability to discern the appropriate course of action to take to address those features. The development of these abilities, which are essential to moral wisdom, is an indispensable part of moral cultivation.

Intellectualism

I do not deny that the study of moral philosophy is a valuable means for understanding what is involved in moral cultivation. I do not deny that the ethical works of the ancient Greek philosophers contain many valuable insights into the nature of moral wisdom. I do not deny that one might be inspired by the reading of these works to embark on a program of moral cultivation. This was the effect, or one of the effects, their authors hoped for them. I deny, however, that these works can provide, in themselves, an adequate guide to one seeking moral enlightenment. No such guide is possible; there is no set of general principles, philosophical or otherwise, the learning of which can constitute moral wisdom. Moral wisdom is not reducible to such a set of rules. The development of moral wisdom is not exclusively, and I think not even primarily, a matter of the internalization of principles. It is more like the development of a skill. The error of thinking that the development of moral wisdom is primarily or exclusively a matter of theoretical understanding I shall call "intellectualism." I shall try to show, by adverting to certain examples from ancient Greek philosophy, why I think intellectualism is mistaken. This has, or should have, rather large implications for the way in which ethics should be taught.

One ancient philosopher, Aristotle, makes the case explicitly for the insufficiency of moral philosophy, construed as the inculcation of abstract moral principles, for moral cultivation. The argument I shall make in this paper owes a great deal to Aristotle's position.[1] It is not clear to me to what extent other ancient philosophers recognized this point in theory. They may have recognized it, however, in practice, and in a couple of different ways. One of these ways involves the use of examples of the sage in their works (and here I have in mind in particular Plato's portrait of Socrates, which I shall discuss below). Another involves the nature of moral education in ancient philosophical schools.

The Teaching of Ethics in Contemporary and Ancient Higher Education

The teaching of ethics in contemporary American colleges and universities is predominately intellectualistic. Students are introduced to the rudiments of moral theories—utilitarianism, Kantian deontology, virtue ethics, and the like—in a way that is intended to be normatively neutral, with no attempt made to get them to make one of these theories their own. They may be asked to apply these competing theories to certain moral problems, but the practice here is purely intellectual and the intended outcome is understanding, not moral growth.

This practice is defended on the ground that intellectual understanding is the only legitimate goal of classroom instruction, or is all that can be achieved in the classroom. Sometimes the practitioners of this approach to ethics argue that it does lead to the moral improvement of students, but the connection between developing an ability to argue about the application of various moral theories and moral transformation is tenuous, to say the least. All who have taught moral philosophy in this way are familiar with the student who has mastered the material of the course and yet remains to all intents and purposes unaffected by them.

In the classrooms of the ancient Greek philosophical schools there was no pretense to neutrality. If one went to study with a Stoic or an Epicurean philosopher, one did so with the intention that the principles of Stoic or Epicurean philosophy would become ingrained in one's character. As Pierre Hadot has argued, philosophy was understood by the ancients as a way of life.[2] The promise made by the teachers of these schools was, "Come here for instruction and you will attain wisdom." In order for this promise to be realized, both student and teacher understood, the student had not merely to come to an understanding of the principles of the school; he or she had to adopt and internalize them.

It *may* be that the philosophers who taught in these schools thought that the inculcation of moral principles was sufficient for the acquisition of moral wisdom. In that case, they would be intellectualists, though intellectualists of a different sort than those described above with regard to contemporary American higher education. Some of the works of these schools, such as the *Principal Doctrines* of Epicureanism, read like intellectualist tracts. But it also may be that one purpose of teaching principles of moral philosophy in schools was so that the students could benefit from the personal example of a teacher who, if he was not a sage, was nevertheless advanced in moral wisdom. The ethical treatises of these schools, which *we* read as intellectualist tracts, may have served a different purpose in them. They may have supplemented, rather than replaced, the kind of personal instruction I shall describe below. If that is the case, then the ancient approach to the cultivation of moral wisdom would have been Aristotelian in practice, if not always explicitly so in theory.

The Role of Principles in Moral Education

When I argue that the inculcation of principles is insufficient for the cultivation of moral wisdom, I do not mean to deny that principles have a valuable, indeed an indispensable role, in ethics. There is a part of ethics in which the inculcation of principle is virtually everything. In this part of ethics, the right thing to do can

William J. Prior

be summarized in a simple prescription or prohibition: "Tell the truth," "Don't lie." A minimal amount of interpretive skill is needed to apply such principles in particular situations, but they are, as moral principles go, fairly self-explanatory. There are more general principles, such as "Respect humanity," and "Love your neighbor as yourself," that require more by way of interpretation, but the principles themselves are of primary importance.

I consider these principles to be the "elementary school" portion of moral development. They are what one must know, what one must have adopted and internalized, even to be admitted to the more advanced levels of moral cultivation. I do not wish to deny that there can be very sophisticated moral theories developed to justify these moral principles. I only deny that the learning of these theories is an essential element in moral cultivation. Consider the remark of Epictetus, critical of even the ancient practice of moral education:

> The first and most necessary department of philosophy deals with the application of moral principles; for instance, "not to lie." The second deals with demonstrations; for instance, "How comes it that one ought to lie?" The third is concerned with establishing and analyzing these processes; for instance, "How comes it that this is a demonstration? What is demonstration, what is consequence, what contradiction, what is true, what is false?" It follows then that the third department is necessary because of the second, and the second because of the first. The first is the most necessary part, and that in which we must rest. But we reverse the order: we occupy ourselves with the third, and make that our whole concern, and the first we completely neglect. Wherefore we lie, but are ready enough with the demonstration that lying is wrong. (*Manual*, 52; P. E. Matheson, trans.)

The Inculcation of Principles vs. the Development of Judgment

It does not matter for the purposes of my argument whether we treat these principles as the first stage of moral education or as a propaideutic to it. I do not wish to deny that these principles have a valid place; the later stages of moral cultivation, however, do not much resemble this initial stage of the inculcation and internalization of principle.

This is a point that was recognized by Kant.[3] In the *Groundwork* Kant distinguished between moral principles, which were derivable from the categorical imperative, formulable in propositions and could be applied without much difficulty, and what he called "counsels of prudence." Kant doesn't say this explicitly, but he must have thought that ancient Greek moral philosophy consisted primarily of such counsels. These counsels were concerned with happiness; but happiness, Kant thought, was far too vague a goal to yield universal principles. Instead, he noted, it yielded maxims that were at best rules of thumb:

the concept of happiness is so indeterminate a concept that although every man wants to attain happiness, he never can say definitely and in unison with himself what it is that he really wants and wills. The reason for this is that all the elements which belong to the concept of happiness are without exception empirical—that is, that they must be borrowed from experience; but that none the less there is required for the Idea of happiness an absolute whole, a maximum of well-being in my present, and in every future, state. Now it is impossible for the most intelligent, and at the same time most powerful, but nevertheless finite, being to form here a determinate concept of what he really wills. Is it riches that he wants? How much anxiety, envy, and pestering might he not bring in this way on his own head! Is it knowledge and insight? This might perhaps merely give him an eye so sharp that it would make evils at present hidden from him and yet unavoidable seem all the more frightful, or would add a load of still further needs to the desires which already give him trouble enough. Is it long life? Who will guarantee that it would not be a long misery? Is it at least health? How often has infirmity of body kept a man from excesses into which perfect health would have let him fall!—and so on. In short, he has no principle by which he is able to decide with complete certainty what will make him truly happy, since for this he would require omniscience. Thus we cannot act on determinate principles in order to be happy, but only on empirical counsels, for example, of diet, frugality, politeness, reserve, and so on—things which experience shows contribute most to well-being on the average. From this it follows that imperatives of prudence, speaking strictly, do not command at all—that is, cannot exhibit actions objectively as practically *necessary*; that they are rather to be taken as recommendations (*consilia*), than as commands (*praecepta*), of reason; that the problem of determining certainly and universally what action will promote the happiness of a rational being is completely insoluble; and consequently that in regard to this there is no imperative possible which in the strictest sense could command us to do what will make us happy, since happiness is an Ideal, not of reason, but of imagination—an Ideal resting merely on empirical grounds, of which it is vain to expect that they should determine an action by which we could attain the totality of a series of consequences which is in fact infinite.[4]

For this reason Kant, at least in the *Groundwork*, dismissed the part of ethics that was concerned with human happiness. (The conception of happiness that Kant makes use of, a conception that defines happiness in terms of the satisfaction of desire or inclination, is quite different from the ancient conception of human flourishing or *eudaimonia*.) When he attempts to apply his theoretical understanding of moral principle to the subject matter of ancient ethics, in *The Doctrine of Virtue*, the results are, to my mind, unsatisfactory. Though Kant is wrong to dismiss the discussion of happiness, or to relegate it to a secondary role, he is right to think that it differs in a fundamental way from the discussion of moral principle.

Aristotle also recognizes in a way the difference between the part of ethics that is concerned with principles and the part that is concerned with the cultivation of *eudaimonia*. In *Nicomachean Ethics* II.6, after defining moral virtue in terms of a mean between two vices, he writes:

> Not every action nor every emotion admits of a mean. There are some actions and emotions whose very names connote baseness, e.g. spite, shamelessness, envy; and among actions, adultery, theft, and murder. These and similar emotions and actions imply by their very names that they are bad; it is not their excess or deficiency which is called bad. It is, therefore, impossible ever to do right in performing them: to perform them is always to do wrong. In cases of this sort, let us say adultery, rightness and wrongness do not depend on committing it with the right woman at the right time and in the right manner, but the mere fact of committing such action at all is to do wrong. (1107a8-17; Martin Ostwald, trans.)

Aristotle here makes a distinction similar to that made by Kant between a part of ethics that is concerned with exceptionless principles and a part concerned with measure and proportion. Unlike Kant, he has no theoretical account of what makes those actions wrong that are always, without exception, wrong. This is almost the only passage in the *Ethics* in which he considers such actions. He agrees, with Kant, however, on the distinction between the two parts of ethics, and on the fact that the part that is concerned with happiness cannot be reduced to a set of exceptionless principles.

The Wisdom of the Sage: Knowing What Is Valuable

The ancients saw the acquisition of moral wisdom as a process whereby the student is gradually transformed into the sage, or someone like the sage. Part of what this involves is coming to know what the sage knows. What is it that makes the sage wise, if not moral principles alone? Part of the answer to this question lies in the fact that the sage knows what things in life are most valuable. The following paragraph from Philippa Foot's essay, "Virtues and Vices," illustrates this point:

> One of the things a wise man knows and a foolish man does not is that such things as social position, and wealth, and the good opinion of the world, are too dearly bought at the cost of health or friendship or family ties. So we may say that a man who lacks wisdom "has false values," and that vices such as vanity and worldliness and avarice are contrary to wisdom in a special way. There is always an element of false judgement about these vices, since the man who is vain for instance sees admiration as more important than it is, while the worldly man is apt to see the good life as one of wealth and power.[5]

Foot claims to find this part of moral wisdom "curiously elusive"; she says, "I have never seen, or been able to think out, a true account of this matter."[6] In contrast with Foot, I think this aspect of moral wisdom fairly straightforward. It is true, as she says, that "most men waste a lot of their lives in ardent pursuit of what is trivial and unimportant,"[7] and it is tempting to infer that many who do so fail to recognize certain truths that the sage recognizes. But the truths themselves are simple and easy to formulate, as Foot's own remarks show. Money doesn't buy happiness. It profiteth not a man if he gain the entire world, and lose his soul. One ought not to sacrifice friends or family for worldly success. Such statements, I think, would be accepted in the abstract by most people, even those whose lives seem to us to be at odds with them. This makes one wonder whether those people who spend their lives, or large parts of them, in ardent pursuit of the trivial have failed to understand the abstract point or have rather failed to make that point a practical, operational part of their lives. Though they would assent to the claims of the sage about what is of greatest value, their lives betray what I shall call a lack of *practical*, as opposed to abstract or theoretical, comprehension.

The life of the sage seems different from the life of the ordinary person. Take, as an obvious example from the Greek tradition, Socrates. Socrates neglected the practical pursuits of wealth and political power popular among his fellow Athenians in favor of the pursuit of philosophical, and specifically ethical, wisdom. This pursuit was, by his own admission, and by his own criteria, spectacularly unsuccessful: he claimed that he had attained no moral wisdom at all beyond the awareness of the extent of his own ignorance. (Yet Socrates was the least controversial example of a philosopher who lived the life of a sage in ancient Greek philosophy. Even members of schools such as the Stoics that were rivals to the Platonic school saw Socrates as a sage, perhaps as the only sage. Later in the paper I shall attempt to explain why Socrates' wisdom could be seen as distinct from any particular set of philosophical moral principles.) Plato in the dialogues shows Socrates in conversation with a number of people who reject this pursuit of philosophical wisdom as the pathway to happiness: Callicles and Thrasymachus are examples that spring to mind. Most of Socrates' interlocutors, however, don't raise questions about the value of philosophical wisdom; they just seem unable to incorporate this pursuit, whose value they don't question, within their lives. Alcibiades, who speaks more eloquently about the allure of Socrates than any other character in the dialogues also describes the practical conflict between the attractions of the philosophical life and the (theoretically inferior but, for him, practically more insistent) attractions of political power (cf. *Symposium* 215a-222a).

One part of the wisdom of the sage, then, is a recognition that is more than theoretical of the relative value of various goods. We might say that the life of the sage shows a level of practical commitment to certain goods, goods that we find of central importance to living the good life. The fact that people whose lives are characterized by "ardent pursuit of what is trivial and unimportant" may nonetheless find the sage an admirable figure without being able to emulate him or her very closely indicates that one may possess a certain amount of abstract theoretical appreciation of certain goods but be unable to live in accordance with that appreciation. This is probably the way life is for most of us, most of the time, or so I suspect. We might wish we were more like Socrates, or Jesus, or Gandhi, but wishing doesn't take us very far.

The Wisdom of the Sage: Knowing What to Do

Still, this part of the wisdom of the sage is, as I have indicated, relatively easy to formulate and to understand, if not to exemplify. The difficult part of the wisdom of the sage, in my view, is his or her ability to put this understanding of what is valuable into concrete action. This part I shall call the practical wisdom of the sage. Practical wisdom is the ability to find the right or best thing to do in each and every concrete situation, or at least to do so a high percentage of the time. Human judgment being inherently fallible, and practical matters being inherently uncertain, the ideal of an error-free life seems to be just that, an ideal. If we are not to assert that it is impossible for anyone at all to become a sage, we must describe a sage as one who comes closer to this ideal than others, not as one who achieves it perfectly over the course of an entire life.

Why is the practical attainment of right action so difficult to understand? As I have indicated up to this point, it is because the reasoning of the sage is not reducible to universal principles that can be clearly stated and transmitted to another. That is not to say that the sage may be unable to formulate such principles. When Aristotle defines virtue as the mean between two extremes he states that this mean is "defined by a rational principle" (*E. N.* II.6, 1107a1). This principle, however, is not a universal one, applicable to all persons in all situations. It is specific to the person and the situation involved. In contrast with universal principles such as the wrongness of lying, the practical principles of virtuous conduct *are* concerned with finding the right amount or degree in relation to the right person at the right time:

> We can experience fear, confidence, desire, anger, pity and generally any kind of pleasure and pain either too much or too little, and in either case not properly. But to experience all this at the right time, toward the right objects, toward the right people, for the right reason, and in the right manner—that is the median and the best course, the course that is the mark of virtue. (II.6, 1106b18-23)

Aristotle famously regards virtue as a mean, but the mean is not an arithmetic one:

> By the median relative to us I understand an amount neither too large nor too small, and this is neither one nor the same for everybody. To take an example: if ten is many and two is few, six is taken as the median in relation to the entity, for it exceeds and is exceeded by the same amount, and is thus the median in terms of arithmetic proportion. But the median relative to us cannot be determined in this manner: if ten pounds of food is much for a man to eat and two pounds little, it does not follow that the trainer will prescribe six pounds, for this in turn may be much or little for him to eat; it may be little for Milo and much for someone who has just begun to take up athletics. (II.6, 1106a31-b4)

A rule or principle that applies in one situation or in regard to one person may not apply in another. Aristotle brings this out by means of several examples. I shall mention only two: one that is concerned with the situation, and one that is concerned with the person. Considering the issue of voluntariness in action, Aristotle make use of the example of cargo jettisoned in a storm "Considering the action itself, nobody would throw away property," he writes; "but when it is a matter of saving one's own life and that of his fellow passengers, any sensible man would do so." (III.1, 1110a9-11) One might object that this action can be brought under a general rule, such as the following: "When faced with loss of life at sea, which can be prevented by jettisoning cargo, then jettison cargo." Such a rule is of little help in practice, however, for it does not tell us what situations are life-threatening. The practically wise individual is the one who neither throws away the cargo unnecessarily, nor holds onto it to his or her own misfortune, but who does what the circumstances require.

Consider now the matter of individual differences. As Aristotle acknowledges, people are differently endowed by nature with the basis for the virtues (VI.13, 1144b34-45a1), just as we are have different physical endowments. One of the ways in which we differ is in our susceptibility to temptations, the matters in which we feel pleasure and pain. As Aristotle notes (II.3), pleasure and pain are closely connected to virtue. Still, our susceptibilities in these matters may differ. Alcohol may have for you a strong allure, and leave me cold; I may, in contrast, be easily tempted by food, which has little attraction for you. Part of what is involved in the development of virtue, then, is the identification and regulation of those temptations that are particularly troublesome for us individually:

> We must watch the errors which have the greatest attraction for us personally. For the natural inclination of one man differs from that of another, and we each come to recognize our own by observing the pleasure and pain produced in us [by different extremes]. We must then draw ourselves away in the opposite direction, for by pulling away from error we shall reach the middle, as men do when they straighten warped timber. In every case we must be especially on our guard against pleasure and what is pleasant, for when it comes to pleasure we cannot act as unbiased judges. (II.9, 1109b1-9)

It is because of the variability in our natural temperament as well as in the situations we face that we are unable to define virtuous activity in terms of abstract, universal principles alone:

> Any discussion on matters of action cannot be more than an outline and is bound to lack precision; for as we stated at the outset, one can demand of a discussion only what the subject matter permits, and there are no fixed data in matters concerning action and questions of what is beneficial, any more than there are in matters of health. And if this is true of our general discussion, our treatment of particular problems will be even less precise, *since these do not come under the head of any art which can be transmitted by precept, but the*

agent must consider on each different occasion what the situation demands,
just as in medicine and in navigation. (II.2, 1104a1-10; italics added)

Perception

If Aristotle's description of the process of moral decision-making is correct, no
knowledge of universal principles *by itself* will lead us to act ethically. We require, in addition, both self-knowledge, knowledge of our own strengths and
weaknesses, and knowledge of the particular situation. How is such knowledge
attained? Aristotle has a short answer to this question: by perception. Consider
this remark:

> [I]t is not easy to determine in what manner, with what person, on what occa-
> sion, and for how long a time one ought to be angry. . . . However, we do not
> blame a man for slightly deviating from the course of goodness, whether he
> strays toward excess or toward deficiency, but we do blame him if his deviation
> is great and cannot pass unnoticed. It is not easy to determine by a formula at
> what point and for how great a divergence a man deserves blame; but this diffi-
> culty is, after all, true of all objects of sense perception: determinations of this
> kind depend upon particular circumstances and the decision rests with our
> [moral] sense. (II.9, 1109b14-23)

The word that Ostwald translates "[moral] sense" is *aesthesis*, normally
translated "perception." In the passage above Aristotle links this kind of *aesthesis* with sense perception, but later he distinguishes them:

> [P]ractical wisdom has as its object the ultimate particular fact, of which there
> is perception but no scientific knowledge. This perception is not the kind with
> which [each of our five senses apprehends] its proper object, but the kind with
> which we perceive that in mathematics the triangle is the ultimate figure. For in
> this direction, too, we shall have to reach a stop. (VI.8, 1142a 25-29)

The comparison with mathematical knowledge is worth considering. If
Ostwald is correct,[8] Aristotle is talking about the ability to "see" that a geomet-
rical figure can be resolved into a number of triangles. This is a form of intuition. It is not the same as the insight into basic principles that Aristotle calls
nous, and which he discusses elsewhere in Book VI of the *Nicomachean Ethics*
(chiefly in Chapter 6). What it has in common with *nous*, however, and for that
matter with practical wisdom, is that it is a grasp of something ultimate from an
explanatory point of view. (That is why we "reach a stop" when we grasp it.)
We may remember being puzzled when studying geometry in school by some
construction or other, and suddenly "seeing" the solution. (The phenomenon is
the one that produces the conviction, "Now I can go on," as Wittgenstein notes.)
We might contrast this quasi-visual experience with performing the same construction in accordance with a set of instructions ("Given a line AB, first bisect

it, then construct a line CD perpendicular to AB from the midpoint of AB." And so on.) According to Aristotle, the perception involved in practical wisdom is similar in nature. One may be puzzled by a practical problem, then suddenly perceive the solution to it, and be able to "go on" by performing the appropriate action. Of course, not every solution reached by practical reason is preceded by puzzlement, nor is every problem equally difficult. In some cases the solution is obvious at once. In others, it eludes the deliberative faculty of the wisest people after prolonged consideration. Still, there are cases of the sort Aristotle describes: the sage "sees" the right thing to do in the situation at hand. The mental phenomenon is akin to a gestalt shift; it is what Wittgenstein refers to as the dawning of an aspect. What distinguishes the sage from ordinary people is that the sage has these moments of insight more regularly than others, and that the discernment is more often genuine rather than spurious.

What is the nature of this perceptual ability? Aristotle does not say a great deal about it. Two contemporary philosophers who do are John McDowell[9] and Lawrence Blum.[10] They describe it as the ability to perceive certain "salient" features of a particular situation. I think there are two possible ways of describing this "perception of salience." It might be a purely cognitive, normatively neutral apprehension of a particular feature of a situation. In one of Blum's examples, the perception is that a woman standing on the subway is uncomfortable.[11] It is at least theoretically possible, I think, that one could perceive this fact without feeling called upon to respond in any way, even if an appropriate response, such as surrendering one's seat to her, were within one's power. On the other hand, we might understand this perception as providing a reason for action, though perhaps not an overriding one. Contrast the situation in which Bob, seated on the subway, sees that a woman passenger who is standing is uncomfortable, but is not motivated to respond to her discomfort, with that of Charles, who sees the woman's discomfort as a morally relevant fact that calls for action. Charles may be unable to do anything practical in the situation: perhaps he is standing himself, or riding with a small child on his lap; but he "feels the tug" of the morally salient fact in a way that Bob does not. Contrast both Bob and Charles with Roger, who simply does not notice the woman's discomfort at all, though he is in the same perceptual situation as they.

Blum, I think, tends to understand the perception of salience in the normatively neutral way, whereas McDowell understands it in the normatively laden one. For Aristotle, I think, the situation is complex. I believe he would say that the cognitive component of perception is theoretically separable from the conative, but that in practice they are generally found together. It is the virtuous person who sees what is morally salient in most situations, and the virtuous person sees the morally salient fact as a reason for action because he or she already is predisposed by virtue to act appropriately. Still, it is possible for someone to know, or at least be able to say, that a certain feature of a situation is morally relevant and yet not be motivated to act on it: consider the morally weak person, for example.

Let us suppose, then, that the purely cognitive perception of morally salient facts is theoretically separable, but perhaps only rarely psychologically separable, from motivation to action. Both the virtuous and the vicious or morally weak person may be able to perceive the morally salient facts in a given situation, though only the virtuous person sees these facts as a reason for action. Still, there is more involved in perception. For Aristotle, recall, moral perception was like the visualization of a construction in a mathematical example. It is more than a perception of a problem: it is the perception of a solution, indeed the best solution, to the problem. As Blum notes, one may perceive a morally salient feature of a situation, and see this feature as one demanding some response, and yet not know how to respond. To cite another of his examples: a cab driver passes by a black mother and child to pick up a white male passenger. The passenger, Tim, sees this as a racially based slight of the woman, and he is opposed to racism. But what is he to do? Blum notes: "Tim could be entirely and sincerely committed to opposing racism and injustice (and for the right reasons), yet be a poor judge of what doing this actually involves in this or other particular situations."[12]

The sage is distinguished not only by his or her ability to perceive the morally salient features of various situations, but also by the ability to see what is to be done to rectify the situation. Beyond this, the sage is distinguished by the fact that this perception leads directly to right or good action. The sage is a moral agent, not just a commentator on the actions of others. Philippa Foot captures this fact in a passage from "Virtues and Vices," in which she quotes from a novel by John Hersey:

> Thus it seems right to attribute a kind of moral failing to some deeply discouraging and debilitating people who say, without lying, that they mean to be helpful; and on the other side to see virtue *par excellence* in one who is prompt and resourceful in doing good. In his novel *A Single Pebble* John Hersey describes such a man, speaking of a rescue in a swift flowing river: "It was the head tracker's marvelous swift response that captured my admiration at first, his split second solicitousness when he heard a cry of pain, his finding in mid-air, as it were, the only way to save the injured boy. But there was more to it than that. His action, which could not have been mulled over in his mind, showed a deep, instinctive love of life, a compassion, an optimism, which made me feel very good."[13]

The relevant feature of the action described above is not only the fact that it was lightning-quick, almost instinctive, but that it was the *right* action in the context, "the only way" to save the injured boy. The tracker's action required more than moral virtue; it required a set of physical skills that not all virtuous agents might possess. But the ability to find the right course of action in a situation where moral goods are at stake is definitely a part of moral virtue; and it does not seem unreasonable to describe it, in cases of this sort at least, as a matter of *perception*.

How Is Perception Developed?

How is this complex ability first to discern morally salient features in particular situations and second to find the correct course of action in those situations acquired?

There seem to be two possibilities: the first, that it is a mysterious natural endowment that one either has or lacks; the second, that it is a skill that can be developed. Aristotle favors the latter answer. If the former were the case, there would not be any point in trying to develop moral education beyond what I have called the "elementary school" stage of the inculcation of principles. Society would consist of two kinds of people: those with insight and those without it. The latter would have to defer to the former in all matters involving complex decision-making. Plato at times seems to invoke this model when he speaks of "the moral expert," as at *Crito* 47c-48a. Aristotle, in contrast, thinks that the capacity for virtue, and thus for happiness, is virtually universal among people of normal psychological capacity (I.9, esp. 1099b18-20).

Let us pursue the second possibility, since the first offers virtually no hope for advanced moral education. If practical wisdom is a skill that can be acquired, what is the process by which it is acquired? An Aristotelian answer would focus on at least two aspects of moral education. The first is moral training. One develops the moral aspects of virtue, the parts that apply specifically to one's character, by practice. As Aristotle says in II.2 and 4, we become virtuous by performing virtuous acts. Aristotle compares this moral habituation to the development of artistic skill. His focus in these passages is on the training of character rather than on the development of cognitive discernment. Still, we might well think that, just as the artist's cognitive abilities are sharpened in the course of practice, so might the moral agent's be. By performing repeated just acts the agent might develop not only a disposition to be just but superior discernment of the nature of just actions themselves.

Experience

Moral discernment might be enhanced, however, by a second method as well, a method that focuses on the cognitive aspects of moral wisdom. Perception, says Aristotle, is shaped by experience.

> While young men do indeed become good geometricians and mathematicians and attain theoretical wisdom in such matters, they apparently do not attain practical wisdom. The reason is that practical wisdom is concerned with particulars as well [as with universals], and knowledge of particulars comes from experience. But a young man has no experience, for experience is the product of a long time. (VI.8, 1142a 12-16)

Experience, as Aristotle explains in *Metaphysics* I.1, is a certain kind of knowledge of particulars:

Now from memory experience is produced in men; for the several memories of the same thing produce finally the capacity for a single experience. . . . [T]o have a judgment that when Callias was ill of this disease this did him good, and similarly in the case of Socrates and in many individual cases, is a matter of experience. . . . With a view to action experience seems in no respect inferior to art, and men of experience succeed even better than those who have theory without experience. The reason is that experience is knowledge of individuals, art of universals, and actions and productions are all concerned with the individual; for the physician does not cure *man*, except in an incidental way, but Callias or Socrates or some other called by some such individual name, who happens to be a man. If, then, a man has the theory without the experience, and recognizes the universal but does not know the individual included in this, he will often fail to cure; for it is the individual that is to be cured. . . . [M]en of experience know that the thing is so, but do not know why. (980 b28-981 a1; a7-9; a12-28; W.D. Ross, trans.)

Not all experience is specifically moral, but experience in moral matters is what gives the sage knowledge of what to do in particular cases. Now long life by itself does not suffice to give one experiential knowledge, but Aristotle clearly regards such knowledge as the exclusive possession of those who have lived a long time. That is not to say, however, that it can only be acquired "first hand"; one can pick up a certain amount of experience, school oneself in moral judgment, by associating with those who already have this sort of wisdom: "[W]e ought to pay as much attention to the sayings and opinions, undemonstrated as they are, of wise and experienced older men as we do to demonstrated truths. For experience has given such men an eye with which they can see correctly." (VI.11, 1143b 11-14)

The implications for moral cultivation of the account just outlined seem clear. The very best way to become a sage oneself would be to enter, when young, into a relationship of discipleship with one who is already a sage. As I mentioned at the outset of the paper, this may be what ancient schools of philosophy offered their students. (Of course, the prospective students faced difficulties in identifying wise teachers before they had become wise themselves; such difficulties face everyone who seeks advanced moral education, both then and now.) The sage might be able, if he or she were a philosopher, to transmit to the student principles of moral conduct. More important, however, the sage would be able to discuss both his or her own moral actions and the actions of the student. By the discussion of particular cases, whether accompanied or not by moral precept, the sage would instruct the disciple in the act of moral discernment. Much of this discussion, but by no means all, would be retrospective. "What was it you saw in that situation," the disciple might ask, "that enabled you to reach the decision you did?" And the sage would reply with an account of the case that revealed its salient moral features. Moral education, on this account, is in part learning to see what the sage sees.

Even more important than the discussion of cases, however, might be the moral actions of the sage. It is for these that the sage would acquire a reputation for ethical wisdom, and a following among the young. Sometimes, indeed, the sage might be unable to explain exactly why a certain action seemed or did not seem right. Still, the disciple might find observing the sage in action in these cases to be morally edifying.

Suppose for a moment that the sage has no moral principles to transmit, no teaching. Suppose further that he has, on occasion, nothing to say about particular actions that is helpful to the disciple. This was the condition of Socrates, whose only explanation for refusal to act on some occasions was that his divine sign forbade him. Still, a disciple of Socrates might benefit from associating with him precisely by observing Socrates' actions. He would see Socrates acting bravely in battle, resisting the seductive attractions of Alcibiades, refusing to apprehend and turn over to the Thirty Leon of Salamis, refusing to try the generals *en masse* after the battle of Arginusae, refusing to leave Athens to escape the death penalty. Most important, perhaps, he would see Socrates every day conducting philosophical inquiry as if it were the thing that mattered most in life. Sometimes Socrates has a rational defense of his actions (as in the *Crito*); sometimes he has, or at least offers, none. One might debate concerning particular actions whether Socrates' choice was actually the wisest one possible. Still, the many young people who followed Socrates must have been drawn to him by the integrity of his actions, and indeed of his life. If they came to Socrates hoping that he would transmit to them a set of moral principles, or a method of moral reasoning that would enable them always to choose rightly (something of the sort that at least some Sophists offered to provide) they would be disappointed; for Socrates had no such set of principles or decision procedure to give. What he had was his own example. For those relatives of Socrates' disciples who offered to defend Socrates in court, the beneficial effect of his association with their relatives must have been clear. Socrates improved the youth by exhibiting moral virtue in action, not by precept.

The example of the sage is more important than his or her precepts. The precepts might be wrong, or at any rate inaccurate, incomplete or misleading, though the life of the sage is exemplary. Still, the association with the sage is valuable. It is the sage's ability to make those precepts real in life, or at any rate to find the right course of action, that may "rub off" on the disciple. If it were not so, we would not be envious of those who had the opportunity to know the great sages, such as Socrates and Jesus, or in our day Gandhi and Schweitzer, to name just a few, at first hand. Each of these wrote down, or had disciples who wrote down, the essential principles of their moral philosophies. If the experience of the example of the sage did not add something vital to the set of principles, we might be able, by the study of those principles, to attain the wisdom of these four persons. It has been the argument of this paper that we cannot.

Socrates, I claimed above, is the clearest example in antiquity of the sage. I suspect, though I cannot prove, that other philosophers who attracted students to their schools did so at least as much by example as by precept. (Consider in this context the remark of Aristotle in *E.N.* X.2 about Eudoxus, who made hedonism seem philosophically respectable because he was himself an admirable human being. I think this point was recognized by Plato, and was one reason for his writing in the way he did.)[14] If Plato recognized that the influence of Socrates on him was not just a matter of Socrates' moral doctrines (for Socrates claimed to have none), but of his moral example, that would explain why Plato attempts in his dialogues not just to present Socrates' moral reasoning but to present the person of Socrates himself. Many young people come to philosophy through Plato's dialogues. They become students of philosophy not just because they share a set of views with Socrates or Plato, but because they are inspired by the life and actions of Socrates. (For the same reason many readers of the Gospels become Christians.) If the argument I have been making so far is correct, this personal attachment is far from irrelevant to one's moral development. In a discussion of the *Symposium* my friend Giovanni Ferrari criticizes Alcibiades for his erotic attachment to Socrates: "Instead of falling in love with wisdom," he writes, "he falls in love with the wisdom-lover."[15] If Alcibiades' love for Socrates is based, as I believe it is, on the moral quality of Socrates' life, such love is anything but a mistake. It is an invaluable aspect of moral development.

What are we to do if we do not have access to a sage? One answer would be to study the sage at second-hand, through the writings, for instance, of Plato. Related to this would be what I shall call the "moral" study of literature. Most moral philosophy, I have claimed, gives us abstract principles. Though it may apply these principles to examples, the examples usually abstract from the character of the agents who figure in them. We hear about Smith and Brown, or Jim and Pedro, but the framer of the example does little or nothing to help us understand their particular motivations and character. In literature, on the other hand, the representation of character is a major part of the writer's task. We get to see how a certain sort of person, whom we get to know well over the course of the work, would respond to various serious challenges of the sort we meet in life. Here examples of error and failure can be as instructive as examples of correct decision and success.

Such study of literature, which views the characters of a novel, story or play as if they were real people, is out of fashion at present. Part of the reason for this unpopularity is the failure to distinguish the moral study of literature from what I shall call the "moralistic" study of literature: the kind of approach that attempts to reduce the moral "point" of a work of art to a single "lesson" that can be formulated in words, perhaps even as an abstract moral principle. This reduction of great art to a sampler formula is of course objectionable, and ought to be discouraged; but it is exactly the opposite of what I am recommending. I am seeking instead a complex appreciation of the characters of works of narrative art, one that brings out the many features that enter into the decisions made by the characters. This form of discussion may violate a canon of literary study by treating the characters as if they were real people, rather than according to the canons of one aesthetic approach or another; but it is not simplistic in its aim.

A second aid to moral development along the same lines would be the moral study of history and biography. Here the problem of treating characters as real people does not arise, because it is real people we are concerned with. Here again I must distinguish what I have in mind from the kind of sanitized presentation of historical figures of history and literature that used to be (and for all I know may still be) offered in schools. What I have in mind, rather, is the detailed and complex study of individual lives, seen in historical context, that was offered in the ancient world, for example, by Thucydides and Plutarch. The portraits offered by these authors of such people as Pericles, Nicias and Alcibiades were of course influenced by the authors' conception of the nature of their project. The historian undoubtedly has a view, which the moral philosopher may not accept, of the power of individual decisions to influence historical events. Even if the moral philosopher does not share all the presuppositions of the historian, however, there is much to be learned from the historian's presentation of his or her understanding of the character and actions of a given historical individual. One of the ways in which the study of such works could be valuable is in making the younger reader, who is thinking, perhaps of embarking on a career that follows in the footsteps of that of Socrates or Nicias, of the possible costs of such a career. One might be inclined to see only the attractions; the historian points out the pitfalls as well. This has application to the question of moral character, with which we are concerned. Integrity is undoubtedly a virtue, but one who undertakes to be a person of integrity should be aware that his fellow citizens may require him to take poison. Piety is also a virtue, but one who sets out on the religious life must realize that the military campaign one undertakes as a general may come to grief as a result of it. (This is not to discourage development of these virtues, or any others, but only to make the point that the world is not made in such a way as to ensure that virtue is always appropriately rewarded.)

Practical Conclusion

I conclude with a practical observation. If what I have argued so far is correct— that is, if the best way to provide advanced moral education is by the close association of a disciple or group of disciples with a person who exemplifies practical wisdom—the university that intends to be an instrument of moral education should aim at the creation and sustaining of these relationships. It should hire faculty who are morally experienced and as morally wise as possible and put them in close contact with the students who are admitted to the university, so that these students have the opportunity to learn from the moral decision-making of their elders. It should further encourage these faculty members, and indeed all of its faculty, to act as mentors to students who present themselves for moral education.

Faculty should not eschew, as many now do in the name of protecting the moral freedom of youth, or diffidence, or for some other reason, the task of moral education. We need not be sages; it is sufficient that we are somewhat further down the road of moral experience than the students we seek to educate (as Protagoras claims, and to my mind truthfully claims to be in Plato's *Protagoras*, at 328a-b). We need not actively seek the role of mentor; if we cultivate our own moral wisdom, students will seek us out. All that is necessary is that we accept the role of moral educator when it is imposed on us, in the realization that the moral wisdom of young people can be developed in no other way than by our example.

If this understanding of the nature of moral education, or the part of it that goes beyond what I earlier called the "elementary school" phase in which people learn basic moral principles, were accepted by universities, and if those universities who accept the moral education of the young as a goal were to institutionalize the practices implied by that understanding, I think the modern university would be changed almost beyond recognition. The change, however, would not be one that brought about something that never existed before; it would, rather, be one that restored something that existed in the philosophical schools of antiquity and, to a lesser extent, in the colleges and universities of Western Europe and the United States until fairly recently. So my practical proposal is for a return to the practices of the past, but of course with the proviso that they must be adapted to the circumstances of the present. That would be enough, I think, to keep us busy for some time.

Notes

1. I make rather extensive use of Aristotle, and in particular of the *Nicomachean Ethics*, in this paper. This use reflects my conviction that Aristotle's account of the nature of ethics is, at least in its outlines, true. My aim is not to offer a scholarly interpretation of Aristotle's text, but to philosophize from an Aristotelian perspective.

2. Pierre Hadot, *Philosophy as a Way of Life: Spiritual Exercises from Socrates to Foucault* (Oxford: Blackwell Publishers Ltd., 1995).

3. I thank Scott LaBarge for reminding me of this point.

4. Immanuel Kant, *Groundwork of the Metaphysics of Morals*, tr. H. J. Paton (New York: Harper & Row, 1964), 85-86 (418-19).

5. Philippa Foot, "Virtues and Vices," in *Virtues and Vices and Other Essays in Moral Philosophy* (Berkeley: University of California Press, 1978), 7-8.

6. Foot, "Virtues and Vices," 7. Note that Foot's problem lies with the difficulty of providing an account of the matter; she does not question the truth of the wise person's values.

7. Foot, "Virtues and Vices," 7.

8. Martin Ostwald, translator, Aristotle, *Nicomachean Ethics* (New York: Macmillan, 1962), 161, n. 37.

9. "Virtue and Reason," in *Virtue Ethics*, ed. Roger Crisp and Michael Slote (Oxford: Oxford University Press, 1997), 141-62.

10. Lawrence Blum, "Moral Perception and Particularity," *Ethics* 101 (1991): 701-25.

11. Blum, "Moral Perception," 702-4.

12. Blum, "Moral Perception," 709.

13. Foot, "Virtues and Vices," 4-5.

14. Scott LaBarge has made this point for me on numerous occasions.

15. G. R. F. Ferrari, "Platonic Love," in Richard Kraut, ed., *The Cambridge Companion to Plato* (Cambridge: Cambridge University Press, 1992), 262.

Chapter Four

Moral Self-Improvement

Brad K. Wilburn

One purpose of moral categories and moral judgment is to facilitate thinking about moral self-improvement. That is, many people who worry about the rightness of action and the goodness of character have these worries because they are concerned with doing the right actions and having good character. It is their hope that by thinking about their world in moral terms, they can become better people and lead more fulfilling lives.

Attempts at moral self-improvement are an important part of our moral experience, and yet such attempts rarely get explicit attention in moral philosophy. In this paper, I will take on three tasks. First of all, I will defend this claim that moral self-improvement is an important part of our moral experience that moral philosophy should address. Secondly, I will present an account of moral self-improvement that I believe accommodates the richness and variety that exists in our attempts to make ourselves better. This account will describe moral self-improvement as potentially having three aspects: a cognitive aspect, a practical aspect, and an affective aspect. Finally, I will apply this account to an example of moral self-improvement, pointing to some of the philosophical issues that this account raises. In the end, I hope that I will have established the fruitfulness of thinking philosophically about moral self-improvement in general and of my account in particular.

The Importance of Moral Self-Improvement

Let me begin by setting out two examples. Imagine a person engaged in a conversation with an acquaintance. In an attempt to make a joke, she makes a comment that hurts the feelings of the other person. She notices this and apologizes to the acquaintance, but the conversation breaks apart, and she continues to think about her actions. "I do that too often," she tells herself, "I'm too careless in my remarks, and I end up hurting people." She remembers the hurt look on the face of her acquaintance, and she resolves to choose her remarks more carefully in the future.

This resolve, I take it, is a basic and familiar attempt at moral self-improvement. We might describe this case as follows: the woman believes that it is wrong to hurt others with thoughtless comments, she examines her own behavior and sees that her carelessness leads her to violate this principle, and so she resolves to monitor her remarks more effectively. She is a person who acknowledges a moral principle, a rule for correct behavior, and who tries to improve her own adherence to that principle. This example is expressed easily in terms of the principles to which someone adheres and her attempts to live up to those principles.

Now consider a different sort of example. Imagine a man with a sister whom he loves very much. Imagine also that this man harbors prejudice against people of another race. When his sister announces to their family that she plans to marry a man of that race, he is conflicted between his love for his sister and his prejudice. After much soul-searching and after getting to know and even like his sister's fiancé, he eventually comes to see his prejudice as mistaken and the varied behavior that sprang from that prejudice as wrong. He begins to realize how deep-seated that prejudice is, and as a result of this experience, he resolves to change this attitude, along with the behavior that it generates. In the beginning, his attempts to change are linked fairly closely to the reactions of his brother-in-law. When his brother-in-law reacts negatively to something he says or does, the man tries to change his behavior. His attempts at change broaden and deepen, however, as time goes on. Instead of being linked to the reactions of this particular person to whom he is personally attached, he eventually develops a sensitivity to the reactions of people to whom he is not personally attached. And instead of making these changes in response to the reactions of others, he eventually develops his own negative reactions to prejudicial behavior. He feels guilty when he engages in prejudicial banter with friends of his own race, even when no one of the other race is present to be offended. Eventually, he feels offended when these friends try to draw him into their banter. At this point, the change has been etched deeply into his character.

Obviously, I have made a long story very short. I am not suggesting that all or very many internal conflicts of the sort I have described will have this sort of a happy ending. What I am claiming is that this sort of soul-searching, this recognition of the need for a restructuring of value, is at least possible. Dramatic change of this sort, though perhaps rare and certainly difficult, does seem possible. Further, a concern with bringing about this sort of change in oneself does seem like a paradigmatically moral concern.

What we have here is an example of a more complex attempt at moral self-improvement than in the first example. One added complexity is that we have a moral agent going beyond an evaluation of his ability to live up to his moral code—that is, the principles of right action to which he would assent. Instead, we have an agent evaluating his system of values, judging it to be flawed in certain ways, and trying to construct a better system. It is challenging to live up to moral principles, but it is also challenging to figure out proper ones.

A second way in which this second example reveals the potential depth of an attempt at moral self-improvement is that even describing the changes involved as changes in his principles is somehow inadequate. Change in principle is certainly involved in this example. Prior to his sister's engagement, the man regarded certain behaviors as acceptable that he eventually came to see as unacceptable. Talk of principles is not necessarily out of place, but it does not seem to capture all that is going on. The man's moral outlook consists of more than the principles to which he would assent. That outlook includes the attitudes he has towards people of the other race and the feelings he has in various situations: hatred, fear, superiority, inferiority, resentment, discomfort, guilt, or any of a wide variety of other responses. To make the moral improvement described, he needs to change these responses as well as the principles by which he guides his conduct. Given this concern with character, as well as action, one way to describe his project is as an attempt to develop virtues: tendencies of emotional and behavioral response that are informed by an understanding of what is important in life.

Many philosophers write about virtues, however, without focusing on these sorts of attempts to improve morally. One reason for this is that other models of virtue acquisition get focused on instead. For instance, Hume's account of virtue stresses how our judgments of character are linked to natural sentiments and mental mechanisms.[1] As another example, Plato spends much of *The Republic* describing the sort of education that would produce virtuous people.[2] Aristotle echoes this concern when he claims that the proper upbringing is a prerequisite for being able to successfully pursue knowledge of the good.[3] These issues about the extent of our natural endowment towards virtue and about the best way to raise people so that they become virtuous are certainly important. My goal in this section will be to show that issues about attempts to shape and develop one's own character are important as well.

One way of bringing out this importance is to look at the factors of natural endowment and education in order to see their connections with moral self-improvement. Looking at natural endowment, we can see that, unless we are willing to defend the strong claim that our endowment completely determines what sort of character we will end up with, we will want to have something to say about how different processes of development can shape that endowment in different ways. For instance, Mencius, the ancient Chinese philosopher, insists that we all possess certain natural, paradigmatically moral reactions such as sympathy, but he also stresses the importance of us cultivating and extending these reactions in order to develop a full-fledged virtue such as benevolence.[4]

Of course, if the need here is for some account of how natural endowment develops into virtue, focusing on moral education fills that need. A concern with moral education can itself lead to a concern with moral self-improvement, however, and it can do so in two ways. First of all, many accounts of moral education stress the importance of role models. On a practical level, then, if one is concerned with being a good role model, and if one's character is not flawless, one has reason for thinking about how to improve one's character.

Secondly, the ability to correct and improve oneself is one of the characteristics that we raise our children to have. We would consider a child's scientific education to be incomplete if the result of it were simply that she had mastery of the current state of scientific agreement. We would also want her to understand what it is to practice science and how to move that practice forward by revising and extending our scientific understanding. Similarly, we would be disappointed if our children turned out simply to be moral replicas of us, warts and all. We also hope that they will develop the capacity for self-criticism, a capacity that allows them to identify prejudices and blind spots that are a result of their moral upbringing. When we conceive of a person with a thriving moral character, I would suggest, part of that conception should be the idea that such a person is able to identify ways in which his character might be improved. Given these various connections, even those who focus on the effect of upbringing and those who focus on the natural basis of our characters will still want to have something to say about attempts by people to make themselves better.

Also, projects of moral self-improvement can be a manageable way of directing one's moral attention. For one thing, the focus of such projects is on improving *oneself*, not passing judgment on others and trying to get them to change. While not an illegitimate activity, the latter is certainly challenging and sometimes counter-productive. When trying to improve someone else, we face hurdles in getting those others to accept our judgments and convincing them that our motives for getting them to change are not self-serving. These hurdles are not there when we try to improve ourselves. Secondly, the focus of such projects is on *improving* oneself, not developing infallible judgment or impeccable character. Moral perfection is likely out of our reach. Indeed, I would argue that ideals of perfection are valuable insofar as they help us achieve the more limited results that are within our grasp. Our inability to achieve moral perfection, or even to understand and describe it adequately, should not dissuade us from making those changes that are within our grasp. Thinking about improvement rather than perfection can sometimes help cut the challenges of morality down to size.

Further, we can see the importance of moral self-improvement if we consider the purposes of moral concepts. We use these concepts when we judge actions to be right and wrong and when we judge characters to be admirable or despicable. Obviously then, if we are going to use these concepts properly, we must know when we are justified in making these various judgments. Thus, moral philosophy should be concerned with the appropriate application of these concepts, with figuring out when an action is right and when a character is admirable. However, we can press further here and think about why we make these judgments. One of our purposes for doing so is often to point out the need for moral improvement. If we judge that someone is doing something unkind, we probably hope that the person would recognize this and change her behavior. Alternatively, we might be holding such a person up as an example of things we want to avoid. If we never had any expectation that anyone, ourselves or others, would ever improve as a result of moral discourse, the importance of this discourse would be much reduced. Since we often do have these expectations when using moral concepts, helping us to think about how we might improve ourselves is one purpose for using these concepts, and so this sort of project is a fitting subject of moral philosophy.

Indeed, I would argue, not only is our use of moral concepts linked to moral self-improvement, but so is the practice of moral philosophy itself, since part of that practice is the analysis of those concepts. Aristotle makes this point when he describes his project in the *Nicomachean Ethics*: "The purpose of our examination is not to know what virtue is, but to become good, since otherwise the inquiry would be of no benefit to us."[5] One reason for engaging in conceptual analysis, for trying to figure out what a virtue is or what makes an action right, is to sharpen our use of those concepts and thereby to make our lives go better. This does not mean that I think that every instance of philosophical inquiry is or should be carried out with the explicit goal of improving our lives. However, philosophy is one example of the important capacity we humans have to evaluate and improve the concepts we use when we view the world.

Finally, my claim that attempts at moral self-improvement are an important part of our moral experience does not commit me to various stronger claims that might be made in this area. For example, this claim is consistent with acknowledging limits to our abilities to change our character; I do not need to claim that we can always and easily reshape our characters at will. Even when attempts at improvement are difficult, long-range projects, they are not necessarily futile. It is important to be able to tell when such a project is futile, but it is also important to identify the opportunities for change that are present. Also, discussing the possibility and importance of moral self-improvement does not commit me to any claim about whether there is a *duty* to engage in such projects, or how strong such a duty might be. My hope is that my account is compatible with a wide variety of positions on these issues.

The Three Aspects of Moral Self-Improvement

Given the potential richness of a project of moral self-improvement, as illustrated by the example of the man trying to overcome his racism, an account of moral self-improvement should consider, not just rules of conduct, but states of character. If we are concerned with doing right actions, we must recognize that simply deciding to act rightly is not always enough. Quite often we have to change our character in order to be able consistently to act as we believe we should. Our concern goes beyond acting well on some particular occasion. We are concerned with acting well consistently, with taking joy in those actions, and with minimizing the temptation of immorality. Thus, a project of moral self-improvement can be seen as aiming at the development of excellences of character, or virtues. I will be working within an Aristotelian framework, and so I will begin my account with a brief description of what Aristotle takes a virtue to be.

In a typically Aristotelian style of categorization, Aristotle tells us what a virtue of character is by giving us its genus and species. Generally, a virtue is a state of character. A state of character is "what we have when we are well or badly off in relation to feelings."[6] Examples of feelings are "appetite, anger, fear, confidence, envy, joy, love, hate, longing, jealousy, pity, in general, whatever implies pleasure and pain."[7] Specifically, a virtue is being well off in relation to a particular feeling. If we tend to have that feeling when it is appropriate to have it, we have the virtue that corresponds to that feeling. We can fall away from virtue by having either an excess or a deficiency in relation to a particular feeling, that is, by having a feeling when it is not appropriate or not having it when it is appropriate to do so.[8] This appropriateness is determined by right reason, as so having our feelings accord with right reason in this way is one way in which we display rational excellence. As rational beings, engaging in activities that manifest rational excellence is what constitutes living a good life, according to Aristotle.[9]

In Book VII of *Nicomachean Ethics*, Aristotle discusses two states of character that are intermediate between the virtue of temperance and the excessive vice of intemperance.[10] The feelings that all these states of character have to do with are feelings of bodily pleasure. A continent person is one who has desires like those of the excessive person, but who recognizes that those desires should not be acted upon and so acts in accordance with virtue. An incontinent person is one who has similarly excessive desires and who has a similar recognition that those desires should not be acted on, but who is unable to act in accordance with virtue. Though Aristotle's main use of this distinction between different ways of falling short of full virtue is related to his discussion of temperance, he also makes more general use of this distinction, and it is this general use that will concern me here.

Consider the following rough classification of people. The virtuous person is one whose feelings are ordered by a correct understanding of the good human life and who, therefore, does the right thing, taking pleasure in doing so. The vicious person is one who deliberates incorrectly concerning the good life, fastening on things that are not really constituents of the good life and, thus, wrongly taking those false constituents as ends in later deliberations. The feelings of such a person will be inappropriate, misguided by this faulty conception of the end. In between these two extremes are those who have a correct conception of the end, but who also have unruly feelings, feelings not properly part of the good life. The strong-willed are those who act correctly despite these inappropriate feelings, and the weak-willed are those who are unable to do so.

By calling this a rough classification, I mean that I do not expect it to allow us to sort people neatly into these four categories. Indeed, it would be hard to find someone whose feelings were all perfectly in order and who could therefore be called completely virtuous. Additionally, completely vicious people, with completely misguided reasoning about the good and with the accompanying unruly feelings, are also rare. Most of us, I take it, are somewhere in between, and not neatly in between. We all have various moral strengths and weaknesses. In some areas, our conception of the good may be accurate; in other areas our understanding of the good may be misguided. In some areas, our feelings may be well ordered, while in others, our feelings may be disordered. In some of these areas in which our feelings are disordered, we may well act appropriately; in other areas such as this, our actions may go astray.

Given our concern with moral self-improvement, however, this account does provide us with an understanding of the pieces we must have in place to acquire virtue, or at least to bring ourselves closer to it. First of all, we must be able to recognize what the right thing to do is, what the good consists in, and how best to achieve it. This corresponds to a move from being a vicious person to being merely a weak-willed person. Secondly, we must be able to do the right thing once we have identified it. This corresponds to a move from being a weak-willed person to being a strong-willed person. Finally, we must develop feelings appropriate to living a good life. This corresponds to a move from being a strong-willed person to being a virtuous person.

Once again, just as the four categories being discussed do not crisply divide humanity, so these three sorts of change are not stages that we pass through in an orderly manner on our way to virtue. This is the case for two reasons. First of all, this description of the process suggests that first we acquire an understanding of the good life, then we begin to act in accordance with that understanding, and then we eventually develop feelings appropriate to that life. There is little reason to suppose that actual cases of moral improvement must follow this pattern. It seems possible that an improved understanding of a flourishing human life might not lead immediately to a change in action. Perhaps it would lead first of all to a change in feelings, while patterns of behavior would be more recalcitrant. Also, it does not seem necessary that the improvement be triggered by an improvement in understanding. For instance, circumstances might lead someone to develop certain patterns of sympathetic response, and it might only be later that understanding and behavior would change to match these new patterns of feeling. Alternatively, certain patterns of behavior might develop before a person understands how these patterns fit into a flourishing life and before her feelings change to match these patterns of behavior. The process of moral self-improvement is not a rigidly defined process. Any of these three sorts of character development might occur first and might be followed by any of the other two sorts. I am not arguing that any particular pattern of development is more desirable or more common.

Secondly, this talk about the different possible orderings of a process of self-improvement should not obscure the fact that what often happens is that the types of change are inextricably mixed. That is, a fuller understanding, more virtuous behavior, and more appropriate feelings often go hand in hand with each other, sometimes all together, sometimes in smaller combinations, and usually to varying degrees. Changes in character are not always the result of epiphanies and often take place over long periods of time. The three aspects of moral improvement are usually intermingled, rather than sequential.

If we consider the example of the man who works to shed racist attitudes, we can easily imagine this to be the case. He might recognize that his new brother-in-law deserves his respect, and he might develop feelings of respect, and yet still engage in abusive talk when his brother-in-law is not around. He might eventually become sensitive to the danger of racist language and change his behavior accordingly, and yet still believe isolated parts of the stereotype that he used to believe in total. He might have a falling out with his brother-in-law, and some of his earlier attitudes might resurface. As he continues to examine his thoughts, feelings, and behavior, he might see more and more of the deep-rooted nature of his racism. Actual moral self-improvement is an often messy and convoluted process. Thus, the structure of the three aspects should be seen as a vehicle for the discussion of relevant issues, and the richness of our moral experience should be acknowledged and maintained.

If we are interested in improving ourselves morally, however, we will probably be concerned with each of these types of improvement in some or another area of our lives. In some areas, we struggle to figure out more accurately what flourishing consists in. In others, we struggle to act according to this conception of what makes life good. In others, we struggle to develop appropriate feelings. In many, we will be working on all three.

This, then, is the basic framework within which I will work. A project of moral self-improvement is an attempt by someone to do at least one of these three things: to come to a better understanding of what the good is and how to achieve it; to develop better patterns of action; or to develop better tendencies of affective response. Improving one's moral understanding I will call the cognitive aspect of moral self-improvement. Improving one's actions I will call the practical aspect. Improving one's tendencies of affective response I will call the affective aspect.

Applying the Account

I would now like to apply this account to an example of someone engaged in another project of moral self-improvement to illuminate some of the philosophical issues involved in such projects. Consider a father who loses his temper too easily with his children. In Aristotle's terms, he does not show anger at the appropriate times, in appropriate ways, and to the appropriate degree. Imagine that he begins to judge this facet of his character as something he should try to change. Perhaps he sees his son playing house with other children, ranting and raving in the role of the daddy. Perhaps he gets mad at his daughter mistakenly, and his apology does little to change her sullen, hurt mood. He begins to see this tendency in himself, not as an appropriate part of his attempts to discipline his children, but as a potentially damaging tendency, and he begins to think of ways to change. This realization would be the beginning of cognitive improvement.

One thing that is philosophically interesting is the potential depth of this thinking. What might start out as a simple piece of means-end reasoning about how best to get his children to behave properly could be extended to include reflection on the practice of child-raising in general, on how this practice should fit into a whole human life, and on how social influences, some of which may be criticizable, shape our attitudes and expectations surrounding this practice.[11] He might think about the ways his angry tendencies affect his relationship with his children, about what other sort of relationship with his children might be possible and preferable, and about what sorts of tendencies of response would be consonant with and constants of that better sort of relationship. He might consider how the unwanted tendencies displayed in this area of his life are reflected in other areas as well. What all this brings out is the rich complexity involved in answering the perennial philosophical question, "What sort of life is best for humans to lead?"[12] This complexity comes into sharp relief when we approach this question from the perspective of actual challenges within our actual lives. Thus, I would argue, thinking about moral self-improvement leads us to these complex issues in a way that helps us keep our philosophical musings grounded in practical concerns.

Perhaps the father's realization that he does not want to react in an angry manner, along with his subsequent reflection, will serve to reduce the number of times that he does so. It is likely, however, that his ingrained tendencies of behavioral response will still exert their pull, especially if the feelings that underlie these tendencies are still present. Given our human potential for acting contrary to our best judgment, we need to do more than simply make sure we make the right judgments. Because of this, the father in our example might focus directly on changing his behavior. Doing so would be the practical aspect of moral self-improvement.

One philosophical challenge that can be made against this practical aspect is that it is a superfluous category in that practical improvement is actually reducible to the other two aspects. If one accepts a desire-belief model of action, then it would seem that once one desires and believes the right things, one's actions will fall into line as well. Indeed, philosophical accounts of weakness of will usually point to some sort of cognitive or affective flaw. For instance, at one point Plato claims that when one seems to act contrary to what one knows to be best, there is actually something incomplete about one's knowledge.[13] Cognitive improvement would seem to be in order. In his discussion of the subject, Aristotle distinguishes between having knowledge and attending to it, and he suggests that our appetites are one factor that can make our attention waver in cases of weakness of will.[14] Affective improvement seems to be in order. Basically, if actions spring out of various sets of desires and beliefs, broadly construed, then it seems that if we want to change our actions, what we need to focus on is changing the desires and beliefs that generate the problematic action.

My response to this challenge is that even if we accept a desire-belief model of action, there is still a role for distinctly practical improvement. I will make this point by examining some of the mechanisms we might use to make this sort of change. For instance, a friend of the father in our example might suggest that when he feels angry at his children, he should write an angry letter and then tear it up as a way to express that anger in some other way. The same feeling is there, but it is expressed differently. The focus is on behavioral change, not immediately on affective change. Another suggestion might be to resolve to pay an arbitrary penalty every time he flies off the handle. Once again, the direct focus is on changing the behavior.

It might be argued that, in fact, the father does change his set of desires and beliefs by employing these mechanisms or others like them. He brings into play a desire to write an angry letter, a desire linked to a belief that this activity would be a less destructive way of expressing his anger. If the desire-belief model for explaining action is correct, then different behavior in similar circumstances always implies some sort of change in one's set of desires and beliefs. I do not wish to challenge this view, but I would argue that many of these changes cannot plausibly be considered *improvements* independent of the changes in behavior. If the father wrote the angry letter, tore it up, and then still exploded at his children, we would not consider the mere addition of the desire to write such a letter to reflect any sort of progress. If the resolve to pay the arbitrary penalty upon exploding did not deter the father from making his outbursts of temper, the presence of that resolve would not be considered improvement. There may be cognitive and affective *change* involved in these mechanisms, but these changes should not necessarily be seen as cognitive or affective *improvement*. There would only be improvement if the behavior actually changes, and this would be practical improvement. Thus, the practical aspect of moral self-improvement is indeed separable from the other two aspects.

In addition to reflecting on how best to interact with his children and working to act appropriately towards them, we can also imagine that the father in our example might have an additional concern with developing appropriate feelings, with not feeling anger so readily in the first place. This concern might be there even if he was very confident about his ability to avoid acting on these feelings.[15] This concern is an example of the affective aspect of moral self-improvement. At this point, a further problem arises. A traditional view of feelings is that we are passive with regard to them. The term "passion" itself reflects this sort of view. We do not decide on how we will react emotionally like we decide what we will do. This feature of our feelings would seem to limit our ability to change our feelings.

My strategy here will not be to deny that this standard view has much to recommend it. Rather, I will try to make two points. First of all, even if our ability to direct our current emotional reactions is limited, we can provide at least some direction. Secondly, even given these limits on directing our current responses, we still have ways of shaping our emotional tendencies, and these tendencies are crucial to the development of virtue. One may find it difficult in a particular situation to simply decide not to be angry, but there are things one can do to develop appropriate tendencies with regard to anger.

To make these two points, I will describe certain features of our emotions, features grouped into three main areas. First of all, there are important links between our emotions and our thoughts. Secondly, there are important links between emotions and action. Finally, emotions play an important social role, connecting us to each other and giving us insight about each other. By looking at these features, we can identify ways in which we can shape our feelings.

Turning to the first feature, there are two sorts of linkage between thought and feeling that I have in mind. Hume speaks of "passion plac'd betwixt two ideas, of which one produces it, and the other is produc'd by it."[16] This suggests that there are at least two ways in which thoughts can be linked with feelings: certain thoughts are crucial for entering certain affective states, and those affective states influence our thought processes in characteristic ways. An example of the first sort of linkage would be the way that feelings of pride depend on judgments that something closely connected to one is valuable.[17] Examples of the second sort of linkage would be the way that feelings of jealousy are characterized by certain obsessive thoughts about the person of whom one is jealous,[18] or the way that anger is characterized by thoughts of retaliation.

This suggests that we might have some ability to direct our feelings by directing our thoughts. Since some thoughts contribute to the production of certain feelings, one way to bring about a feeling would be to bring to mind the appropriate thoughts. Since some feelings are characterized by certain thoughts, one way to whittle away a particular feeling would be to whittle away the characteristic thoughts. Descartes provides an example of the first sort of redirection in *The Passions of the Soul*, saying that to arouse boldness one could "consider the reasons, objects or precedents which persuade us that the danger is not great; that there is always more security in defence than in flight; that we shall gain glory if we conquer, whereas we can expect nothing but regret and shame if we flee; and so on."[19]

Redirection of the second sort may be more difficult. Ronald DeSousa also points out the linkage between thought and feeling, but argues that we can exploit this linkage to produce an emotion much more easily that to eliminate an emotion. We can bring certain thoughts to mind more easily than we can keep certain thoughts out of our mind. "It does me no good to tell myself how foolish I am to miss her: for the thought is an enemy agent, calculated to fix my thoughts on just what I should forget."[20]

One thing we can do in this second sort of case is to make use of the first sort of redirection. We do not simply try to push out one thought; we try to put in another.[21] For instance, the redirection in Descartes' example could be seen as a way of combating fear as well as inciting boldness. Thus, in trying to lessen his feelings of anger, the father in our example might try to redirect his thoughts.

Perhaps his wife advises him that when she feels angry or frustrated with one of the children, she looks at their baby pictures on the wall, which reminds her of their vulnerability and their need for love and protection. Thoughts such as these might serve to deflect his anger as well.

The second feature I would like to discuss is the way our feelings are linked with characteristic actions and reactions. As an example of bodily reactions, an accelerated heart rate is characteristic of fear and anxiety. Examples of actions characteristic of certain feelings include fleeing out of fear and helping someone out of compassion.

This link between feeling and behavior points to other possible ways for us to influence our emotional responses, by controlling our behavior. William James makes a strong claim in this regard when he says, "Refuse to express a passion and it dies."[22] I would not be willing to defend a claim this strong, but we do have some capacity for influencing our feelings by controlling our behavior. If someone is depressed, we might tell him to keep his chin up or to put on a happy face. Someone trying to keep up her confidence might stand tall. One can whistle past a graveyard to try to allay fear. Robert Roberts writes, "If I am afraid of someone, one way to handle the fear is to stand up straight, look him in the eye, and speak clearly in an even, strong voice. The fear may not disappear entirely, but it will certainly be less than if I shrink back, speak in a weak mumble, and generally present myself as one who is in an oppressive situation."[23]

Some of the bodily reactions characteristic of certain feelings, though they normally occur without our deliberating on them, also have the potential for being consciously controlled, and we do seem to use this potential to moderate our feelings. If someone is overly excited due to panic or anxiety, we tell them to take deep breaths, relying on the connection between physical and emotional relaxation.

Beyond this possibility, however, paying attention to the actions we perform can have an impact on our tendencies to feel certain ways, on our patterns of emotional response, if not on our actual emotions at the time of performance. Aristotle, who regarded habituation as the way in which virtue, indeed any state of character, is acquired, famously makes this point.[24] To become virtuous, to have the proper direction of feelings that is virtue, we need to act as the virtuous person acts. By acting properly, by engaging in the proper pursuits, we become accustomed to those actions, become attached to those pursuits, begin to appreciate their value, take that value to heart, and eventually we find that the proper feelings can develop. An awareness of this connection between action and character development might help the father trying to lessen his anger maintain his resolve. Behaving as he thinks he should will not always be a difficult matter of fighting off violent feelings. As he becomes habituated to that sort of behavior, the contrary feelings are likely to lessen, and the desired behavior will become more and more second nature.

The third and final feature of our feelings that I would like to discuss is the way they are linked to our relations with others. The communicability of feelings is very important to the roles they play in our lives. Expressions of feelings are used to convey information about what matters to us by conveying information about our emotional states. Evidence for the importance of the communicability of feelings can be found in the work of psychologist Paul Ekman. Ekman has performed a number of experiments that provide convincing evidence that, for certain basic emotions, facial expressions of these emotions and the ability to identify these emotions are cross-culturally universal.[25] Other researchers point out ways in which infants rely on their perceptions of these expressions in their parents as a means of receiving feedback on their activity.[26]

Given this third feature, an important technique for adjusting our feelings and reshaping our patterns of affective response will be to participate in more explicit communication concerning those feelings. When sighs and grimaces, smiles and raised eyebrows do not say enough, it is often helpful to say more verbally. Doing this can serve to allay concerns that may be bothering us and to nurture concerns that we may be developing. This sort of communication can influence our emotions in at least two ways. First of all, by getting the insights of others, especially those close to us, we can increase our understanding of the situation that is generating the emotion. This increased understanding can, in turn, influence the course that emotion takes. Secondly, given that emotion plays a role in communicating with others, engaging in explicit verbal communication can affect the strength of an emotion. For example, a nervous speaker might make herself more comfortable by letting her audience know that she is nervous. The father in our example might be able to ameliorate his anger by identifying the concerns that underlie that anger and developing alternative techniques for communicating those concerns to his children.

What should be clear is that he will not be engaging in a completely futile project once he takes on the task of trying to reshape his feelings. Once again, there are certainly limits to how much they can be reshaped. By capitalizing on certain features characteristic of feelings, however, he will be able to exert some influence on both his feelings as they occur and on his tendencies of emotional response.

One theme that I hope has emerged throughout this section is that there are deep interconnections between the various components of character. Our thoughts arise from and direct our ways of life in crucial ways. Our actions are produced by our beliefs and desires, even as they influence the ways in which those beliefs and desires change. Our feelings channel our thoughts and influence our actions, and in turn our feelings are influenced by what we believe and do. In light of these interconnections, I would like to stress three points to conclude this section. First of all, as pointed out above, by dividing projects of moral self-improvement into three separate aspects, I do not mean to claim an extreme independence of these three aspects. My claim is that these projects often involve improvement along a variety of dimensions, and any adequate account needs to speak to these various dimensions. Secondly, as a practical matter, recognition of these interconnections can help us to make changes more successfully. If we attempt to adjust our beliefs without acknowledging how beliefs get embedded in our feelings and influence our actions, those attempts are less likely to be effective. Similar points can be made about our attempts to change actions and feelings. The third point I would like to stress is that moral self-improvement provides a productive context for examining these issues about the richness and complexity of character. By examining character in flux, the interconnections that make up this richness and complexity are brought into focus.

Conclusion

I believe that the possibility of projects of moral self-improvement is a major source of the value of moral thinking. Thus, I have argued, our moral theorizing should be able to accommodate the richness that such projects can exhibit. I have presented an account that incorporates this richness through the aspects of thought, action, and feeling, and I believe that each of these aspects is unique, important, and able to be improved. In carving out the theoretical space necessary to talk about moral self-improvement, I hope that I have also succeeded in providing a sense that such projects are indeed meaningful and deeply valuable.

Notes

I would like to thank Rachel Cohon, Philip J. Ivanhoe, Anne Tarver, Robert Audi, and Michael Meyer for extensive comments on earlier drafts of this paper, as well as an audience at Union College for illuminating feedback. In addition, I would like to thank Amélie Rorty and the participants in her 1992 NEH Summer Seminar for College Teachers on "Virtues and Their Vicissitudes," as well as participants in the Northern California Virtues Discussion Group, for much general conversation on virtue ethics. Special thanks in this regard should go to William Prior, who was a consistent contributor to both of the groups just mentioned, and to Elizabeth Radcliffe, who has been a consistent contributor to the latter group. Finally, I would like to thank Stanford University, Santa Clara University, California Institute of Technology, Washington University, and the National Endowment of the Humanities for institutional support.

1. David Hume, *A Treatise of Human Nature*, edited by L. A. Selby-Bigge, 2nd edition, revised by P. H. Nidditch (Oxford: Clarendon Press, 1978). For a recent discussion of Hume's views on this issue, see Annette Baier, *A Progress of Sentiments* (Cambridge, MA: Harvard University Press, 1991), especially 185-88. See the paper by Elizabeth Radcliffe in this volume for an account of how projects of moral self-improvement can be integrated into a Humean framework.

2. Plato, *Republic*, tr. G. M. A. Grube, revised by C. D. C. Reeve (Indianapolis: Hackett Publishing Company, 1992), especially Books II-VII.

3. Aristotle, *Nicomachean Ethics*, tr. Terence Irwin (Indianapolis: Hackett Publishing Company, 1985), 6, 1095b5-10. See M. F. Burnyeat, "Aristotle on Learning to Be

Good," in *Essays on Aristotle's Ethics*, ed. Amélie Oksenberg Rorty (Berkeley: University of California Press, 1980), 69-92.

4. Mencius, *Mencius*, tr. D. C. Lau, (London: Penguin Books, 1970). See, for instance, pp. 162-163. This aspect of Mencius' thought is brought out very thoroughly and clearly in Chapter 2 of Philip J. Ivanhoe, *Confucian Moral Self Cultivation* (New York: Peter Lang, 1993).

5. Aristotle, *Nicomachean Ethics*, 35, 1103b28-30. Early on in *Nicomachean Ethics*, Aristotle uses a metaphor with archery to make a similar point. The goal of the work is to provide an account of *eudaimonia*, or human flourishing. The hope is that a better understanding of *eudaimonia* will improve our chances of achieving this flourishing: "Will not knowledge of this good, consequently, be very important to our lives? Would it not better equip us, like archers who have a target to aim at, to hit the proper mark?" (p. 4, 1094a22-24) Moral theorizing is grounded in a concern with improving our lives.

6. Aristotle, *Nicomachean Ethics*, 41, 1105b26.

7. Aristotle, *Nicomachean Ethics*, 41, 1105b23.

8. Aristotle, *Nicomachean Ethics*, 42-46, 1106a16-7a33.

9. Aristotle, *Nicomachean Ethics*, 16-17, 1097b34-98a17.

10. Aristotle, *Nicomachean Ethics*, 172-98, 1145a15-52a35.

11. Alasdair MacIntyre develops an account of virtue that brings out this potential depth in thinking about how to live. See *After Virtue*, 2nd edition (Notre Dame, IN: University of Notre Dame Press, 1984), 187 in particular and Chapters 14 and 15 in general.

12. I do not mean to suggest that one, narrowly defined form of life can be presented as the best human life. Other ways of asking the question might be, "What sorts of lives are best for humans to lead?" or "What constitutes living well for humans?"

13. Plato, *Protagoras*, tr. C. C. W. Taylor (Oxford: Clarendon Press, 1976), 46-52, 352d-357e.

14. Aristotle, *Nicomachean Ethics*, 178-82, 1146b33-47b20.

15. One reason for this concern might be to avoid the internal struggle that is involved in avoiding acting on these feelings. Another reason might be that the value of close relationships is bound up in the feelings we share with those close to us, not just in the activities we share with them.

16. Hume, *Treatise*, 278.

17. See Hume, *Treatise*, 275-328.

18. Jerome Neu makes this point in "Jealous Thoughts," in *Explaining Emotions*, ed. Amélie Rorty (Berkeley: University of California Press, 1980), 432.

19. René Descartes, *The Passions of the Soul*, translated by Stephen Voss (Indianapolis: Hackett Publishing Company, 1989), 43, AT 363.

20. Ronald DeSousa, *The Rationality of Emotion* (Cambridge, MA: The MIT Press, 1990), 243.

21. DeSousa makes a similar suggestion in the passage cited above.

22. William James, "What Is an Emotion?" *Mind* 19 (1884): 28-29.

23. Robert C. Roberts, "Will Power and the Virtues," *The Philosophical Review* 93 (1984): 245.

24. Aristotle, *Nicomachean Ethics*, 35, 1103b21.

25. Paul Ekman, *The Face of Man* (New York: Garland Press, 1980).

26. Two examples of this sort of research are Daniel Stern, Lynne Hofer, Wendy Haft, and John Dore, "Affect Attunement: The sharing of feeling states between mother and infant by means of inter-modal fluency," in *Social Perception in Infants*, ed. T. Field and N. Cox (Norwood, NJ: Ablex Publishing Company, 1985), 251-68, and James F.

84 Brad K. Wilburn

Sorce, Robert N. Emde, Joseph J. Campos, and Mary Klinnert, "Maternal Emotional Signaling: Its Effect on the Visual Cliff Behavior of 1-Year-Olds," in *Contemporary Readings in Child Psychology*, ed. E. M. Hetherington and R. D. Parke (New York: McGraw-Hill, 1988), 183-89.

Chapter Five

Self-Cultivation and Relations with Others in Classical Rabbinic Thought

Jonathan W. Schofer

Should we engage in practices of moral self-cultivation? The answer may seem obviously to be "yes" if we focus upon the *goal* of becoming better people. Self-cultivation ideally would lead to the development of virtues and skills enabling both individual excellence and improved ways to encounter and interact with others.[1] It may also enable relationships that are not possible otherwise, as is asserted in the view that certain forms of friendship are only available for virtuous people. If we focus upon the *process* of becoming better people, however, then difficult questions may arise. David Wong has elegantly argued that relations with others are crucial to defining human identity, and those relations include duties and responsibilities.[2] Moral self-cultivation, even if done in solitude, often requires time and resources that could be devoted to other activities (including productive labor) and other people (including but not only family members). If one's development requires entering a particular community, then the very act of entering a new social world can cause tensions with others in one's life, especially if it requires the dislocation of moving to a distant place. Moral self-cultivation, then, may conflict with one's responsibilities towards others, even if the ultimate goals include compassion and benevolence.

Key questions to consider in relation to a given form of self-cultivation concern how that process fits into the rest of one's life. This paper will examine one subset of these issues—the interplay of self-cultivation and relations with others. Specifically, in what ways are others necessary for, implicated in, or hindrances to one's self-cultivation? In what ways does self-cultivation enhance or create

difficulties for relations with others? My work will center on a descriptive study
of classical rabbinic sources from Late Antiquity. Rabbinic self-cultivation centers upon immersion in a particular disciple circle of study and learning, and
their writings reveal a strong sensitivity to the interpersonal nature of their ethical development. I will present and analyze sources in which they prescribe a
communal approach to self-cultivation, and in which they struggle with the tensions and dangers in such a process. My key argument is that their focus upon
community as a crucial element of ethical development leads them to identify
difficulties in their relations with those outside the community, and it also leads
them to be concerned to address, among the members of the group, vices that
may be inspired by yet detrimental to the disciple circle itself. While these
points are in many respects specific to the ancient and foreign context of early
rabbinic Judaism, I will conclude with reflections on the relevance of these issues for moral self-cultivation in the modern or post-modern West.[3]

The Sources

The classical rabbis were a movement of Jewish religious elites in late ancient
Palestine and Babylonia that probably coalesced in the late first or second century C.E., though our earliest textual sources begin somewhat later. Rabbis
claimed they inherited a tradition that they called the Torah, which in their view
had its origins in the revelation to Moses at Sinai, and their creative work to develop that tradition resulted in a tremendous volume of texts.[4] Rabbis did not
compile systematic treatises on ethics and self-cultivation, but certain anthologies contain a large amount of relevant material, often conveyed through short
sayings with commentary upon those sayings.

   In this paper I will focus on teachings from a large collection known as *The
Fathers According to Rabbi Nathan*. This text is a commentary upon maxims
that are found in a highly influential corpus known as *The Fathers*, which was
ultimately placed in the Mishnah (a canonical anthology of rabbinic law) and included in Jewish liturgy.[5] As many have observed, *Rabbi Nathan* is our best
source for understanding how these sayings were employed in the context of the
classical rabbinic period. Despite the attribution to "Rabbi Nathan," *Rabbi Nathan* is not a single authored work but a family of anthologies created by
anonymous editors over centuries, probably starting in the second or third century and continuing after the sixth. We now have the text in two major recensions—commonly labeled as "Version A" and "Version B"—and my analysis
will center on the one that was included in printed editions of the Babylonian
Talmud, Version A.[6] Despite its size and significance, though, we should not
take *Rabbi Nathan* to represent all of rabbinic thought. I make a point to avoid
using the definite article before the word "rabbis" in order to signal that *Rabbi
Nathan* represents a strand and not the totality of rabbinic views: *Rabbi Nathan*
reveals what certain rabbis state, but not what all of "the rabbis" believed.

For philosophers, rabbinic literature presents challenges in interpretation for at least two reasons. First, the forms of expression are highly concrete rather than abstract. Rabbis convey ideas through tropes, narratives, and pedagogical instruction, and often the conceptual issues have to be inferred. Second, large portions of rabbinic thought are generated through a form of biblical exegesis known as midrash. Midrash has a distinct poetics and set of hermeneutical methods that are very different than philosophical reasoning, and it is based on theological claims concerning the divinity of the Hebrew scriptures that today's philosophers would not accept. I will not enter into these latter issues very deeply in this paper, but it is worth noting that passages and interpretative moves that may seem odd to the academic reader are likely part of a complex and well-developed world view that is very distant from our own.

Self-Cultivation, Family, and Material Well Being:
The Example of Rabbi Akiva

A key pedagogical motif in *Rabbi Nathan* is the figure of the sage—the rabbi who appears in narratives as an exemplar of correct comportment and action. Three of the most prominent sages in the text are Rabban Yohanan ben Zakkai, the legendary founder of rabbinic Judaism, his student Rabbi Eliezer ben Hyrcanus, and his student Rabbi Akiva. They flourished roughly between the mid-first and mid-second centuries, though the stories about them were transmitted and developed for generations afterwards. In a late rabbinic compilation such as *Rabbi Nathan*, accounts of these men probably reveal much more about the ideals of the anonymous transmitters than they do about the early sages themselves.

Rabbi Nathan includes two large narrative compilations presenting the careers of Rabbi Eliezer and Rabbi Akiva. The stories have certain themes in common—the man starts his study in adulthood, goes to learn from a great sage, overcomes obstacles, shows great brilliance, and ends up wealthy. These features imply a rhetorical purpose of persuading the listener or reader to follow the rabbinic path of study and practice, countering the responses that one is too old, the process is too difficult, or the results not economically worth the effort (in one passage, as we will see below, this persuasive goal is quite explicit). Each story also has certain motifs that are particular to the broader rabbinic legends that are associated with each sage, particularly Rabbi Eliezer as having ascetic tendencies, and Rabbi Akiva as starting his study at age forty and having a great deal of support from his wife Rachel in the process.

A central concept in the stories is the rabbinic Torah. The word *torah* literally means "teaching," and it can denote the first five books of the Hebrew Bible, the full Hebrew Bible (also known as the "Written Torah"), or the entire rabbinic tradition of study and practice that rabbis assert to be derived from scripture (also known as the "Oral Torah"). The latter inclusive sense is probably most relevant for these stories. As a tradition, the Torah has all of the functions in rabbinic ethics that Alasdair MacIntyre emphasizes in his theoretical account: it is continual rabbinic discussion and debate concerning the nature and ideals of the tradition itself, setting out norms for practices as well as the narratives that underlie and frame those practices.[7] For rabbis, though, the Torah is not only an intellectual foundation but a way of accessing their deity. Also, and more specifically relevant for our topic, rabbis believed that the study and practice of Torah would have direct impact on the self, shaping and transforming emotions and desires.

The stories appear as part of the commentary to a maxim attributed to a first century sage named Yose ben Yoezer, "Let your house be a meeting place for the sages, sit in the very dust of their feet, and drink with thirst their words." (*Rabbi Nathan*, Version A, ch. 6; also *Fathers* 1:4) The maxim itself implies a social setting in which teaching and learning occurs in people's houses rather than an institutionalized school, and teachers seem to depend on the hospitality of their students and other supporters for the very space in which they taught. The saying also calls upon the student to respect the teacher, embodied in the image of sitting "at the dust of their feet," and it presents sagely teachings as nourishing and quenching.

After a series of comments upon the call to make one's house a meeting place, the text states, "Another opinion: Sit at the dust of their feet—this is Rabbi Eliezer. And drink with thirst their words—this is Rabbi Akiva." (*Rabbi Nathan*, Version A, ch. 6) What does this mean? The editors present a story of the latter, younger sage:

> What were the beginnings of Rabbi Akiva? They said: He was forty years old and had not studied anything. One time [Akiva] would stand at the mouth of a well. He asked, "Who chiseled out that rock?" They said, "The water, which continuously falls upon it, every day." They said, "Akiva, do not you read in Scripture, 'Water carves away rocks . . .'" (Job 14:19) Rabbi Akiva reasoned on his own from the minor to the major case, "Just as the soft wears away the hard, how much the more so that the words of Torah, which are hard as iron, will hollow out my heart, which is flesh and blood." (*Rabbi Nathan*, Version A, ch. 6)

The story opens by presenting Akiva (not yet with the status of "Rabbi Akiva") as an uneducated man who understands neither the workings of nature nor the text of the Torah. He sees a rock that has been worn away by water, wonders how it came to be this way, and others respond by citing the first part of a verse from the Book of Job, "water carves away rocks." (Job 14:19) The full verse says, "Water carves away rocks, its torrents wash away earth, so You destroy human hope," yet Akiva interprets the verse in a way that brings him hope for his own transformation.

The new aspirant draws from the words an ethical teaching that centers upon the possibility of shaping his heart through Torah: "the soft [water] wears away the hard [stone]." If this metaphor were applied directly as an analogy for self-cultivation through tradition, it would imply that the process involves a slow wearing away of a hard and unformed heart. However, he sets out an *a fortiori* argument asserting that the heart is not hard stone but soft flesh and blood, and Torah is not soft water but hard iron. If water can wear away the rock, then this iron-like Torah has more than enough power to "hollow out" a fleshy heart. According to these metaphors, Torah is a powerful agent, the heart is very receptive, and the process of cultivation is rapid. What does it mean, though, to hollow out one's heart? In rabbinic literature the heart is a site of thought, emotion, and desire, and in several sources it is the location of the "impulse" (*yetzer*) towards transgression. The shaping of the heart through Torah, then, describes the forming of character through tradition, redirecting transgressive tendencies to create desires and actions in accord with rabbinic ideals.[8]

The story begins, then, by framing Torah as central to moral self-cultivation and then shows how a forty-year-old man should immerse himself in this tradition. In the next sections, we find extensive discussions portraying his prodigious learning and persistence, and a key element is that he goes to study with others, particularly great sages. Not even being literate, "He went with his son and they sat with the teacher of children." Later, "He sat before Rabbi Eliezer and Rabbi Yehoshua." (*Rabbi Nathan*, Version A, ch. 6) Rabbinic self-cultivation through Torah requires the right teacher and quite literally locating oneself in the correct place.[9]

The next scene, though, examines some of the difficulties involved in the process:

> Every single day he should gather a bundle of straw[10]—half of it he would sell to provide for himself, and half of it he would use to adorn himself.[11] His neighbors would stand against him and say, "Akiva, you are going to make us perish from smoke. Sell it to us and get oil with the money, and study by the light of a candle." He said to them, "There are many benefits that I generate from it: I study with it, I warm myself by it, and I sleep on it." (*Rabbi Nathan*, Version A, ch. 6)

This passage presents the study of Torah as economically unproductive time that requires at least a minimal expenditure for a light source in order to study at night. Rabbi Akiva finds a solution that is efficient but also inconsiderate, and the story appears to uphold his choice. The broader point is that the pursuit of traditional learning may lead one to cause a certain degree of discomfort or inconvenience to others, but one should do it nonetheless.

The next passage shows a rare moment in rabbinic discourse, where the text discusses the pedagogical significance of its own narratives:

> In the future, Rabbi Akiva will make all the poor guilty of judgment, for if one says to them, "Why did you not study?" and they say, "Because we are poor," then one can say to them, "But look, Rabbi Akiva was even more poor, and poverty stricken." And if they way, "Because of our children," one can say to

them, "But look, Rabbi Akiva had sons and daughters." (*Rabbi Nathan*, Version A, ch. 6)

In this reflexive moment, the compilers of *Rabbi Nathan* tell the reader how to draw upon the story of Rabbi Akiva in their lives. The sage sets a standard for right behavior. One should "look" at the case of Rabbi Akiva whenever considering reasons for not studying Torah. The first obstacle—poverty—continues the theme that Torah study is not economically productive and may cost resources, and the other is that the demands of being a parent could impinge on the time and energy needed for study. For both cases, though, the story of Rabbi Akiva should be cited in persuading oneself or other people to study Torah.[12]

The issue of children touches on a much broader tension in rabbinic literature. On one hand, the rabbinic movement took very seriously the biblical command that one should "be fruitful and multiply." Rabbis upheld marriage and child rearing, and they did not develop ideals of celibacy or monastic communities. More generally they tended to set out a religious and ethical path that centered on life in towns and cities, amidst larger communities of Jews as well as non-Jews. In this sense they contrasted with the earlier groups that went out to the area surrounding the Dead Sea to pursue life separate from Roman society, and also with Christians who began to develop communities in the Egyptian desert starting in the fourth century. On the other hand, there were rabbis who embraced ideals of sexual renunciation to varying degrees, and more generally, their Torah study in a community of men competed with their time devoted to family.

This constellation of commitments underlies the picture of an ideal spouse in the next part of the narrative:

> But they say about them [the sons and daughters]: it was from the merit of Rachel, his wife.[13] At forty years old he went and studied Torah, and at the end of thirteen years he taught Torah in public. They say: He did not leave the world until he had tables of silver and gold, and went up to his bed on ladders of gold. His wife would go out with shoes and a tiara of gold. His students said to him, "Master, you embarrass us with what you did for her." He said to them, "She suffered much with me for the Torah." (*Rabbi Nathan*, Version A, ch. 6)

This fragment is only one of several rabbinic accounts describing Rabbi Akiva's wife Rachel supporting his study.[14] Other narratives present her as the daughter of a wealthy family that disowned her because of marrying a poor aspiring rabbi, yet she sent him away for years to study, supporting the family through the process. Through the figure of Rachel rabbis uphold the androcentric ideal of a woman who is strong, productive, and channels her energies into support for her husband's rabbinic pursuits.[15] At the same time, in these stories and particularly this version, rabbis reveal a strong awareness that much of their religious practice—including their moral self-cultivation—competed with their family lives, and they were dependent upon their wives to uphold their dual ideals of procreation and study.

Self-Cultivation, Family, and Material Well Being:
The Example of Rabbi Eliezer

The next story, centering on Rabbi Eliezer, begins with a different kind of conflict between study and family responsibilities. Ideals of filial piety are canonized in Judaism through the Ten Commandments, which uphold honor of one's parents, but here the son has to evade his father in order to enter the rabbinic community:[16]

> What were the beginnings of Rabbi Eliezer ben Hyrcanus? He was twenty-two years old and had not studied Torah. Once he said, "I will go and study Torah with Rabban Yohanan ben Zakkai." His father Hyrcanus said to him, "You will not taste [food][17] until you have plowed an entire furrow." He woke early and plowed an entire furrow. (*Rabbi Nathan*, Version A, ch. 6)[18]

Again we see a tension between the time required for study and the time needed for productive labor. This economic issue is linked with the responsibilities that a son has to his father and more generally to his family of origin—Eliezer is told he has to work before he can study. He attempts to do both, plowing the field and then, in subsequent sections of the story, going to study with Rabban Yohanan ben Zakkai in Jerusalem. The bulk of the ensuing narrative compilation portrays his trip, his stay, and his ascetic tendencies expressed through fasting.

Rabbi Eliezer's extended trip apparently was not acceptable to his father Hyrcanus, and the concluding sections of the narrative focus on the father and the teacher:

> Hyrcanus his father heard that he was studying Torah with Rabban Yohanan ben Zakkai. He said to himself, "I will go and ban Eliezer my son from my possessions." They said: On that very day Rabban Yohanan ben Zakkai was sitting and expounding in Jerusalem, and all the great ones of Israel were sitting before him. He heard that [Hyrcanus] was coming, and he sent guards and said to them, "If he comes do not let him sit down." [Hyrcanus] came, and they did not let him sit. He advanced up and back until he arrived at the places of Ben Tzitzit Hakeset, Nakdimon ben Gurion, and Ben Kalba Savua. He sat between them and trembled. (*Rabbi Nathan*, Version A, ch. 6)

Hyrcanus intends to disinherit his son in public. Somehow Rabban Yohanan ben Zakkai knows this and arranges that the father be led to sit with men who (at least in the discursive world of *Rabbi Nathan*) are wealthy, influential, and supporters of the sages and their students. Hyrcanus, who throughout the story is associated with material concerns (the field, his possessions), appears to be intimidated among these men.

The next scene presents a public initiation of Rabbi Eliezer as a sage. He is called upon to perform a sermon even though he is not ready, he expresses his doubt, and then he succeeds triumphantly:

They said: On that same day Rabban Yohanan ben Zakkai looked at Rabbi
Eliezer and said to him, "Begin a sermon and expound." He said to him, "I
cannot begin." He pushed him, and his students pushed him. [Rabbi Eliezer]
stood, began, and expounded about matters that no ear had ever heard. At every
single word that came out from his mouth, Rabban Yohanan ben Zakkai stood
and said to Rabbi Eliezer, "My master, truth you have taught me." (*Rabbi Nathan*, Version A, ch. 6)

The support from the teacher clearly contrasts with the near rejection by the
father. Rabban Yohanan ben Zakkai may also be performing for Hyrcanus, affirming Rabbi Eliezer's excellence in front of the entire public, including the influential figures in the audience. The strategy is successful: "Before it was time
to leave, Hyrcanus his father stood on his feet and said, 'My masters, I came
here only to ban Eliezer my son from my possessions, and now all of my possessions will be given to Eliezer my son. All of his brothers will be disinherited and
will not get anything.'" (*Rabbi Nathan*, Version A, ch. 6)

As in the story of Rabbi Akiva, the conclusion is that the sage ends up rich
and reconciled with his family. The happy ending is a rhetorical flourish in stories structured to persuade the reader to take on the study of rabbinic tradition.
For the purposes of this paper, however, the crucial point is the conflicts raised
earlier: study of Torah, and the moral self-cultivation that is associated with it,
may conflict with both one's familial relations and with one's material well being.

The stories of Rabbi Akiva and Rabbi Eliezer, then, expand and develop
the instruction of Yose ben Yoezer, "Let your house be a meeting place for the
sages, sit in the very dust of their feet, and drink with thirst their words." The
young adult Eliezer sits in the dust of Rabban Yohanan ben Zakkai's feet and
drank his words with thirst, and the forty-year-old Akiva does the same with
Rabbi Eliezer and his peer Rabbi Yehoshua. The sages' words transmit the rabbinic tradition of Torah, which among other things is central to rabbinic moral
self-cultivation. The study of Torah depends on the student-teacher relationship,
but it also poses challenges for material prosperity, relations with families of
birth and marriage, and also relations with others nearby (such as neighbors).[19]
The stories reveal rabbinic concerns both to sustain those relationships and to
pursue the rabbinic path even if it means putting them at risk.

Relations with Teachers and Peers

Participating in a proper rabbinic community of study and practice is highly valued in *Rabbi Nathan* and emphasized in a number of ways. In the above stories,
we saw that part of Rabbi Akiva's excellence as a sage is that he had numerous
students. Although the story of Rabbi Eliezer does not focus on this point, it
culminates with his public exposition of his learning, and in the story of Rabbi
Akiva, Rabbi Eliezer appears as a sage teaching a new generation of students.
Some maxims in the text emphasize the importance of teaching to others what
one learns and practices. (*Rabbi Nathan*, Version A, ch. 13) Others speak in

more general terms, upholding those whose actions bring merit to the larger group, or asserting that the very act of spending time with those who observe the commandments is like observance itself (and spending time with transgressors like a transgression). (*Rabbi Nathan*, Version A, ch. 23, 25, 30, 40; *Fathers* 5:18) One of the worst consequences, however, for those who engage in improper teaching is that they would be exiled to a place of "bad waters," far from the nourishing words of the sages who teach Torah. (*Rabbi Nathan*, Version A, ch. 11)

What more can we say about this community, at least the ideal one presented in the pedagogical discourse of *Rabbi Nathan*? The sages who appear in the text teach a small circle of disciples, making up an urban or semi-urban community centered on the study of traditional materials.[20] Relations between teachers and students are a central concern. Teachers are instructed to "raise up many students," and to "be careful" with their words in their teaching of Torah. As we have seen, students are told, "Let your house be a meeting place for the sages, sit in the very dust of their feet, and drink with thirst their words," and another passage commenting on this maxim specifies the student's ideal comportment towards a sage: "For every word that emerges from your mouth, let him receive it upon himself in awe, fear, trembling, and shaking." (*Rabbi Nathan*, Version A, ch. 6) This fourfold emotional response appears earlier in *Rabbi Nathan* to describe Moses' state when receiving the Torah at Sinai (ch. 1). The student, then, is to take on the same relation toward his teacher as Moses took before God during revelation.[21]

A crucial maxim for this issue is attributed to Yehoshua ben Parahyah, a sage of the Second Temple period, "Appoint for yourself a teacher, acquire for yourself a fellow (*haver*), and judge every man with the scales weighted in his favor." (*Rabbi Nathan*, Version A, ch. 35; *Fathers* 1:6) The word "fellow" (*haver*) is a technical term that has a range of meanings in rabbinic literature centering on sharing, friendship, and fellowship in maintaining piety, righteousness, or Torah study.[22] In *Rabbi Nathan*, one commentary upon "acquire for yourself a fellow" states: "How so? This teaches that a man should acquire a fellow for himself, that he will eat with him, drink with him, study scripture with him, study Oral Torah with him, sleep with him, and reveal to him all his secrets —secrets of Torah and secrets of the way of the world." (*Rabbi Nathan*, Version A, ch. 8)

As is evident in the philosophical schools of Roman Late Antiquity, we see here a prescription for an all-male community practicing an interpersonal spirituality: men work together to cultivate themselves and follow divine precepts. The fellowship of peers continues through day and night: students are to eat together, worship together, study together, and, if they were unmarried, sleep together. The community also appears to have its version of peer counseling, as students are to have intimate communication with each other that includes their personal and perhaps mystical secrets.[23]

The relations among fellows in a disciple circle are major concerns in *Rabbi Nathan*. Students are instructed to honor their fellows' "glory" (*kavod*); they are told how to respond to their fellows in times of anger, mourning, and other points of difficulty; and they are given guidance in how to deal with disagreement. (*Rabbi Nathan*, Version A, ch. 14, 15, 29; *Fathers* 4:15) At the same time, it may be the case that the very context of the study house contributes to tensions among the students. Within *Rabbi Nathan* there are numerous passages in which students are labeled, categorized, and set in hierarchical relations,[24] which could easily generate competition between them. Ideals of harmonious relations may in part be attempts to counter competition and jealousy that are generated by the elite community itself. For example, consider the following teaching about envy:

> Rabbi Joshua says, "The evil eye, the evil inclination, and hatred of human beings cast a person from the world." The evil eye, how so? This teaches that just as a person views his house, so too he should view the house of his fellow. Just as he desires that a bad name not go forth regarding his wife and children, so too a man should desire that a bad name not go forth regarding his fellow's wife and his fellow's children. Another opinion: The evil eye, how so? This teaches that a person's eye should not be distressed regarding his fellow's [knowledge of] Mishnah. There is a story of a person whose eye was distressed regarding his fellow's [knowledge of] Mishnah: his life was shortened, and he died. (*Rabbi Nathan*, Version A, ch. 16)[25]

The passage centers on two cases, one concerning family life (wife and children) and one specific to ideals of study (one's "Mishnah"). Both give us a hint that, in a close circle of peers, jealousy and envy can easily arise. In the second case, the very practice of learning, which is central to rabbinic moral self-cultivation, itself can inspire and be corrupted by "the evil eye."

A communal context of study and self-cultivation may require distinct virtues to sustain itself, and it is vulnerable to certain vices. Humility and patience are highly valued in *Rabbi Nathan*, and the text gives tremendous weight to the control of speech, condemning in strong terms those who gossip and slander.[26] One passage states that that "plagues" come upon those who engage in malicious speech (*Rabbi Nathan*, Version A, ch. 9) and another presents it as greater than other sins: "Four things for which the person who does them will be punished in this world and in the world to come: idolatry, incest, and murder. Yet malicious speech (*lashon ha-ra'*) is greater than all of them." (*Rabbi Nathan*, Version A, ch. 40)

Idolatry, incest, and murder often appear in rabbinic literature as paradigmatic sins, the most extreme of religious, sexual, and misanthropic transgressions. This numerical list places malicious speech above them in significance, hyperbolically emphasizing the dangers of improper speech.[27]

A communal context for moral self-cultivation, then, provides certain significant resources and influences, including teachers who may impart great knowledge, exemplify ideals, and offer guidance; peers who share the process and offer support and fellowship; and also varying degrees of separation from outsiders who may distract from the ethical path. At the same time, rabbinic literature reveals a concern with problems generated by this context, and sages both uphold specific virtues (such as patience and humility) and warn against certain vices (including envy and malicious speech).

Contemporary Reflections

What is the significance of these late ancient rabbinic sources for contemporary reflection on moral self-cultivation? Rabbis embraced certain forms of moral self-cultivation as absolutely crucial to their religious and social ideals, yet they identified and tried to respond to conflicts in the process. Ideally sages would honor their parents, support their spouses and children, and respect their neighbors. However, rabbis acknowledged that their practices might draw an aspiring sage from his family and lead to distant or tense relations with those outside the rabbinic fold. Teachers, peers, and ultimately students are necessary for self-cultivation, yet the very community of study can also generate internal tensions.

At least two broad issues are at stake here. The first is the role of conflict in the ethical life. Do both private and public life pose for us a series of irreconcilable conflicts, such that ethics is a matter of managing them as best as possible, or are ethical conflicts only apparent, and a true understanding of a good life will find a way to reconcile or move beyond them?[28] The second issue is the role of self-cultivation as a human activity in relation to the rest of life—how much importance should it have in our deliberative priorities?[29] There are several options for responding to these questions. One is to emphasize that most forms of self-cultivation require time and resources. Given that humans are both social creatures and are finite, then there are necessarily conflicts between the process of self-cultivation and other forms of right action. Whatever importance we assign to self-cultivation, we should acknowledge that such activities come at a cost, and at best we can aim for a "lopsided" character, with some virtues more developed than others. Striving to be a wise sage may mean being a mediocre parent, for example.[30]

Another approach is to try to eliminate conflicts such as those addressed by the rabbinic sources, and this could be done in a number of ways. First, one could uphold only practices that can be fully integrated into other aspects of life. Everyday life provides constant opportunities to exercise one's virtue, whether in relations with parents, children, and other family members, or in the course of a workday, or even in public space. Self-cultivation, then, could be envisioned as constantly striving to improve oneself at all times in and through one's relations with others. The efficacy of this approach, however, turns on questions such as: Is there something distinctly efficacious about forms of self-cultivation that require time, resources, and community, such that they enable forms and degrees of change that cannot be done in the course of ordinary life? For example, the late ancient rabbis who compiled *Rabbi Nathan* might answer that the study and practice of Torah impacted the self in ways that other activities could not. Also, is the assimilation of self-cultivation into daily life something that all people can do? The issue may not only vary between cultures and persons, but across the lifetime of an individual. Perhaps at early or volatile stages of one's development, immersion in a process of self-cultivation is necessary or particularly valuable, while at other moments integration is much easier.

One way to reduce conflicts between self-cultivation and relations with others, then, is to streamline the process of cultivation. Another way is to eliminate one's relations with others. Retreat from social life into the desert, or to a mountain, or to other places of solitude have been cultural options in many times and places. If one does not marry or have children, and one moves far from any neighbors, then problems raised in the story of Rabbi Akiva are not relevant. If one is not in a communal context of study and learning, then vices like envy and slander are not temptations. Yet, as long as the members of one's family of birth are still alive, the challenges faced by Rabbi Eliezer are likely present, and religious communities that advocate a separation from society often struggle in complex ways with filial piety and familial responsibilities.[31]

The passages I have examined from *Rabbi Nathan* give immense weight to Torah and the rabbinic community in the priorities of an aspiring sage, counseling him to take on traditional learning even if it may risk harm to his well being or that of his family, and even if it may engender its own vices and obstacles. At the same time, the narratives of Rabbi Eliezer and Rabbi Akiva present an optimistic picture (likely implying the action of a deity) that ultimately the sage who follows the rabbinic path will be rewarded with a happy and prosperous end.[32] They do not attempt to reconcile the conflicts between their form of self-cultivation and their relations with others, but they carry on with the hope that the world, and their God, will reconcile the conflicts for them.

I am not calling for a hermeneutics of retrieval such that today's scholars would take up rabbinic practices as their own, and the development of contemporary Jewish ethics is a very different project than the one I present here. I do hold, though, that many of the possibilities and challenges raised in the late ancient sources are salient for modern and post-modern Western forms of self-cultivation. There are numerous contexts through which people seek to join with others in order to develop themselves, and these contexts can foster moral development in ways that may be difficult to achieve in ordinary life. Generating resources, time free from productive work and family responsibility, and appropriate social spaces for these communities is a constant challenge, as is the cultivation of virtues that help sustain the communities themselves. Such problems need to be understood and addressed by those upholding moral self-cultivation in its varied and complex forms.[33]

Notes

1. Definitions of excellence and improvement of course vary within and across cultures, but in this paper I will not address the problems for ethical theory that arise from this point.

2. David Wong, "On Flourishing and Finding One's Identity in a Community," *Midwest Studies in Philosophy, Volume XIII. Ethical Theory: Character and Virtue*, ed. Peter A. French, Theodore E. Uehling Jr., and Howard K. Wettstein (Notre Dame, IN: University of Notre Dame Press, 1988), 324-41. I thank P. J. Ivanhoe for pointing out this article to me.

3. This article builds from and extends my larger study on rabbinic ethics and self-cultivation, *The Making of a Sage: A Study in Rabbinic Ethics* (Madison: University of Wisconsin Press, 2005). Some of the translations herein appear also in the book, along with more extensive references and discussions of textual variants, and I will cite the appropriate pages when relevant.

4. Catherine Hezser characterizes the rabbinic movement as a network "in which each rabbi had direct contacts to a limited number of colleagues and through them indirect contact to other rabbis whom he could consult in case of need." See *The Social Structure of the Rabbinic Movement in Roman Palestine* (Tübingen, Germany: Mohr Siebeck, 1997), 228-39. Seth Schwartz makes a strong argument for the lack of rabbinic influence among Jews during the classical rabbinic period, particularly from 135-350 CE but also from 350-640 CE; see *Imperialism and Jewish Society, 200 BCE to 640 CE* (Princeton, NJ: Princeton University Press, 2001), 175-76, 199-202, 238-39, and generally 101-289.

5. The Mishnah was completed in the early third century in Roman Palestine, though *The Fathers* was likely reworked and edited over a much longer period; see M. B. Lerner, "The Tractate Avot," in *The Literature of the Sages*, ed. Shmuel Safrai (Philadelphia: Fortress Press, 1987), 263-81.

6. I will cite from *Rabbi Nathan* by version (A or B) and chapter, so the reader can look up citations either in the original Hebrew or translations. The current critical edition of the text is Solomon Schechter and Menahem Kister, *Aboth de Rabbi Nathan, Solomon Schechter Edition* (Hebrew), (New York: Jewish Theological Seminary of America, 1997). All translations of Hebrew and Aramaic texts in this paper are my own. A recent and crucial textual study that informs my analysis is Menahem Kister, *Studies in Abot de-Rabbi Nathan: Text, Redaction, and Interpretation* (Hebrew) (Jerusalem: The Hebrew University Department of Talmud, 1998). Both versions A and B of *Rabbi Nathan* appear in reliable English translations that have excellent notes and scholarly commentary: Judah Goldin, *The Fathers According to Rabbi Nathan* (New Haven, CT: Yale University Press, 1983); Anthony Saldarini, *The Fathers According to Rabbi Nathan (Abot de Rabbi Nathan) Version B* (Leiden, The Netherlands: E. J. Brill, 1975).

7. See Alasdair MacIntyre, *After Virtue*, Second Edition (Notre Dame, IN: University of Notre Dame Press, 1981), esp. 220-23.

8. See Schofer, *Making of a Sage*, 5-7 for a treatment of this story with references, and 69-119 for an extensive discussion of rabbinic views concerning the impact of tradition upon the self. For a different interpretation of this passage, see Ivan Marcus, *Rituals of Childhood* (New Haven, CT: Yale University Press, 1986), 49-50 and my comments in *Making of a Sage*, 177-78, n. 12.

9. Rabbinic religiosity is locative, in the sense that "fulfillment occurs when people locate themselves within a complex social order that is thought to be sacred"; see Lee Yearley, *Mencius and Aquinas* (Albany: SUNY Press, 1990), 42. Both rabbinic Judaism and classical Confucianism are examples of such locative religions. Yearley develops the distinction of Jonathan Z. Smith, who characterizes locative religions as affirming and celebrating a cosmic order that is created by bounding that which is chaotic. Such religions charge humans with finding a "place" that harmonizes with that order; see J. Z.

Smith, "The Influence of Symbols on Social Change," in *Map is Not Territory: Studies in the History of Religions* (Chicago: University of Chicago Press, 1978), 129-46; also Alasdair MacIntyre, *Three Rival Versions of Moral Inquiry* (Notre Dame, IN: University of Notre Dame Press, 1990), 196-203. On people going to study with the sages in *Rabbi Nathan*, see also Schofer, *Making of a Sage*, 40-41, 50-52.

10. Following manuscript witnesses; see Schechter and Kister, *Rabbi Nathan*, 29 n. 22 and Goldin, *Rabbi Nathan* 42. The printed edition states that he gathers wood.

11. The meaning of *mitqashshet* ("adorn himself") here is unclear. Goldin's translation states that he sells half to provide himself with wood and half to provide himself with clothes ("part he would sell to provide for his food and part for his clothing"), but this leads to problems in accounting for the material Rabbi Akiva uses to burn (Goldin, *Rabbi Nathan*, 42 and 184 n. 15). My reading is that he sells half and burns half, but the text is difficult. Tal Ilan translates "Half of it he would sell for sustenance and half of it he would use for other needs"; *Mine and Yours are Hers: Retrieving Women's History from Rabbinic Literature* (New York: Brill, 1997), 42-43.

12. Schofer, *Making of a Sage*, 49.

13. It may be appropriate to emend the text to read, "because Rachel, his wife, provided for them." For a full treatment of this point, see Ilan, *Mine and Yours are Hers*, 78-82; also Kister, *Studies*, 49; Schechter, *Rabbi Nathan*, 138; Goldin, *Rabbi Nathan*, 42 and 184, nn. 16-19.

14. Most stories and fragments focus on his late start, how he became rich, and his relation with Rachel his wife—both her devotion to him and his study, and his gifts to her after he became successful. See *b. Shabb.* 59a-b; *b. Ned.* 50a-b; *b. Ketub.* 62b-63a; *y. Shabb.* 6:1; *Sifre Deut.* 357; Louis Finkelstein, ed., *Sifre on Deuteronomy* (New York: The Jewish Theological Seminary of America, 1993), 429. For an analysis of this story as an ideal for relations between rabbis and their wives, see Daniel Boyarin, *Carnal Israel: Reading Sex in Talmudic Culture* (Berkeley: University of California Press, 1993), 134-66. Also note Jacob Neusner, *Judaism and Story* (Chicago: University of Chicago Press, 1992), 79-86, 118, 134, 147-49.

15. In characterizing rabbinic thought as androcentric, I follow the analysis of Charlotte Fonrobert, who writes, "On a most basic level, an androcentric perspective on the world and human culture is one in which the literary subject as the projecting center of perceiving is gendered male, explicitly or not. In other words, we are not merely dealing with a textual culture that creates explicit hierarchies, but one that imagines a certain directionality of perceiving. The male subject may be qualified in multiple ways, but in an androcentric body of literature the imagining, perceiving, speaking, and knowing subject is predominantly marked as male. Often, this marking is hidden or only implied, which may make it much more powerful and convincing." See *Menstrual Purity: Rabbinic and Christian Reconstructions of Biblical Gender* (Stanford, CA: Stanford University Press, 2000), 8.

16. Ideals of filial piety in religious ethics are a crucial point of study. Philip J. Ivanhoe examines early Confucian concerns with filial piety in "Filial Piety as a Virtue," in *Working Virtue: Virtue Ethics and Contemporary Moral Problems*, ed. Rebecca Walker and Philip J. Ivanhoe (New York: Oxford University Press, 2007).

17. The text just has "taste." I follow Goldin in focusing on food (*Rabbi Nathan*, 43), since is the most literal reading and since the motif of fasting appears later in the story.

18. For a full analysis of the story concerning Rabbi Eliezer, addressing all the recensions in rabbinic literature, see Z. Kagen, "Divergent Tendencies and their Literary

Moulding in the Aggadah," in *Studies in Aggadah and Folk Literature. Scripta Hierosolymitana*, Vol. 22, ed. J. Heinemann and Dov Noy (Jerusalem: Magnes Press, 1971), 151-70; Neusner, *Judaism and Story*, 79-86, 119-22, 134, 147-49.

19. The account of difficult relations with neighbors may be part of a broader tension in rabbinic literature between the rabbis as aspiring elites and other Jews, who are often labeled as "people of the land" (*'am ha-'aretz*); see Schofer, *Making of a Sage*, 38-9; Hezser, *Social Structure of the Rabbinic Movement*, 353-404 (she highlights rabbis teaching in people's homes on page 356, focusing on passages from *Rabbi Nathan*).

20. As Anthony Saldarini writes, the text "does not give a complete description of the Rabbis nor does it recount how they lived, but rather how they ought to live as members of a school"; Anthony Saldarini, *Scholastic Rabbinism: A Literary Study of the Fathers According to Rabbi Nathan* (Chico, CA: Scholars Press, 1982), 82, and also 79-92, 135-42. On the sages as a small, urban community, see Hezser, *Social Structure of the Rabbinic Movement*, 157-65; Seth Schwartz, "Gamaliel in Aphrodite's Bath: Palestinian Judaism and Urban Culture on the Third and Fourth Centuries," in *The Talmud Yerushalmi and Graeco-Roman Culture*, Vol. 1, ed. Peter Schäfer and Catherine Hezser (Tübingen, Germany: Mohr Siebeck, 2000), 203-17; Hayim Lapin, "Rabbis and Cities: Some Aspects of the Rabbinic Movement in its Graeco-Roman Environment" in Schäfer and Hezser, *Talmud Yerushalmi*, Vol. 2, 58-80.

21. Schofer, *Making of a Sage*, 30-33; Hezser, *Social Structure of the Rabbinic Movement*, 335-39, and on status differences among students, drawing upon these lists, 209-210, 339-50.

22. Saul Lieberman, "The Discipline of the So-Called Dead Sea Manual of Discipline," *Journal of Biblical Literature* 71 (1953): 199-206; Catherine Hezser, "Rabbis and Other Friends," in Schäfer and Hezser, *Talmud Yerushalmi*, Vol. 2, 202 and generally 189-254.

23. Schofer, *Making of a Sage*, 32-33; also Hezser, *Social Structure*, 351-52; she quotes this passage along with others outside of *Rabbi Nathan* that present students fulfilling some of these ideals. D. Boyarin and C. Hezser both discuss this intimacy and its relation to sexual practices. Neither one equates homosocial ideals with homosexuality, but Boyarin's analysis gives greater weight to the possibility of there being erotic dimensions. D. Boyarin, *Unheroic Conduct: The Rise of Heterosexuality and the Invention of the Jewish Man* (Berkeley: University of California Press, 1997), 16-17; Hezser, "Rabbis and Other Friends," in Schäfer and Hezser, *Talmud Yerushalmi*, Vol. 2, 245-47. Edward Watts discusses the intense intimacy of Roman schools in "The Student Self in Late Antiquity," in *Self-Revelations: Religion and the Self in Antiquity*, ed. D. Brakke, M. Satlow, and S. Weitzman (Bloomington: Indiana University Press, 2005).

24. Schofer, *Making of a Sage*, 32-33.

25. This formulaic expression appears several times in a cluster of teachings in *Rabbi Nathan*, Version A (ch. 15, 16, and 17; Kister, *Studies*, 165). On the manuscript variants regarding the last sentence, see Kister, *Studies*, 256.

26. Schofer, *Making of a Sage*, 32.

27. Schofer, *Making of a Sage*, 136-37 on this passage, and 71 on the three paradigmatic sins.

28. A sustained argument that "ineliminable" conflicts are a central part of ethics appears in Stuart Hampshire, *Innocence and Experience* (Cambridge, MA: Harvard University Press, 1989), esp. 150-51, 189.

29. This question, and the specific terminology of "importance" and "deliberative priority," are inspired by Bernard Williams, *Ethics and the Limits of Philosophy* (Cambridge, MA: Harvard University Press, 1985), esp. 21, 117, and 182-86.

30. For a strong claim concerning the "lopsidedness" of virtue, see Hampshire, *Innocence and Experience*, 134.

31. Charles Hallisey has emphasized the importance of this issue among Buddhist monks in his conference paper "Grieving Children and Abandoned Parents" (n.d.).

32. Not all rabbinic texts are like this, however, and there are cases that uphold the study of Torah even under the threat of execution by the government. One well known example is the story of Rabbi Akiva's martyrdom in the Babylonian Talmud *Berakhot* 61b. On these issues in general, see Michael Fishbane, *The Kiss of God* (Seattle: The University of Washington Press, 1994) and Daniel Boyarin, *Dying for God* (Stanford, CA: Stanford University Press, 1999).

33. Comments by Brad Wilburn and P. J. Ivanhoe on earlier versions of this paper were very important in my developing this final section.

Chapter Six

Moral Naturalism and the Possibility of Making Ourselves Better

Elizabeth S. Radcliffe

Is it possible for ordinary persons with well-formed dispositions to undertake a project of moral self-development? Virtue ethics seems a good home for a discussion of becoming better people, since it makes the notion of character primary, and changing one's character (for the better) appears to be what moral improvement is about. Improving judgment can also be a part of moral improvement, but it cannot be all there is to making oneself better. Character ethics comes ordinarily out of the naturalist tradition, which makes empirical observation primary and demands that theories about persons and their behavior be consistent with our account of the rest of the natural world. However, it is within naturalism itself that questions about the possibility of making ourselves better persons are raised. On the one hand, if our character is itself the product of causal forces, as all things in nature are, it looks like *we* can do nothing to change ourselves. On the other hand, on a view advocated by some sociologists and philosophers (among them Gilbert Harman and John Doris[1]), there is no reason to think there are such things as character traits or dispositions; they say that the behavioral evidence doesn't support belief in them.

One theoretical alternative to virtue ethics makes right action rather than good character the most important element in living morally. On a view like Kant's, doing actions that fulfill one's duty is the morally crucial thing; on the utilitarian view, doing actions that create the greatest happiness is morally primary. So, some perspectives might generate disagreement about what constitutes moral improvement, since, on these views, to make oneself better is to make it such that one does right actions more consistently, which is to say that one does them from certain formed dispositions. However, the question then becomes what it is to make an agent "such that" she does right action more frequently. On a plausible psychology, I would contend, right actions become more typical for an agent only as the agent develops in certain ways that make the actions results of some enduring mental set or mental readiness. So, even for utilitarians and Kantians, moral improvement must be improvement of persons primarily, and actions secondarily. Contemporary utilitarians, for instance, can allow that there are utilitarian virtues, those features of a person that make it natural for him to choose the actions that produce happiness. Ordinary benevolence would be a virtue of this sort, although universal benevolence, if it exists, would be an even better trait on this perspective, since universal benevolence would lead us to consider the happiness of even those remote and unknown to us, as a utilitarian would recommend.

In this chapter, I will argue for the possibility of self-improvement in the context of moral naturalism. The next section explains why I choose to deal with this issue in a naturalistic context. The section after that studies a systematic effort to undertake a practical project of self-improvement. The next two sections then present a theoretical explanation of this practical project in the context of a strict naturalistic theory, that is, one derived from Hume. If Hume's moral theory, which lacks a robust notion of agency, can make sense of self-betterment, then we have all the more reason to believe in the possibility that we might change our characters. The last section finally takes up the issue of whether we have reason to believe there is such a thing as character at all, the notion on which the possibility of self-improvement, I argue, ultimately depends.

Why Moral Naturalism?

As I have indicated, I talk about self-betterment in the naturalist's framework of character building, with character composed of dispositions that produce action. I presuppose this view rather than the naturalistic picture in which a person's actions are said to be caused and yet undetermined by character, or a non-naturalist picture in which a person's actions somehow "stem from" her rational commitments, but in a non-causal way (as exemplified by some Kantian views). For the most familiar Kantian position, actions are a consequence of the agent's uncaused adoption of maxims or policies reflecting her rational commitments. On a typical Kantian view, talk of actions as the causal results of character is eschewed in favor of talk of adopting maxims that somehow govern or give rise to actions. The worry about character here is that rational agency seems to imply the freedom to choose from among alternative maxims governing one's conduct, no matter what one's settled commitments or psychological dispositions.[2] Nonetheless, surely any notion of moral improvement for this view would still have to say something about the development of the agent—into someone who has the judgment to make the right commitments and the determination to carry through on them.

The optimistic implication of the Kantian view is that because I am free, it is always possible for me to choose to do my duty, no matter what else I want, or what I have committed myself to in the past. My freedom should also allow me to choose not to do my duty, no matter what I have committed myself to in the past. Yet my commitments or maxims are supposed to matter somehow, although not in a way that compels me to act in any particular way in the moment.[3] I'm not sure a view can recommend coherent methods for moral improvement if it implies that committing myself now to always doing the right thing can have no determining effect on my future free choices. If there is any plausible Kantian notion of character development, therefore, it can only be one where freely acquired virtues causally determine morally good actions, which seems to mean that in choosing to perform those actions we are not free.

I need to put aside one more related topic: I do not intend this discussion to be an essay on free agency. I needn't try to settle that issue in order to talk about moral self-improvement. It seems to me that what is necessary for the possibility of moral cultivation is not that we be able to claim in the libertarian's sense that we have the free choice to change who we are. If human beings are subject to causal conditions in the way the rest of nature is, then their motivations, dispositions, settled desires, intellects, and other factors that enter into character are formed by such things as their original endowments and external environments. The question is how *we* can interject change into those circumstances that exercise control over us. The possibility of moral self-improvement requires only that there be some non-arbitrary way in which we can play a role in inducing character changes in ourselves. From where the original impetus for making the changes derives, I am not prepared to say. There is a very plausible view in metaethics, moral internalism, which says that to accept any beliefs at all about what is good or about how one ought to behave is to have at least some kind of motivation to conform one's behavior to the beliefs.[4] This thesis has substantive implications for what the content of morality could be. On internalism, morality has to consist in some feature or features of the universe we can conceive moral agents to be moved to promote, on some plausible conception of how they are motivated. If the proponents of moral internalism are right, then anyone who sees that she ought to be better than she in fact is has a motivation to engage in self-improvement.

But in whom this motivation will actually produce action, outweighing other contrary motivations, like laziness or the attraction of immediate pleasures, it is difficult to say. The naturalist will have to take a cautious stance here. Perhaps there are persons who will never be drawn strongly enough by the content of morality to do anything about their moral deficiencies. The crucial question, however, is whether everyone might be incorrigible by nature, so that no one is a possible candidate for self-cultivation. In other words: Is it possible for people to care enough about making themselves better such that they will actually take steps to improve on who they are? If we can find even just one case in which someone has attempted a project of moral enhancement of his or her character, then we can at least hold out for the possibility of moral self-improvement. If we can construct an argument that the case we find is typical, or at least not atypical, and we have some systematic or theoretical explanation how the process works, then we have reason to think many of us can follow suit. I frankly think there are many examples of attempted self-improvement—people who quit smoking or start an exercise program, who try to be more patient with their kids or more understanding of their parents' attitudes, and so forth. But Ben Franklin's description in his autobiography of his attempt to arrive at "moral perfection" is a striking and detailed narrative of such a project with an explicit theory of human psychology as its ground.

The Case of Benjamin Franklin

Franklin points out that since he knows the difference between right and wrong, why not think he might always do the former and avoid the latter? This does not seem an unreasonable expectation, believing as he did that virtues are excellences of character that contribute to our self-interest. So, he thought he should have sufficient motivation to be virtuous. Interestingly enough, Franklin discovers that his presumption was wrong:

> But I soon found that I had undertaken a task of more difficulty than I had imagined. While my care was employ'd in guarding against one fault, I was often surpris'd by another. Habit took the advantage of inattention; inclination was sometimes too strong for reason. I concluded at length, that the mere speculative conviction that it was in our interest to be completely virtuous, was not sufficient to prevent our slipping, and that the contrary habits must be broken and good ones acquired and established, before we can have any dependence on a steady, uniform rectitude of conduct.[5]

Consequently, since Franklin identified force of habit as his chief obstacle to acting even on what he thought in his best interest, he devised a method for altering his habits in favor of the virtues. First, he devised a list of necessary virtues, compiled from his reading of various sources and from his desire to make some finer discriminations among traits than some writers made. Franklin's list, along with corresponding injunctions that explain each virtue, included:[6]

1. TEMPERANCE. Eat not to dullness; drink not to elevation.
2. SILENCE. Speak not but what may benefit others or yourself; avoid trifling conversation.
3. ORDER. Let all your things have their places; let each part of your business have its time.
4. RESOLUTION. Resolve to perform what you ought; perform without fail what you resolve.

5. FRUGALITY. Make no expense but to do good to others or yourself; i.e., waste nothing.

6. INDUSTRY: Lose no time; be always employ'd in something useful; cut off all unnecessary actions.

7. SINCERITY. Use no hurtful deceit; think innocently and justly, and, if you speak, speak accordingly.

8. JUSTICE. Wrong none by doing injuries, or omitting the bene-fits that are your duty.

9. MODERATION. Avoid extremes; forbear resenting injuries so much as you think they deserve.

10. CLEANLINESS. Tolerate no uncleanness in body, clothes, or habitation.

11. TRANQUILITY. Be not disturbed at trifles, or at accidents common or un-avoidable.

12. CHASTITY. Rarely use venery but for health or offspring, never to dulness, weakness, or the injury of your own or another's peace or reputation.

13. HUMILITY.[7] Imitate Jesus and Socrates.[8]

Franklin reasoned that it was futile to try to acquire the habits indicative of all of these virtues at once, so he devised a plan to work on one each week, in a sequence such that the acquisition of one might facilitate the acquisition of the next. Starting with temperance, for instance, could make one more clear-headed, which makes it easier to keep one's guard up against temptation in general. Acquiring the habits of silence and order would afford him more time, which would make it easier to attend to his entire project. Resolution was crucial to keeping him determined to practice the rest of the virtues on the list. Franklin set up a book in which each page was allotted for one week and one virtue. On each page, he drew a chart that cross-referenced the days of the week with his thirteen virtues; on the chart, he recorded infractions of all the virtues, but his concentration was on the virtue of the week:

> Thus, if in the first week I could keep my first line, marked T [Temperance], clear of spots, I suppos'd the habit of that virtue so much strengthen'd and its opposite weaken'd, that I might venture extending my attention to include the next, and for the following week keep both lines clear of spots. Proceeding thus to the last, I could go thro' a course complete in thirteen weeks, and four courses in a year. And like him who having a garden to weed, does not attempt to eradicate all the bad herbs at once, which would exceed his reach and his strength, but works on one of the beds at a time, and, having accomplish'd the first, proceeds to a second so I should have, I hoped, the encouraging pleasure of seeing on my pages the progress I made in virtue, by clearing successively my lines of their spots.[9]

Franklin reports that he had some success with his plan, although he was surprised to find how many faults he actually possessed. He had the greatest problem, he explains, with the virtue of order, and his difficulties in that regard made him wonder whether attaining the ideal of moral perfection was really the best thing to do after all. His career as a printer did not lend itself to order, given that he often had to meet clients at odd hours and given that he had a good memory anyway for locating things that were out of order. He found himself giving up on the virtue and related a story to explain his change of attitude. A man bought an ax and decided he wanted the whole surface to be as bright as the sharp edge; the smith agreed to grind it into a shiny surface if the man would turn the wheel.

> The smith press'd the broad face of the ax hard and heavy on the stone which made the turning of it very fatiguing. The Man came every now and then from the wheel to see how the work went on; and at length would take his ax as it was without farther grinding. "No," said the smith, "turn on, turn on; we shall have it bright by and by; as yet 'tis only speckled." "Yes," says the man, *"but I think I like a speckled ax best."*[10]

Franklin observed himself concluding that imperfection might be best after all, with the reasoning that others might find him intolerable or ridiculous were he to have a perfect character. But ultimately, he thought he was rationalizing, as the man with the ax was doing, in light of the fact that achieving the virtue of order required more than he could muster. He concludes, however, that although his project of acquiring all of the virtues fell short of its goal, "I was, by the endeavor, a better and a happier man than I otherwise should have been if I had not attempted it," just as the person who tries to perfect her handwriting by imitating engraved copies acquires a better style even though not reaching the perfection of the engraved writing.[11]

We might find Franklin's approach naïve in some ways. He doesn't seem to doubt that he knows what to do in each instance to create the particular virtue for which he is striving. For instance, sincerity requires no "hurtful" deceit—but it surely takes sound judgment to discern what sort of deceit is not hurtful. Likewise, industry requires that one do no unnecessary actions, but deciding when an action is "necessary" is certainly a complicated process of considering alternatives and the importance of one's aims, etc. Nonetheless, Franklin's example is a clear case of someone striving for moral self-improvement, so we do have empirical grounds on which to claim it possible for persons to try to introduce new factors into their circumstances and attempt to change their own habits, and with some success. While the extensive stratagem and scope of the plan Franklin used is surely not typical, his initiating an attempt at all seems not unusual. As I've remarked, people try to change their eating habits, their dental habits, their exercise habits, their work habits, and so on. Furthermore, one might simply try to improve by making one's lapses less frequent, with no intention of achieving the sort of perfection Franklin had in mind. A speckled ax may be better than a dull one, although in the case of character, unlike axes, the effort required to maintain the degree of improvement will be continuing. In any case, the motivation to change ourselves in various ways is prevalent, even though we don't always succeed.

On what theoretical grounds can we explain how character traits are changed by this sort of concentrated effort to habituate oneself to a certain way of behaving? One theory that offers an explanation is Aristotle's, since he argues that virtues are traits of character acquired by conscious effort that enable us to live well. Franklin obviously subscribed to Aristotle's theory that practice builds character. But Aristotle offers an account of virtue based on a theory of the good life that requires acceptance of teleological considerations that may actually undermine a strict naturalistic rendition of virtue. He argues that rational activity is the most characteristic function and, so, the purpose of human life; the virtues are defined therefore in terms of their exemplifying reflection and conscious practice. There are, for Aristotle, no virtues by nature. Natural talents, for instance, are to be distinguished from virtues, even though we find the latter admirable.[12]

In the eighteenth century, David Hume (incidentally, a friend of Ben Franklin's) offers a moral theory closer to a purer naturalism that identifies a different basis for virtue. Hume recognizes that his empirical and scientific starting points cannot support a theory of the good based on speculative teleology; instead he defines virtue in terms of the human proclivity of admiring certain traits in others. Because Hume is the stricter naturalist, I ultimately want to ask how far his theory can take us in an account of moral self-improvement. This is an interesting question to ask of Hume, since his theory of morality is a third-person "spectator" theory, having no easy account of agency and no obvious account of self-cultivation. Hume actually says little about changing our characters, but I will argue that a theory of self-improvement can be constructed from the elements of his view.

Hume on Virtue and Vice and on Character

Hume famously argues that our distinctions between virtue and vice are not made entirely on the basis of reason, as some philosophers prior to him maintained, but rather require experience. He argues that the experiences that give us our notion of what virtue and vice consists in are feelings—emotive states rather than intellectual ones. This conclusion is based on his observing that our accepting moral distinctions at all has a practical influence on us (at least on our motives, and often on our behavior), and he is convinced that what we know by reason alone has no such influence. Reason gives us beliefs about the way the world is, and beliefs about math and geometry, but such beliefs are inert without passions that give us ends for which we strive. Our beliefs about the world, of course, are necessary for us to achieve the things our passions set their sites on.[13] It follows from Hume's view that our regarding, say, malice, as a vice is a result of an emotional reaction, not a conclusion of a line of reasoning.

Hume's procedure as a philosopher applying the scientific method to a study of human nature is to observe and then to generalize to principles that explain his observations. One principle of human nature fundamentally responsible for our emotions is sympathy (itself *not* an emotion, but a "mechanism"): Human beings react to the world by taking on feelings like those felt by others with whom they come in contact. Hume writes,

> No quality of human nature is more remarkable, both in itself and in its consequences, than that propensity we have to sympathize with others, and to receive by communication their inclination and sentiments, however different from, or even contrary to our own. . . . A good-natur'd man finds himself in an instant of the same humour with his company; and even the proudest and most surly take a tincture from their countrymen and acquaintance. . . . Hatred, resentment, esteem, love, courage, mirth and melancholy; all these passions I feel more from communication than from my own natural temper and disposition.[14]

Sympathy also explains how we come to make the distinctions between virtue and vice, which are based on our feelings. Obviously, we can only observe actions, but since we experience the world in terms of causes, we assume that actions are caused by passions, which are the motives underlying the behavior. We take actions that people do as signs of their motivations. But we approve or disapprove of their motivations based on the actions' effects on those with whom we sympathize; these feelings give us our categories of virtue and vice. Sympathy, however, is not the only quality of human nature on which we rely when we draw up these moral distinctions. We also utilize our tendency to generalize and standardize our experience.

This tendency to generalize is expressed in two ways when we make moral judgments. First, we realize that the strength of our sympathetic feelings varies along with the connections we have to others; that is, we feel more intensely about those closer to us in space and time—our neighbors and acquaintances—and about those to whom we are connected—our family—than we feel about those strange and distant. We don't, however, make our moral discernments of people's motives based on these personal connections. Instead, Hume notices that we take up a "general or common point of view" in which differently situated observers can find agreement among their emotional reactions toward others' actions. That point of view is one in which we sympathize, even if only in thought, with those directly affected by the actions of the person (character) in question, and we set aside our own connections. "We blame equally a bad action, which we read of in history, with one perform'd in our neighbourhood t'other day: The meaning of which is, that we know from reflexion, that the former action wou'd excite as strong sentiments of disapprobation as the latter, were it plac'd in the same position."[15] The second way in which we generalize when we make moral discernments is that we regard a person who has regularly exhibited a tendency to benefit others as good, despite the fact that he is now incapacitated and prevented from producing those consequences or that his actions have accidental results. "Virtue in rags is still virtue."[16] Consequently, Hume concludes that the natural sentiments are refined by our practices before we regard them as indicative of virtue and vice.

Hume describes the virtues in general as those traits that are useful or agreeable to oneself or to others. Examples of features useful to the self are discretion, enterprise, economy, prudence, temperance, patience, considerateness, and order; qualities immediately agreeable to us include cheerfulness, tranquility, and serenity. Among qualities useful to others are generosity, gratitude, kindness, and courage; features immediately agreeable to others include politeness, wit, ingenuity, modesty, decency, cleanliness.[17] I think it is no coincidence that Ben Franklin's list of virtues from his 1784 biography is reminiscent of Hume's. Hume's more popular version of his moral views, *An Enquiry Concerning the Principles of Morals*, was first published in 1751, with other editions to follow, and Franklin visited Hume after Hume retired to Edinburgh in 1769.

Even though Hume has a systematic account of how we arrive at our ideas of the virtues and the vices, he actually lacks a well-developed account of character. He certainly countenances the notion of character and suggests that character consists of those durable and constant qualities of mind that allow others to hold us morally responsible for the actions that proceed from them. He says more than once that we are only objects of moral praise and blame insofar as we have such enduring qualities.[18] This might seem problematic, since it suggests that no one ought to be punished for doing wrong actions that aren't part of a discernible pattern of behavior. But this leaves open the possibility that parents, educators, or authorities might still intervene in such cases, not to punish, but to direct the course of the perpetrator's future actions. Hume says a bit about where our character comes from and something about how external influences can affect a person's moral development, but only a little about whether we can do anything to initiate changes in ourselves. It is true that many of the steady features of persons about which he writes seem determined by inherent temperament and cultural influences. Hume includes in the discussion of character the traits, some of which mentioned above, we consider virtues and vices, but also natural talents that we generally admire and one's delicacy of taste or lack of such. There are characters distinctive to individuals, but we also possess general temperaments determined, he thinks, by ethnic origin.[19] There are also traits of character we have in virtue of being human, such as curiosity, ambition, and friendship. So, character for Hume is a broad notion, including what many theorists would call personality, which they would distinguish from character by the former's involuntary nature.

In the reply to the complaint that his theory cannot make a distinction between moral virtues, which are voluntary, and natural talents, which are not, Hume makes some telling remarks about the ability to change some aspects of our character. First, he observes that many of the features that ancient moralists considered virtues were equally involuntary, citing constancy, fortitude, and magnanimity. In this context he makes the comment that it is "almost impossible for the mind to change its character in any considerable article, or cure itself of a passionate or splenetic temper, when they are natural to it."[20] Second, he requests a reason why virtue and vice must be voluntary, since we take pleasure as spectators in many features of persons (e.g., grace and beauty), without a concern for their being voluntary. Third, he confirms his view that freedom is not a feature of human actions or qualities, and those who believe that voluntariness implies liberty are mistaken. More important are his comments about a genuine difference between natural abilities and what many see as distinctively moral virtues:

> that the former are almost invariable by any art or industry; while the latter, or at least the actions, that proceed from them, may be chang'd by the motives of reward and punishment, praise and blame. Hence legislators, and divines, and moralists, have principally applied them-selves to the regulating these voluntary actions, and have endeavor'd to produce additional motives for being virtuous in that particular. They knew, that to punish a man for folly, or exhort him to be prudent or sagacious, wou'd have but little effect; tho' the same punishments and exhortations with regard to justice and injustice, might have a considerable influence.[21]

Hume adds that this distinction has not been kept in mind, however, since it is natural to praise whatever we approve and blame what we disapprove; hence, traits like prudence, which are not directly affected by threat of punishment, are generally denominated virtues nonetheless.

The purpose for which I find his discussion interesting is to highlight that while Hume appears to be a pessimist about the mind's changing its own character, he does understand the effects of external incentives, like the threat of punishment and the promise of reward, the fear of colleagues' or parents' disapproval and the anticipation of their esteem. Not all potential behavior is subject to such influence; no matter what rewards are offered to me, practice as I might, I will never sing an aria like Beverly Sills or hit a baseball like Babe Ruth. But that some of our conduct is subject to such outside causes gives us a foothold into a view of character change. The strategy I want to suggest here is that if we understand our own motivational psychology and what factors others affect in order to induce changes in our behavior, we can then engineer those changes in ourselves. I want to suggest that persons can be spectators to their *own* behaviors and exercise a third-person-like influence on their *own* actions. If this is so, then we only need a plausible account of how changes in behavior induce changes in character to have a naturalistic model of how we can direct our own character development.

A Naturalistic Account of Moral Self-Cultivation from Hume

On the Humean view I want to develop, actions are caused by internal states (motives, or beliefs and desires, or reasons), and natural dispositions have some role in determining what these are for each of us. This means that a person with an optimistic nature is more likely to believe than a pessimistic person that the current dilemma she faces is solvable, and she is more likely to welcome further perplexities in her life. It is surely also true that factors external to us influence these internal states, contributing to content and the degree of strength with which they are experienced. We don't normally believe *anything* we are emotionally disposed to believe, but also look for evidence provided by our environment. Likewise, our particular emotions are influenced not just by our inherent tendencies to be this way or that (excitable or calm, happy or sad, timid or intrepid, etc.), but also by factors outside of us. The extent to which we can be moved by external influences is delimited by our natural dispositions, of course, but we have no reason to think that the range of possibilities for each of us is exceedingly narrow. An extremely shy person may never become a nightclub singer, and an extremely violent person may never become completely docile, but even a very shy person can have a public life, and a violent person can become less aggressive. Furthermore, on a view that supposes we have many shared dispositions as human beings, as Hume's does, it is plausible to expect that we can be shaped in similar ways by similar circumstances.

Among the "external" influences to which persons are susceptible are the exhortation of authorities, the rhetoric of politicians, education, the threat of punishment and the promise of reward, and the approval or disapproval of others. Hume himself doesn't always indicate explicitly how these things work on us, but we can figure it out by reference to various Humean "principles" inherent in human nature: imagination, sympathy, the force of custom or habit, and various universal passions—for pleasant things, for good reputation, for fellowship. The forceful rhetoric of authorities and politicians arouses the imagination and prompts us to consider the possibilities of better states of affairs and more comfortable lives. Educators can expose us to a broader range of possibilities that expand the imagination's repertoire; they can interject considerations into our thinking of which we were never before aware, broaden our abilities to sympathize by presenting the lives of others through narratives; they can habituate us to certain ways of conceiving of others and of interacting with them. Of course, fear of punishment and prospect of reward are motivating because of our loathing of the unpleasantness of the former situation and our attraction to the pleasantness of the latter. Aversion to the disapproval of others has an effect on us not only because we care very much about how we look in the eyes of others, but also because we sympathize with their reactions and so their unpleasant responses to us are mirrored in our own feelings.

I want to suggest that, even though Hume says little about it, we can use some of these recognized influences in our environment to alter our own actions and eventually to shape our own characters. First, however, we have to be aware of our own moral shortcomings. On a spectator view, this means we must observe ourselves in the way we observe the moral qualities of others. But this feat looks practically impossible, since we would have to sympathize with those affected negatively by our own actions; if we lack caring passions in the first place, it is difficult to think that we'll be able to adjust our sympathies to take on others' feelings, especially when we are the source of their trouble. Hume has an alternative suggestion here about how we notice our inadequacies: "When any virtuous motive or principle is common in human nature, a person, who feels his heart devoid of that principle, may hate himself upon that account, and may perform the action without the motive, from a certain sense of duty, in order to acquire by practice, that virtuous principle, or at least, to disguise to himself, as much as possible, his want of it."[22]

We do become spectators of ourselves, but our feeling of self-disapprobation is based on a comparison of ourselves to others, rather than on our sympathetic feelings with those affected by our own actions. We realize that there are ways in which we ought to be better, not due to a comparison with some ideal of moral perfection, but due to the way we feel when we find ourselves deficient in the approved qualities that many others around us possess. This implies that the best way to detect our own faults is to surround ourselves with those we acknowledge to be good people. This implication seems right. For instance, the experience of finding one's qualities paling in comparison to a generous friend's is common, and the more we are surrounded with people who exemplify generosity, the more likely we are to feel the discomfort of our own stinginess, if only because we are different from them.

The passage cited above is also a rare instance of Hume's suggesting a strategy for self-improvement: Namely, I do the action the virtuous person would do, even without the virtuous motive, but I do it from a different motivation, that is, from a "sense of duty" (a sense that I ought to do it); I do so, either to acquire the proper motive by practice, or "at least" to disguise to myself that I lack the proper motivation. The notion of practicing to become virtuous is common in virtue ethics, as we have already seen. Aristotle offered a developed account of this process, and Ben Franklin employed the strategy also. Hume places great emphasis on habit as a hugely influential feature in our lives. But we can also improve our own character by interjecting into our experience the same kind of causes others introduce in an attempt to influence our behavior. We can extend our own sympathies by exposing ourselves to literature, and we can change our sensibilities by our choices of movies, activities, and companions. The more aware we are of the condition of others, the more likely we are to recognize the content of virtue (a prerequisite to practicing it) and the more likely we are to respond to the needs of others (to exercise the virtue of benevolence itself). If we set before ourselves models of good character, even if only in the imagination, we will respond with admiration, and the feeling of admiration can motivate us to emulate the exemplars we have in mind. We can exhort ourselves with reminders. We can reward ourselves for our successes over our worst temptations. These strategies are attempts to get ourselves to behave in the ways a virtuous person would behave when we lack the proper motivation to qualify as virtuous ourselves.

To make this account of the possibility of self-cultivation more plausible, however, I think we need some explanation how we acquire a virtue, which is a motivation, by practicing a behavior without the motivation. Why should we think that actions can eventually affect motivations? How does the "external" incentive to morality become an "internal" one? Perhaps the answer is simply that the fact that habits of behavior introduce motives is a fundamental principle of human nature, explainable by nothing more ultimate. But I think an analogy can help to answer the question as well: Consider the development of tastes. How do we come to enjoy something that initially tastes bad to us? The experience of a smoker is a good example. The motivation to smoke is not that the nicotine tastes good or that smoking is an enjoyable experience; the first experience or two at smoking is physically unpleasant (causes coughing and gagging, etc.). Rather, the motivation is something like that others one is around are smoking—the social pressure that Hume identifies when he writes about our uneasiness at not being like others. So, one begins from an external incentive. But with repeated instances of smoking, the motivation to do so changes to an internal incentive; the experience becomes an enjoyable one and something the person does at her own prompting, even outside social contexts. Of course, with tobacco, the motive is grounded in a physical dependency. Developing one's taste for certain foods is another example. Many foods we come to regard later as delicacies are foods that we were motivated to try first by external promptings, not because we found the foods attractive ourselves; we were told that we "had" to try this, or we were moved by social pressure to eat or drink what others were having. Developing the taste for fine wine is like this; at first, it tastes unappealing and seems even pungent or bitter. With greater experience, its taste becomes attractive, and with wider experience with various wines, our palate is able to make finer-grained distinctions among the qualities. The motivation to have wine with dinner then consists in our own tastes and dispositions, not the advice of others.

Practicing the actions a grateful person would do when we lack gratitude ourselves can likewise make grateful actions more comfortable to us. I suppose I could be in a habit of doing actions to which I am averse, but on the analogy with taste, it's reasonable to think that my "tastes" for such actions develop until I find myself motivated by my own disposition to grateful actions. However, given that gratitude, the virtue, is a feeling of appreciation toward a benefactor, we also need to ask whether the disposition to grateful actions is itself that feeling of appreciation identified with gratitude. Likewise, is the disposition to generous actions itself generosity? Is the habit of doing actions that benefit others a feeling of kindness? The attitudes of gratitude, generosity, and kindness all involve some kind of caring about the objects involved.

Can we have developed dispositions toward actions whose objects we don't really care about? A child might be trained to say "thank you" every time she's given a gift or a cookie or a piece of candy without actually feeling gratitude for the treat. But I'm inclined to think that this possibility is a function of immaturity rather than something indicative of habits of action and corresponding feelings. Mature individuals who make it habitual to *show* gratitude with no pro-spect of reward or praise are surely *experiencing* gratitude for the benefit they've received, and the experience is the cause of their actions. They are in a position to comprehend the efforts of others, while perhaps a little girl simply can't yet appreciate the trouble her grandma went through to have her favorite cookies ready. The child's sympathies are not yet fully developed in the way an adult's are. In fact, on the analogy with taste, one may eventually develop deep-er and deeper appreciation of the contributions certain individuals make to the quality of one's life and the qualities of others' lives. People can be more appre-ciative (or kinder or more generous) as their experiences widen, just as the wine connoisseur is more discerning as his experience widens. It is simply hard to imagine that we might be in the habit of doing actions that affect other objects or persons in certain ways without our having a genuine regard of some kind for those objects or persons. Consequently, it does make sense psychologically to identify the disposition to action with the motive—the virtue or the vice. Conse-quently, we have reason to think that the strategy Franklin used to increase his virtue, one recommended by Aristotle and Hume, is on a sound psychological basis.

Why Believe There Is Character At All?

I have maintained that the project of moral self-cultivation depends on a notion of character. I have offered some reasons to think that affections develop as we practice certain actions and that we are warranted in positing the appropriate vir-tues and vices that describe those affections according to the habits people exhi-bit. I believe, along with some other traditional virtue theorists, that these vir-tues, vices, and other ingrained traits, whether a matter of natural endowment or conscious practice, are constitutive of a person's character. The notion of char-acter has recently been challenged, however, by those who think that empirical psychology provides evidence against the idea that persons act from enduring and consistent dispositions.

John M. Doris, in his recent book, *Lack of Character*,[23] argues that people do not exhibit the behavioral reliability that virtue ethics requires for attribution of "Aristotelian" traits to them. His discussion centers on Aristotle's theory, but has some application to similar theories like Hume's in which character is thought of as constant qualities exhibited in stable patterns of behavior. Doris offers a description of the Aristotelian view as containing the notion that the per-son of virtuous character will behave appropriately, even when faced with cir-cumstances that contain obstacles to moral success; we can predict that a person who acts courageously in his ordinary life will demonstrate his courage under extraordinary circumstances as well, for instance, as a prisoner of war or on a foundering ship. Although he does not put it quite so bluntly in his book, Doris writes in an article preceding the book,

Unfortunately, experimental evidence . . . suggests that this approach, however commonplace it may be, is inadequate to the facts of actual behavior: trait attribution is often surprisingly inefficacious in predicting behavior in particular novel situations, because differing behavioral outcomes often seem a function of situational variation more than individual disposition. To put things crudely, people typically lack character.[24]

Gilbert Harman affirms a similar line as well, and it has been suggested by social scientists.[25] The sort of experimental evidence to which they appeal is gathered from studies in which people are given opportunities to exhibit the traits expected of them on a positing of their characters, but they instead seem to respond to the circumstances of the situation and behave in ways inconsistent with the expected.

The famous Milgram experiments from the 1970s are such a study.[26] Subjects were asked to send supposedly near-lethal doses of electric shock to other subjects as part of an important conditioning experiment in which they thought they were taking part. Even when those receiving the shocks screamed out in apparent pain, the subjects who thought they were part of a significant experiment continued, on the command of the experimental psychologist in charge, to send the electric impulses. Where the expectation is that normal compassion would typically prevent people from unnecessarily imposing dreadfully painful conditions on others, the Milgram experiment allegedly showed that such character traits do not carry people through situations in which perceived authority exerts pressure to the contrary. In another such experiment, students at Princeton Theological Seminary were told as each arrived that he or she would be giving a talk in another building. Some students were told that they must hurry or they would be late for their talk; others were told that they had just enough time to get to their talk; and others were told that they had spare time. Half of the subjects were assigned to talk on the parable of the Good Samaritan and half on something else. The students' religious and moral outlooks were varied. On the way to their assigned locations, each student encountered a person slumped in a doorway, apparently in need of help. The point of the study was to see which variables, if any, were correlated with students' stopping to help. The only correlating factor that emerged was how pressed one was for time: 63 percent who were not hurried stopped; 45 percent in the somewhat hurried group stopped; 10 percent of those who feared being late stopped.[27] A similar experiment from the 1970s had a poser drop a file of papers in the path of those leaving a phone booth after making a call. We would expect most people to stop and help the person in distress gather up her scattered pages. For one group of callers, a dime was left in the phone's return coin slot, and for another it wasn't. Of sixteen who found a coin in the slot, fourteen stopped to help pick up the papers, and two did not; of twenty-five who did not find a dime in the slot, one stopped to help and the rest did not.[28]

The contemporary analogue to Aristotelian character ethics that Doris maintains is undermined by such evidence he calls "globalism." Globalism holds that runs of trait-relevant behavior "exhibit consistency across situations" and that "runs of consistent behavior will exhibit evaluative affinities with other such runs." Hence, an honest person "will be consistently honest, and will also exhibit consistent behavior indicative of traits related to honesty, such as loyalty and courage."[29] Doris cites evidence from history that supports the rejection of globalism as well, discussing the psychology of the Holocaust, which, he holds, is populated by psyches of a fragmented nature. The Auschwitz doctors, for instance, exhibited both compassionate behavior and brutal behavior; Nazi war criminals issued murderous commands and then drank heavily, some into alcoholism. Torturers are not torturers overnight; they had to be acculturated gradually into their work by an all-encompassing institution.[30]

Doris concludes that situationist social psychology is the viable alternative to globalism. Situationist psychology rejects the notion of robust traits like broad categories of the "compassionate" or the "courageous" in favor of

> temporally stable, situation-particular, "local" traits that may reflect dispositional differences among persons. These local traits may be extremely finegrained: a person might be reliably helpful in iterated trials of the same situation (such as when she finds a dime in a mall phone booth and someone drops a pile of papers in her path), and reliably unhelpful in other, often surprisingly similar, circumstances.[31]

The situationist also suggests that personality is not composed of "evaluatively" integrated traits that produce a unified character of virtue or vice, but rather it is made of fragmented "trait-associations"; so for instance, a local disposition to honesty (a tendency to honest actions in one situation) will often be found with a local disposition to dishonesty (a tendency to dishonest actions in another situation).[32]

Harman (unlike Doris) wants to differentiate character traits from psychological disorders and innate aspects of temperament; schizophrenia is not character, he says, and neither is shyness or being an optimistic person. He writes, "Character traits include virtues and vices like courage, cowardice, honesty, dishonesty, benevolence, malevolence, friendliness, unfriendliness, as well as certain other traits like friendliness [sic] or talkativeness."[33] This means that the conclusions of his arguments are to apply to this group, but not to the traits that are attributable to innate temperament. I am not certain what the underlying idea is here, especially since talkativeness seems, if not the opposite trait to shyness, a consequence of its opposite, sociability. So, why friendliness and talkativeness would be character traits, and shyness not, is unclear. The proposal that biologically-determined traits cannot be part of character seems not to explain this classification, since it may be that all traits are to some degree an outcome of biology; anyway, it would not be crazy to think that friendliness and talkativeness are. Perhaps the distinction is based on Hume's suggestion that what people traditionally call character traits can be influenced by offers of rewards and punishments, while other traits cannot (although Hume does not himself distinguish character traits this way). This is a promising explanation of Harman's distinction, but there are problems here too: Rewards can get one to behave in ways that are not the typical actions of a shy person, just as rewards can coax one into more benevolent-looking behavior. Perhaps Harman presumes that doing the acts an outgoing person would do does not change one's shy temperament, because shyness is, after all, a genuine temperament, while doing benevolent-looking acts says nothing about enduring dispositions one way or the other. This reply would beg the question, though, since the issue is whether there is in fact an underlying disposition that defines the one trait (shyness) and not the other (benevolence).

The main line of response offered to the situationist's argument, at least on behalf of Aristotelian or globalist virtue, is that the various social experiments do not show that there are no character traits, but rather that virtue is not as common as we thought it to be. "The picture of moral development of the virtues is one of gradual development subject to set-backs in the face of extreme difficulty. Virtue requires the right reasoning and the appropriate desire, neither of which are easy to acquire."[34] But neither Harman nor Doris is persuaded by this reply. Harman explains that experiments like Milgram's do not show directly that there are no character traits, but they do show that observers have "a fundamental attribution error": the wrong tendency to infer that actions are due to distinct, robust character traits, rather than to features of the situation. This error is connected to the argument that people have no character traits, however, because the error is an error due to the fact that there is no reason to believe there are character traits. If there is no such reason, then it is irrational to believe they exist. Doris's chief response to the Aristotelian's reply is to inquire about the practicality of an ethics that holds up ideals of virtue that no one attains. Aristotelian virtue ethics is alleged to be practical; he cites Aristotle's claim that "we are inquiring not in order to know what excellence is, but in order to become good, since otherwise our inquiry would have been of no use."[35] Doris claims that situationist moral psychology is better in terms of its practical recommendations, for it implies that the way to do right is to avoid the circumstances that hold the greatest temptations to do wrong. Believing that virtue can carry us through temptation is morally dangerous, since studies have found that belief to be unsubstantiated.

Since the concern in this discussion is over the best explanation of actions, first I want to examine the method of explanation the situationist employs. No one can argue that circumstances alone (that is, external circumstances) determine actions, since if this were the case, all people in the same situation would behave in the same way: 100 percent of those under the impression they have to hurry to give a talk would not stop to help someone in need, not just 90 percent, and so forth. Since the claim can't be that circumstances are the only factor (although it is not clear what counts as "circumstances"), the situationist states that psychological causes are also contributors. Since the event to be explained here is action, then psychological causes have, at the least, to be seen as dispositions to action. The internal causes of actions are, logically, *dispositions to* action. The dispositions the situationist is willing to posit to explain actions are, however, very specific ones, like the disposition to help someone pick up her scattered papers after finding a coin in a phone booth (a dime in the 1970s—would a quarter be necessary now?) or the disposition to stop to help someone who is hurt when one is not pressed by other commitments to hurry along. How satisfying are the explanations that pair circumstances with very specific dispositions?

In answer to the request for an explanation why a particular lump of sugar dissolved in this glass of water just now, we're told that it dissolved because sugar is soluble, that is, it has the disposition to dissolve when put in liquid, and we can explain the disposition to dissolve in liquid in terms of other properties or dispositions as well. When the disposition used in the explanation is wider in terms of what it covers than just the particular case being explained, reference to dispositions has explanatory power. For instance, my disposition to be afraid of going to the fiftieth floor of this building on Tuesdays after I've had a full meal is no explanation of why I'm afraid right now to go to the fiftieth floor of this building today, Tuesday, when I've just had a full meal. But that I am generally disposed to be fearful of heights and that I am generally disposed to stomach upset when I'm afraid is a kind of explanation, since it says something about my psychology and physiology more broadly. Our understanding advances when specific phenomena can be encompassed under general principles.

Doris recognizes this criticism to some degree in his book, but I think his discussion of it is inadequate. His view is that general trait attributions are not obviously more informative than local trait attributions: "saying that Alberta is 'sociable' does little more to explain her office party sociability than saying she is 'office party sociable.' In any such case, a more enlightening explanation appeals to motives, goals, values, attitudes, strategies, or whatever else it is that forms, for a given individual, the psychological context of the trait."[36] While I agree that appeal to all of these factors avails us of a more thorough explanation of behavior, I fail to see how local trait attributions are as revealing as the general. The view defended by the situationist moral psychologist does not allow for wide generalizations about the psychology of individual persons, at least when it comes to what Harman has defined (in a question-begging way, I think) as character traits. While he might allow that we can infer a disposition to be fearful of heights, since that disposition is not a character trait on his view, he will not allow that we can reasonably infer a disposition to care for the welfare of others or even the welfare of one's family, since the evidence would never support, according to the argument of both Doris and Harman, the positing of such a disposition. On their view, the phenomenon of behavior does not allow for broader explanations than very specific dispositions, along with particular goals, attitudes, and so forth, of the moment. The explanatory power of such narrow and transitory states is paltry, however.

A connected methodological problem to which I have already alluded is that it is not clear what constitutes "the situation" to which actions are relative. Why aren't the events that immediately preceded one's entering a phone booth relevant to whether one stops to help someone who has dropped her papers? Why isn't the amount of sleep a person got the night previous to the experiment relevant to whether he stops to help someone? What about the sort of medications the subject is taking or his state of mind? The social scientist's assumption is that we establish the relevance of events to action by achieving a correlation with the action under study. But the circumstances that could be relevant are artificially limited by the experimental situation: Nothing that happened to the subject prior to entering the experimental environment can possibly count as relevant simply because the sociologist hasn't been in a position to observe it.

Second, I want to look at the notion of character purportedly undermined by the empirical data; it will turn out that it is an overly simplistic one. The sort of virtue ethics that Doris and Harman have been discussing, they say, is one in which a person cannot have the virtue if one does not display it consistently in all circumstances, even in the most extreme cases of conflict, which constitute the real test of one's virtue. Whether this is the correct way to understand the Aristotelian view is questionable. (While the person of virtue is expected always to behave according to the mean, this person is, say, not required always to be *fearless*, but always to show fear under the right circumstances and in the right way.) However, putting Aristotle's specific claims aside, do we generally imply that there are never exceptions to one's pattern of behavior when we attribute dispositions to that person? I'm in the habit of brushing my teeth before I go to bed, but I miss doing so one night because I received a very late unexpected urgent call that kept me on the phone past my usual bedtime and distracted me. Have I lost the disposition to brush my teeth every night? Was this case the test of whether I really have formed the habit? Good drivers follow the rules of the road, signal all turns and lane changes, watch out for unexpected moves on the part of other drivers, don't impede traffic by driving too slowly, and so on. If I typically do these things, but neglect a couple of them one afternoon when a friend is getting sick in the back seat of my car, is it correct to conclude that I really am not a good driver after all? I keep my office organized even when I get very busy, but the extraordinarily huge of amount of work that has come in recently has kept me from doing what I usually do, and my desk is a mess. Am I no longer an organized person? The question I'm asking with these examples is whether we are logically forced to give up on attributing habits at all, since behavior is never 100 percent consistent, given the difficult circumstances in which people sometimes find themselves. Sugar, after all doesn't dissolve completely in ice water, either, but it *is* still soluble.

I am suggesting that the cases of severe emotional conflict or conflict of commitments are *not* the cases that test whether or not one possesses a certain disposition. The Milgram experiment has been analyzed over and over again in terms of what it shows about human obedience to authority. Subjects were put in a situation in which they were led to believe that they were part of a very important experiment conducted by a reputable authority, and they were eager to serve. They experienced conflict between obedience and compassion, and many suffered emotionally at the responses of the persons who were subject to the shocks they chose to give out of obedience to authority. (This is not the analysis the Doris/Harman camp gives, of course, since obedience and compassion are character traits.) The view of character that I want to suggest here is based on a Humean analysis, but Aristotelians can accommodate much of it as well, I think. Two points are important. First, Hume's view implies that actions that don't fit into a pattern of consistent behavior are not done from character, and that the actor is not responsible for them. (Nothing in my present discussion turns on this seemingly controversial claim about responsibility, although I think Hume's view on this issue, properly understood, is plausible.) This is not to deny that we have character, but in fact the opposite: It allows that there is such a thing as acting out of, or contrary to, character. That is, one's character is not lost by the exceptions, as long as the exceptions are not so numerous as to obscure the established pattern. None of the psychological studies cited, however, follows a particular individual through the course of his or her recent life to see if there is any established pattern of behavior before coming to the "test."[37]

Second, in cases where there is conflict of formed dispositions, the actor is forced to act against one of those dispositions, but that does not compel us to say that he has lost the disposition against which he is acting, or that he never had it. Had he not had the disposition, the conflict would not have arisen at all. The studies cited from social scientists are all comparisons between groups of individuals caught in conflict circumstances and groups of individuals not so caught; among the latter group, many more choose the better good than among the former. Their conclusion is that no one has character traits, since the presumption is that, were character a cause, equal numbers from the comparison groups would choose the better alternative. This view ignores the complexity of character and the effect on action of conflict between the various dispositions *comprising* a person's character.

The situational psychological experiments suppose that if there is such thing as virtuous character, most people will do the overall best thing in each situation, no matter how difficult; since few people do the best thing, it follows there is no virtuous character. If the only character traits attributable to actors were the disposition to be good and the disposition to be bad, then it could follow from the sociological studies (were their method of explanation not flawed in the first place) that there are no character traits—or that few people are good. The supposedly standard Aristotelian reply, to affirm the second alternative, is to say that few are practically wise enough to know that compassion should prevail over punctuality or over obedience, etc., in these difficult cases. This reply may very well be right, but if few people are practically wise, it is because the complications of character make conflicting dispositions extremely difficult to negotiate. It is because character is not a simple phenomenon that the inconsistent behavior of Nazi war criminals actually makes sense on a character ethics approach. Character ethics does not deny that environmental forces and institutions in which one participates can inculcate new dispositions of character that cause emotional turmoil. Whether one is facing a conflict of commitments is something evidenced by one's emotional reaction to one's choice in these extreme situations. There is a significant difference in the Milgram experiment between the person who suffered emotionally, broke out in a sweat, and begged the experiment be stopped and the person who was indifferent to the effects of the shocks she sent. The latter person, feeling no conflict when we think she ought to, is subject to stronger condemnation than the former, even though both performed the same type of action in similar situations. The character theorist can accord moral significance to feelings of guilt, regret, or remorse in a way that the situational theorist cannot, by appealing to internal conflicts that are a result of one's having character traits in the first place.[38]

Because of deficiencies in the situationist psychologists' method of explanation and in their conception of character, I see nothing in their arguments to undermine the conception of character on which moral improvement depends. The absence of practical wisdom necessary to goodness of character over all, a normative conception of character, does not constitute the absence of personal dispositions, understood descriptively. Taken singly, those dispositions (benevolence, punctuality, gratitude, selfishness, laziness) can be understood normatively as well, as individual virtues and vices, but when two virtues conflict in a certain situation, there is no ground to conclude that such dispositions do not exist because they cannot all be realized in particular situations.[39]

I conclude this section with a general point about theory and observation in moral psychology and philosophy. Moral philosophers are often accused of ignoring empirical data in their work, but the question is "How ought philosophers to use this data?" Scientists do not build their theories by first making observations to see where the data lead them—because they cannot. Data collection can only take place in the context of a theoretical structure within which observations have significance. Likewise, there are no non-theory-laden psychological or moral observations. To borrow an example that arises in the context of a related debate in which Harman is engaged, one's observation of a vapor trail in a cloud chamber is evidence of the presence of a proton, but *only if* one already presupposes the framework of atomic theory.[40] These points raise large questions about the relation of empirical data to moral theory that I cannot pursue here, but my point is that we cannot pretend that we situate ourselves in a vacuum to observe human behavior and then generalize *to* a theory of psychology that our pure observations directly support, whether it be theory of character or lack of such.[41]

Conclusion

I have argued in this essay that the notion of personal moral development requires the notion of character and that we have good reason to think that belief in character as composed of general dispositions or habits to action is justified. Moreover, I have tried to show that the project of moral self-improvement is possible in a naturalistic framework that does not construct the notion of morality out of the idea of agency. (As I have suggested, I'm inclined to think that if non-naturalist conceptions of agency do not allow that characters causally determine actions, they cannot account for personal moral improvement.) The naturalist cannot say, however, whether everyone is able to find sufficient motivation to engage in a project of self-improvement. There may very well be those who are simply lack the requisite psychological constitution. However, most people do try at some time to change themselves in some ways; consequently, such motivation is widespread, and we can conclude that relatively few people are beyond the pale.

I have also argued that the project of character development requires that we understand our characters and our motivations as subject to forces outside of ourselves; this knowledge allows us to interject into the conditions determining our character factors that may alter our habits or dispositions. When we engineer our own character changes by altering the external conditions that affect our habits, we take a third-person stance toward ourselves, but this still counts as *self*-improvement, since the goal is to alter our *own* habits or dispositions. Consequently, nature allows the possibility that we may make ourselves better persons.[42]

Notes

1. John Doris, *Lack of Character* (Cambridge: Cambridge University Press, 2002); John Doris, "Persons, Situations, and Virtue Ethics," *Nous* 32 (1998): 504-30; Gilbert Harman, "Moral Psychology Meets Social Psychology: Virtue Ethics and the Fundamental Attribution Error," *Proceedings of the Aristotelian Society* 99 (1999): 315-31.

2. Onora O'Neill writes, "Kant's account of the intelligibility of action begins with the claim that acts must have maxims, or underlying practical principles. . . . It is these maxims that determine the will . . . but not, of course, in the way that efficient causes determine anything." (Onora O'Neill, *Constructions of Reason* [Cambridge: Cambridge University Press, 1989], 71.) Marcia Baron says, "The problem is that the term 'motive' suggests causation, as if the motive or duty or a desire to help another were a force within us that causes us to act accordingly," and "This is a familiar picture of agency from the empiricist tradition. Kant's theory of agency is very different. Our actions are not the result of a desire or some other incentive that impels us. An incentive can move us to act only if we let it." (Marcia W. Baron, *Kantian Ethics Almost Without Apology* [Ithaca, NY: Cornell University Press, 1995], 189.) Henry Allison states, "Incentives . . . do not motivate by themselves causing action but rather by being taken as reasons. . . . Correlatively, we think of reason as determining the will . . . by providing the laws or principles . . . which govern, without causally necessitating . . . its choices." (Henry E. Allison, *Kant's Theory of Freedom* [Cambridge: Cambridge University Press, 1990], 51.)

3. See Richard McCarty, "The Maxims Problem," *The Journal of Philosophy* XCIV (January 2002): 29-44.

4. For important formulations of internalism, see Robert Audi, "Moral Judgment and Reasons for Action," in *Ethics and Practical Reason*, ed. G. Cullity and B. Gaut (New York: Oxford University Press, 1997), 125-59; W.D. Falk, "'Ought' and Motivation," *Proceedings of the Aristotelian Society* 48 (1947-1948): 492-510, reprinted in *Ought, Reasons, and Morality* (Ithaca, NY: Cornell University Press, 1986), 21-41; and Christine Korsgaard, "Skepticism About Practical Reason," *The Journal of Philosophy* 83 (January 1986): 5-25.

5. Benjamin Franklin, *The Autobiography of Benjamin Franklin & Selections from his Other Writings*, intro. by Stacy Schiff (New York: The Modern Library, 2001), 90.

6. It is probably no coincidence that Franklin's list resembles the sort of virtues one might derive from the eighteenth-century devotional book, *The Whole Duty of Man*.

7. Franklin writes that his original list was of twelve virtues, but a Quaker friend convinced him to add humility. His friend persuaded him that Franklin's pride, an obstacle to virtue, was demonstrated in conversation when he was not merely happy with being right, but was also insolent and overbearing!

8. Franklin, *Autobiography*, 91-92.

9. Franklin, *Autobiography*, 94.

10. Franklin, *Autobiography*, 97.

11. Franklin, *Autobiography*, 98.

12. Aristotle, *Nicomachean Ethics*, 1103a.

13. This is the so-called Humean theory of motivation, on which naturalists typically agree; they say that desires plus beliefs, and not beliefs alone, give us motives to action. The contemporary Humean theory of motivation focuses on desire, but Hume saw desires as only one type of passion that could serve as a motive; there were many others, like gratitude, fear, and benevolence.

14. T 1.2.11.2; SBN 316-17. References to Hume's *A Treatise of Human Nature* designated by "T" are to ed. David Fate Norton and Mary Norton (Oxford: Oxford University Press, 2000); the "T" is followed by book, part, section, and page number. References to the Treatise designated by "SBN" are to the page numbers in the Selby-Bigge/Nidditch edition (Oxford: Clarendon Press, 1978).

15. T 3.3.1.18; SBN 584.

16. T 3.3.1.19; SBN 584.

17. Hume, *An Enquiry Concerning the Principles of Morals*, sections V-VIII.

18. T 2.3.2.6; SBN 411; 3.3.1.5; SBN 575.

19. T 2.3.1.10; SBN 402-3. See also his essay, "Of National Characters," in David Hume, *Essays: Moral, Political, and Literary*, ed. Eugene Miller (Indianapolis: Liberty Classics, 1985), 197-215.

20. T 3.3.4.3; SBN 608.

21. T 3.3.4.4; SBN 609.

22. T 3.2.1.8; SBN 479.

23. See note 1.

24. Doris, "Persons, Situations, and Virtue Ethics," 505-6.

25. Harman, "Moral Psychology Meets Social Psychology." The social scientists Nisbett and Ross hold a similar view in *The Person and the Situation: Perspectives of Social Psychology* (New York: McGraw-Hill), 1991.

26. Stanley Milgram, *Obedience to Authority* (New York: Harper and Rowe, 1974).

27. J. M. Darley and C. D. Batson, "'From Jerusalem to Jericho': A Study of Situational and Dispositional Variables in Helping Behavior," *Journal of Personality and Social Psychology* 27 (1993). Cited in Harman.

28. A. M. Isen and H. Levin, "Effect of Feeling Good on Helping: Cookies and Kindness," *Journal of Personality and Social Psychology* 21 (1972). Cited in Doris.

29. Doris, *Lack of Character*, 23.

30. Doris, *Lack of Character*, 53-58.

31. Doris, "Persons, Situations, and Virtue Ethics," 507. Doris affirms this view in his book as well: see *Lack of Character*, 64.

32. Doris, "Persons, Situations, and Virtue Ethics," 509.

33. Harman, "Moral Psychology Meets Social Psychology," 316.

34. Nafsika Athanassoulis, "A Response to Harman: Virtue Ethics and Character Traits," *Proceedings of the Aristotelian Society* 100 (2000): 215-21.

35. Aristotle, *Nicomachean Ethics*, 1103b.

36. Doris, *Lack of Character*, 66.

37. Joel Kupperman discusses the lack of so-called "longitudinal" studies in psychology. See *Character* (New York: Oxford University Press, 1991), 162-63.

38. A final observation about the Milgram experiments: They also seem not to show what the situational psychologists takes them to show because the subjects were asked to commit in advance to something about which they were systematically misinformed; they were not told that their participation would require (apparent) infliction of pain on someone else. Had the participants been so informed, we can assume that at least some, if not many, would not have taken part. As it is, these people were told that the experiment was of crucial importance and that millions of federal dollars were at stake, and each participant signed a consent form in advance. It's certainly not clear what their behavior under these circumstances shows about their virtue or lack of it.

39. For other critiques of Doris and Harman on various other grounds, see Gopal Sreenivasan, "Errors about Errors: Virtue Theory and Trait Attribution," *Mind* 111 (January 2002): 47-68; Robert Solomon, "Victims of Circumstances? A Defense of Virtue Ethics in Business," *Business Ethics Quarterly* 13 (January 2003): 43-62; and James Montmarquet, "Moral Character and Social Science Research," *Philosophy* 78 (July 2003): 355-68. Harman replies to Solomon in "No Character or Personality," *Business Ethics Quarterly* 13 (January 2003): 87-94.

40. See Gilbert Harman, *The Nature of Morality* (New York: Oxford University Press, 1977).

41. See also Nicholas Sturgeon, "Moral Explanations," in *Morality, Reason and Truth*, ed. David Copp and David Zimmerman (Totowa, NJ: Rowman and Allanheld, 1984), 49-78.

42. I thank Richard McCarty for several conversations about the issues in this paper, and I am grateful to Robert Audi, William Prior, and Brad Wilburn for their very helpful comments.

Chapter Seven

Self-Development as an Imperfect Duty

Robert N. Johnson

"You ought to make something of yourself." That certainly has the ring of truth about it. But is there really any obligation to develop yourself? Those who let abilities lie idle are shortsighted, of course. But are they guilty of anything more than imprudence? It is easy to think that there could be a moral fault in failing to help others such as your children to develop their talents and abilities. But what about not developing your own? And if this is a moral failing, is the fault solely in your having let others down in some way? Or is there fault in having let yourself down as well?

In my view, Kant had the right answers to these questions: "A human being," he argued, "has a duty to himself to cultivate his natural powers," and "owes it to himself" to do so, quite apart from what he might owe to his family, friends or community.[1] There is thus a moral obligation to develop yourself, and, moreover, what makes it wrong to fail in this obligation is not that you will let others down or even that the world will be made worse off, although both might also be true. What makes it wrong is that you have failed to respect your own humanity. These are the right answers, I think, but proving it is a large task. Elsewhere I defend Kant's arguments that your duty is to develop your own capacities, but not anyone else's, and that this is a duty toward yourself rather than to others.[2] The part of the task I take on in this chapter addresses two basic questions about Kant's views: First, what is (and to some extent what ought to be) the nature and extent of the Kantian duty toward yourself to develop your natural capacities, talents, abilities and the like? And, second, what, according to that model, do moral failings with regard to this duty look like?

It will come as a surprise to many that Kant's views on self-development should be worth taking seriously. For instance, Robert Paul Wolff remarks that they are so moralistic that they may be dismissed out of hand.[3] Indeed, it may seem surprising to some that there is any view to defend. But I believe that Wolff's views are based on substantial misunderstandings of Kant's position on these matters. The development and exercise of natural talents or capacities are important parts of one's good, if not parts of one's happiness as Kant conceives of this. And while it is true that Kant holds that a (direct) duty to pursue your own happiness is impossible, he thinks it is a duty to pursue one's own *good* if this is broadly construed to include natural self-development. Moreover, far from being overly moralistic, I think it can be shown that Kant's view that we owe it to ourselves to develop our capacities comports very well ordinary intuitions about what morality asks of us in this regard. The range and significance of this duty of natural self-development shows, surprising as it may seem, that the dissatisfaction with Kant's views expressed by philosophers such as Wolff and Slote is quite unfounded. That, at any rate, is what I hope the following shows.

Before I go further, I want to make my present aims clear. My interest is in obligations regarding our *natural*, rather than *moral*, capacities.[4] Kant agues that we are obligated to develop both, but it is a more interesting question if and why there is a moral obligation regarding our talents and abilities. Of course, given that we should improve our *moral* characters, it would follow that, other things equal, we should develop any abilities required for this. And certainly we ought to develop abilities, if there are such, required to fulfill any of our moral obligations. But Kant's position, and I think common sense morality, goes well beyond valuing natural talents merely as instrumental to, or constitutive of, morally good character or the performance of one's moral duties. One of the famous four examples in the *Groundwork*, for instance, is of a duty to develop talents with no obvious connection to moral ends, and in the *Metaphysic of Morals* Kant argues quite explicitly for a duty of natural perfection regardless of its role in moral perfection. I am interested, then, in the rationale for this *non-derivative* duty to develop oneself in *non-moral* respects.

I recognize that the very idea of an obligation to oneself has itself been controversial. If we had such an obligation, some argue, then, since it is an obligation *to ourselves* we should be able to free ourselves of it at will.[5] Yet an obligation from which one could free oneself at will would be no obligation at all. Kant himself offered a solution to this supposed paradox, but it is not clear that the paradox arises in his own theory. One comes to have a duty toward a person or persons, on his view, once and because one proposes to make use of their rational wills. Hence, although a person's will is an essential component in his account of how we come to acquire duties toward that person, it is not in virtue of that person's actual consent or agreement that this relationship is generated. Duties are thus generated toward yourself, not because of some fanciful prior agreement one has made with oneself, but because human beings must relies on the use of their rational will—rather than relying on instinct, say—to move about and change the world around them.[6]

I also realize that talk of natural human capacities that should be developed will naturally raise suspicions that an outdated teleological conception of human nature is at work.[7] Indeed, Kant's own appeals to the natural purpose of various capacities, and occasional suggestion that these were implanted by God, will reinforce these suspicions.[8] I do not pretend that these ideas can be entirely ignored, nor that they did not influence Kant in his thinking about an obligations to develop talents. But I am convinced that no dubious teleological considerations are actually required by his arguments. Kant nowhere argues that it is *because* our capacities are God-given or that Nature has a purpose in mind for them that we are obligated to develop them. Indeed, his argument is that we owe it to ourselves, not to God or Nature, to develop whatever natural capacities we have (taking other moral obligations into consideration).

To be sure, advocating the development of talents raises questions about, for instance, the justifiability of public standards of excellence in the context of conflicting ideals of the human good (e.g., as they might be found in a liberal educational system).[9] But my project circumvents these questions, being devoted not to what we may or ought to do to promote human development generally, but what we ought to do with regard to our own development. Granted, conceptions of the human good, and hence what counts as genuine human development, may be caught up in complex social contexts with histories and traditions. This adds complexity to the question of which of talents one ought to develop, and how far. But whatever conceptions of human talents we possess, regardless of their origins, the issue I am presently concerned with is not what is or is not "really" a human capacity, but whether we're obligated to develop what, in some sense, we reasonably hold to be our natural capacities.

Another preliminary worry: It will seem to some—as it evidently does to Wolff—to be obviously illegitimate to take a *moral* interest in whether anyone develops his or her own talents. Is it in general anyone else's business if someone prefers, say, watching TV to practicing piano? Perhaps it is not just *anyone's* business, but this isn't enough to undermine my project at the outset. Judgments that a family member has let himself down, or that a friend or a student owes it to herself to "make something more of herself," and so on, are commonplace.[10] When you make such judgments, you are not simply pointing out the direction of his or her well-being. There is an element of moral reproach in your judgment. What if anything justifies this element? Moreover, even if self-development were "not just anyone's business," it wouldn't follow that there are no grounds for moral judgment. What would follow is only that not just anyone is in a position to find fault with a person who refuses to develop herself. Indeed, if Kant's view is right, it can explain this consequence: that this is a duty toward oneself rather than others implies that the only person who will always be in a position to blame you if it is not fulfilled is you yourself. So in the following, when I speak of the failure to develop yourself as a moral failing, it will help to imagine that the person with the failing is, if not yourself, then a family member or close friend.

The Duty of Natural Self-Development

In this section of the paper, I explain the nature and extent of your duty regarding your natural capacities as this is represented in Kant's views. Although the following points focus on the *Metaphysics of Morals*, I aim to reconstruct views also found in the *Groundwork* and elsewhere where noted. Although these views are found in different works, unlike his views on some other topics, there are few apparent discrepancies that need working out between different texts. Thus, I will make the working assumption that these views are elements of a single consistent overall position. Still, at a number of points my account will have to go well beyond anything Kant actually says to fill out the position, and I will mark those points clearly. I want to stress that my main aim is not to argue for Kant's position on self-development, but simply to lay it out as I think it is best understood.

1. Kant holds that the duty of natural self-development is "wide and imperfect."[11] By this Kant means that the development of our natural capacities is an end we are morally obligated to adopt. As such, this duty can determine "nothing about the kind and extent of actions themselves but allows a latitude for free choice."[12] We are not, therefore, morally required to develop particular talents or abilities at particular times. By contrast, perfect duties, such as those forbidding suicide, gluttony, theft and so on, forbid or require particular acts at particular times. Now in setting and pursuing an end, as in performing or omitting an action, we are adopting a maxim (Kant's term for a practical principle, policy or, more generally, a guiding rationale for action), and it is, strictly speaking, these *maxims* that ethics concerns itself with. Any maxims we adopt, whether maxims of performing actions or of pursuing ends, must at the outset qualify for legislation as universal laws of nature.[13] Perfect and narrow duties turn out to be mainly negative duties forbidding certain kinds of behavior without exception or latitude. They forbid us from acting on maxims that cannot even be *conceived* of as coexisting with themselves as universal laws of nature. By contrast, imperfect and wide duties are positive duties, enjoining the pursuit of certain ends. Such duties arise, not because we cannot conceive of maxims of refusing to do so as universal laws (since we can), but because we nevertheless are not supposed to be able to rationally *will* these maxims as such.[14] Although conceivable that these maxims could coexist with themselves as universal laws of nature, human rational wills could not will that they become laws. This is supposed to be because such wills must will, insofar as they are rational, that they be happy and that their capacities be developed.

These are familiar features of Kant's views concerning wide imperfect duties, and I will return to elements of them below. But even these familiar features have significant implications for the extent of our duty of self-development: since one's maxim must be conceivable as a universal law in order to take the further step of willing it as such, it follows that one cannot fulfill a duty of self-development by violating a perfect duty—say, by unjustly harming or stealing from others. Indeed, if we take Kant seriously here, talents developed by knowingly and intentionally trampling human rights, even if they produced some of the world's great cultural treasures and human achievements, would not count as fulfilling anyone's moral obligation to perfect herself, and will even be blameworthy. That they produced treasures and achievements, and represent in some sense the heights of human development, cannot make up for the wickedness of the means used to produce them.[15]

This does not, however, tell us how we should weigh self-development against promoting the happiness of others, our other obligatory end. Intuitively, it seems that helping others ought to be a weightier concern than developing talents, that selfish indifference to the plight of others is a worse fault than idleness. Imagine two people, for instance, who are each equally observant of his moral duties and, in particular, have adopted their own perfection and the happiness of others as their ends. It is likely that they will differ on the amount of time they spend on each of these ends. One may spend more of his time on self-development, while the other spends more on helping others. Though equally free from blame, many will find on balance the latter to be the morally better person. Yet there can be no moral difference between them in terms of observance of their duties for Kant. Are we then simply to use intuition to decide when to leave off helping others in favor of developing ourselves, or vice versa?

Kant's view provides no general moral guideline for deciding this matter. But this is not itself an objection. As long as each person genuinely adopts both ends, neither has done better in performing his moral obligations than the other. This does not make it permissible, for instance, for Nero to fiddle while Rome burns, though not simply because each should spend *more time* on the needs of others. It is impossible to take seriously someone who claims to have taken the well-being of others to heart, yet when their needs are dire, knowingly and deliberately pursues self-development instead. To adopt the well-being of others as your end in any sense that is not a sham requires that you do something to promote it when there is an obvious opportunity, when little or no sacrifice and no violation of other duties is required. So although the person who helps others more than develops himself may seem to some to be a better *person* than the person who does the reverse—perhaps he seems more "saintly"—he has not done better, from a Kantian perspective, than the latter in meeting his moral obligations.

In fact, the choice Kant himself envisaged in his discussions of the duty of self-development is not between, on the one hand, ignoring self-development, and, on the other, lying to an admissions committee, failing to feed one's family or risking one's health and sanity. What is forbidden is "devoting [one's] life to pleasure" rather than "enlarging and improving [one's] fortunate natural predispositions."[16] Moral failing here will thus normally require conditions in which one has, to put it bluntly, some opportunity to loaf. The latitude for free choice allowed in imperfect duties does not imply that the pursuit of any whim or pleasure excuses failure to pursue an obligatory end. But it does show that one cannot

cannot be required to ignore one's own needs. If one does not develop oneself because one lives in life-threatening poverty, for instance, this does not mean that one has failed in one's obligation. To attempt to develop a worthwhile capacity under such circumstances might require violating a perfect duty toward oneself and perhaps others who might depend on you. Therefore, those who are economically disadvantaged or socially oppressed and so lack opportunities for self-development are not morally blameworthy for not developing themselves. Were such people to lack developed human capacities, it would therefore be no moral failing.

One may, of course, prefer to spend all of one's time developing one's capacities, but Kant's standard does not judge those with different preferences to be morally inferior. One has fulfilled one's duty so long as one has sincerely adopted self-development as one's end, and, given extreme needs of oneself or others are not at issue, this will reveal itself when one takes serious and deliberate steps to develop one's capacities when the opportunity presents itself. And although some have suggested otherwise, as I read it, Kant's view does not require maximizing, and so does not imply that self-perfection and helping others must fill up all of the space left in our lives after we have observed our perfect duties.[17]

2. The duty of natural self-perfection differs from the related duty of moral self-perfection, in that, although both are imperfect, the latter, unlike the former, is a "perfect one in terms of its quality" even if "imperfect in terms of its degree . . . because of the *frailty* (*fragilitas*) of human nature"[18] or a "general weakness of the human heart in complying with" moral maxims.[19] Even an honest and complete change of heart can be overcome by competing desires. Moreover, we cannot be certain whether we have ever succeeded in becoming morally perfect, since we cannot "see into the depths of [our] own heart[s]."[20] Nonetheless, one's obligation is "to strive with all one's might that the thought of duty for its own sake is the sufficient incentive of every action conforming to duty."[21] That is, by contrast with natural perfection, the form of our obligation regarding moral perfection is *always* to perform an action that will not vary in kind or extent from individual to individual based their different ends. This maxim, in other words, leaves no playroom for inclinations. The maxim of natural perfection, by contrast, lacks this perfect quality. It explicitly leaves playroom for inclinations, since human ends, and so the natural capacities that might serve those ends, vary from person to person and across cultures and social settings. This leaves it up to each to decide the kind and extent of the capacities to develop.

Nevertheless, because perfection represents an ideal limit, there is presumably no stopping point for the development of talents—a determinate point at which one is permitted to say "I've done enough; now I shall devote the rest of my life to pleasure." Again, this is not because one must aim to *maximize* self-development. One can genuinely have an end without seeking to maximize its realization. But, clearly, to relinquish self-perfection entirely at any point is to give it up as one's end. Therefore, even if the kind and extent of self-development is left up to each to decide for him or herself, that does not imply that one escapes moral blame if he, say, spends a few years fanatically developing his musical abilities, only to stop and spend the rest of his life drinking beer and lying on the sofa.

3. Sometimes we feel disappointed when gifted friends or family do nothing, or at least not enough, to develop or use that gift. And Kant's example from the Formula of the Universal Law of Nature in the *Groundwork* suggests that he is speaking to just this sort of disappointment. There, he refers to the relevant capacities as "talents" and "fortunate natural predispositions."[22] This suggests that our obligation is to develop those capacities with which we are particularly well endowed by nature, as opposed to simply some human capacities, however naturally well-endowed by nature we might be. So, for example, I would on this reading violate my duty of self-perfection if I refuse ever to develop my any gifts I might have and instead, because it happens to interest me, develop capacities that are not gifts at all.

Despite this reference to fortunate predispositions, I think that the Kantian view does not in fact entail that this is a moral failing. For one thing, the mere fact that you are gifted *alone* does not obligate you to develop that gift rather than some lesser ability unless that obligation is somehow based on its really being a gift, say, from God. If someone gives you a gift, perhaps you now owe a debt of gratitude. And perhaps the appropriate way to show gratitude were talents gifts would be to develop them fully. For instance, if someone makes a gift to you of a rare plant, it seems right that you should water and feed it or somehow do something to cultivate it. To let it wither and die seems an offence to the giver. Yet the development of talents is a duty *toward oneself*, while a duty based on gratitude for a gift would be a duty *toward the giver*. Indeed, as I will discuss more fully below, Kant insists that it is impossible for us to have duties toward God or nature, the two most likely candidates for a duty of gratitude. Kant's reasoning, moreover, nowhere appeals to talents being gifts, even if he refers to them as such in his example. Which talents one chooses to develop, he claims, and "in what proportion one against the other it may be a human being's duty to himself to make these natural perfections his end" is left to each to decide, "in accordance with his own rational reflection about what sort of life he would like to lead and whether he has the powers necessary for it."[23] Because of this, it seems clear that Kant's considered position is that even if a person has, for instance, an unusual talent for music or mathematics, there is no moral failing if she decides instead to develops abilities required for auto mechanics. She might decide that a musician's life is not desirable. Or she might love the violin but realize that it would be folly to think that her abilities will ever reach the level required to lead the life of a violinist in the sense desirable to her.

That said, even if there is no moral failing in those who ignore their gifts in favor of other capacities, Kant's view is not that *which* capacities a person should develop can therefore be left up to impulse, whim, or fluke. One's obligation is to develop one's talents based minimally on rational reflection about both the sort of life one wants to lead and whether one's own endowments will be up to the task. That means that a person who, for instance, randomly develops now this, now another, then another capacity, flitting from one to the other without giving any thought to how these capacities will serve some coherent way of life, will not have adopted self-development as a rational end. In particular, this would indicate that she has not sincerely willed her own perfection as her end, given that willing an end requires, at least minimally, following through to some degree in a recognizably coherent direction. Each person has a variety of capacities of various sorts she *could* develop, but some will take rational precedence over others depending on the sort of life she has chosen for herself. If one wants to lead the reflective life of a mathematician, for instance, one should obviously develop mathematical skills. If one wants to live a life creating art, one should develop artistic abilities instead. And if one believes that one's achievement of mathematical or artistic skills will not be sufficient to achieve the sort of life as mathematician or artist that one wants to live, one has good reason to abandon development of those skills and pursue the development of others appropriate for an alternative sort of life one finds desirable.

Therefore, although Kant refers to the failure of self-development as a failure to improve one's fortunate natural predispositions, this does not require us to read this as the view that the gifted have some special obligation to develop their gifts. In deliberation about self-development, one obviously ought to take into account facts about the status of one's endowments. One such fact is that human capacities are not equally, but "fortunately," distributed among persons in such a way that each can become aware in rational reflection with which of these capacities he might be better or worse endowed. Clearly if one's reflection is to be rational, one's fortunes should be factored in when thinking about what sort of life, together with its course of self-development, it would be reasonable to pursue. The point can obviously be generalized without appealing to innate endowments, if such there be: By the time one engages in this sort of reflection about one's capacities, nurture as well as nature has had a large hand in presenting one with one's endowments.

There is thus still room within this view for moral criticism of those who forgo the development of gifts in favor of pursuits at which they are naturally less well-endowed. It is one thing if you possess *nothing* in the way of a talent. Your vain bungling in that kind of case would then be inevitable. But if it could be avoided, and you knew that it could, it seems that you let yourself down by deliberately ignoring your gifts. Imagine someone looking back over a life filled with personal failures that could have been avoided, and blaming himself for it. His self-evaluation would surely appeal to exactly the sorts of considerations Kant refers to, for instance, his failure at the time to be guided by rational reflection on his capacities and future prospects.

It is not merely natural endowments that one must weigh in rational reflection. Projects for self-development may be ruled out, on the Kantian view, because on reflection, they turn out to be immoral, impossible or foolish. It would be impossible for me now to develop skills necessary to be a professional ballet dancer, and not simply because I lack natural endowments to that end. Different talents take different amounts of time and experience to develop, and it would be unreasonable not to take this into account in making decisions about self-development. Thus, by embarking on a quixotic project, I would not thereby be fulfilling my obligation of self-development, since my obligation is to develop myself, taking into account such rational considerations. This is not to say that one may not take reasonable chances. But in order to *will rationally* to develop oneself as one's end (and so to fulfill one's duty) one could not knowingly take only entirely unreasonable or utterly foolish chances, especially when one has other reasonable options.

Further, there is no reason to limit Kant's position in this regard to the young. Throughout one's life one has opportunity to rationally reflect on how far one has developed oneself, on how much further one needs to go to have developed oneself. At that point, rational reflection may include sizing up one's previous goals and achievements, one's capacities as they now stand, the time and energy one could devote to various projects, and the likelihood of success in new goals one sets for oneself. The obligation of self-development should not be thought of as binding only the young; it is an on-going project, always revisable in light of current circumstances.

4. Kant refers to the relevant capacities as "predispositions to greater perfection" in humanity.[24] Neglecting such predispositions, he says, may not "conflict" with treating humanity in ourselves as an end, but it does not "harmonize with" or "further" it. And, again, although we can "conceive" of a world in which no one perfects her talents, we cannot really rationally *will* such a world to come about.[25] We are to conceive of ourselves, then, as possessing a collection of capacities that constitute our "humanity," at least some of which can be more or less "furthered" in any one individual toward some limit of full development or perfection. Although no single individual could even begin to develop *every* determinate human ability, each can develop some to some extent.

Further, one can imagine an ideal future state in which all human capacities are or have been fully developed by sum of all human beings. Here, I think, the best way of understanding Kant's position regarding human natural perfection is as a group rather than individual project. Thus, the complete development of human capacities is not a burden that each must or even could bear, but a task that all are jointly to take part in. Kant refers to such a joint task in various places. For instance, in the *Anthropology*, he writes, "All other animals left to themselves reach as individuals their full destiny [*Bestimmung*], but human beings reach their full destiny only as a species."[26] I take "full destiny" to include the development of all human capacities. If that is right, the *complete* perfection of *all* individual human capacities would be something left for the totality of humanity to achieve in the fullness of time.[27] Thus, although Kant denies that we can have an obligation to perfect others, the obligation to perfect ourselves is in fact an obligation to "do one's part" toward this joint task of humanity as a whole.

Kant's discussion of the capacities that constitute our humanity themselves is brief and in general terms.[28] In the *Groundwork,* he makes no distinction between moral and natural capacities, as he does in the later *Metaphysics of Morals.* Regarding moral capacities, Kant holds that no one who has duties is utterly without them, though all can and should be cultivated and strengthened.[29] Aside from developing self-control and strengthening one's will, moral self-development includes cultivating four moral "endowments" of moral feeling, self-respect, conscience and love of humanity.

One does not find on Kant's list of natural abilities painting, sculpture, poetry, singing, dancing and so forth. He divides natural capacities into three much more coarse-grained categories: powers of mind (including capacities used in the pursuit of mathematics, logic, science and philosophy), spirit (including memory, imagination, learning, and taste) and body (including athletic abilities and "gymnastics in the strict sense").[30] This categorization is meant to be very general. Clearly anything we might ordinarily think of as a "talent" or "ability" will tend to involve the exercise of some complex combination of elements from more than one category. Thus, Kant is not thinking as abstractly as the terms he uses might indicate. These more general terms refer to capacities that are combined in what we ordinarily think of as talents. And so when one develops a talent in the ordinary sense, we will typically be developing many of these more general capacities all at once.

5. Two reasonable worries about my construal of this element of Kant's position. (1) Kant argues that a person cannot rationally will that there be a world in which everyone lets talent rust since "as a rational being he necessarily wills that all his powers be developed, since they are after all useful to him and given to him for all sorts of possible purposes."[31] This apparently implies that complete human perfection is not humanity's collective project at all, but a project to be undertaken by each person because each has a seemingly unlimited set of possible purposes to which to put human capacities. (2) In the second *Critique* Kant goes out of his way to argue that it is rational to hope for the immortality of the soul precisely because we are obligated to perfect ourselves individually, and no finite amount of time is sufficient to achieve perfection.[32]

The second worry is the easier to address. The kind of perfection requiring immortality of the soul is *moral* rather than *natural* perfection, and I am here restricting my concern to the latter. It is consistent to hold that the moral perfection of humanity must be carried out by each and every individual person by perfecting the moral aspect of his humanity in himself, while holding that the natural perfection of humanity must be carried out by the entire human race with each contributing his or her own part.

The first worry, however, is more difficult. Now there is no disputing that Kant's official position was not that we should develop *all* of our capacities *completely.* We are to develop natural capacities "some among them more than others, insofar as people have different ends."[33] The trouble is getting from the premise that insofar as we are rational, we will that all of our capacities be developed, to this desired conclusion. If the argument is simply that since rational wills necessarily will that all of their capacities be fully developed, we imperfectly rational creatures ought to will that "some among them more than others" should be developed, it is hardly worth taking seriously. Perhaps rational wills with an *infinite amount of time, ends and curiosity* will that all of their talents to be developed, but not rational wills *as such*.

Alternatively, one might think his position is that rational wills necessarily will that all of their capacities be developed *somewhat*, however little. But, although the premise is less implausible, the intermediate premise, that if rational wills develop all of their capacities somewhat imperfectly rational wills ought to develop some among them more than others, is at best *ad hoc*.

The context of Kant's claim about fully rational wills is an example of one who "finds in himself a talent that, with a certain amount of cultivation, could make him a useful man for all sorts of purposes."[34] This might suggest that, contrary to my above representation of his position, when he says that as a rational being he necessarily wills that *all* of his powers be developed, he means all of his *talents* or the abilities at which he is particularly gifted. Hence, if I find that I have a gift for music, insofar as I am rational, I will that this gift be developed, that it is irrational for me not to pursue the development of everything for which I have a particular knack. And since no one is talented at everything, this is clearly not impossible.

Charity, however, undermines this reading, and the reasons should put to rest any view of Kant's position that has him focusing on obligations that arise because we possess "gifts." First, although no one is talented at everything, some are talented at far too many things to rationally will that *all* of these talents be developed. Picking and choosing when time and energy are at stake is a virtue of rationality, not a vice. Moreover, if some are talented at many things, but others are talented at a few, those who have fewer talents but develop them all would be more rational than those who have many more talents but develop the same number to the same, or even to a further, degree. Surely we should not take the homily "of those to whom much is given, much is asked" this far. Finally, although many are talented at something, and a few at many things, some are talented at nothing. These agents would then have no duty of self-perfection at all. But even if morality were inequitable in this way, since self-perfection is one of the two obligatory ends, it is just incredible to attribute this view to Kant. It would allow fully one half of these ethical duties not to apply at all to some people.

Kant states that it is because these powers are given to him "for all sorts of possible purposes" that a rational being wills that they all be developed. Perhaps we should then read "all of his powers" as "all of the powers necessary to achieve all sorts of possible purposes." But then the argument would be invalid.[35] It is indeed true that, for any (morally permissible) end (perhaps a limitless number), it *possible* for a rational will to adopt it. Now a rational will must also will the means necessary to achieve or realize any end that he wills. Moreover, for each end he might adopt, that end will require as means in turn some human capacities and talents to achieve or realize it. From this, however, it does not follow that a rational will must will to develop all of his human capacities and talents. What follows is only that for each human capacity or talent, it is *possible* that a rational will must will to develop it. And that is clearly compatible with a rational will actually not developing any talent to any extent.

Although this argument does not show that rational wills develop all or even any of their talents, there is an intuitively plausible idea behind it. Rationality does not require omniscience. Full rationality does not imply knowledge of all of the talents that might be needed to achieve current ends, nor knowledge of the novel ends in the future that one might adopt, nor which new talents these ends might require as means to their realization. Intuitively, it makes sense to develop at least some capacities we might need as a hedge against these contingencies. But of course, this is so only if we are not talking about all of the ends it is logically possible for a rational agent as such to adopt. Take a given person as he is, given details about his background, culture, physical nature, psychology and interests. There are a range of ends that it is psychologically, physically, perhaps culturally possible for him to adopt, and there are talents necessary to realizing them. Given you are who you are, it is in some sense not possible for you to adopt certain ends, but quite possible and perhaps likely that you will adopt other ends. Clearly, this is a graded affair; becoming a professional musician or mathematician may not be *impossible* for some people though perhaps it would take Herculean efforts. Perhaps a rational being develops or at least tries to develop all of the talents he knows are actually necessary to achieve not only the ends he actually does have, but also those that might be necessary to achieve those actual ends, as well as those that are or might be necessary for ends he might adopt in the future. In any case, although this strikes me as plausible, and as perhaps getting at something Kant may have had in mind, I confess that I do not see how the argument according to this line of interpretation can be taken any further.

My suggestion, which admittedly goes beyond the text, is to adopt an alternative way of construing Kant's position that fits with the view I have been setting out so far. As we have seen, he divides natural perfection into mental, spiritual and physical categories. Further, he holds that the destiny of mankind is achieved as a species, which I have read as the position that complete development of the sum total of human potential is not to be undertaken by each alone, but in the sense that in developing oneself one is doing one's part toward a goal that can be reached only by all together. These positions suggest a reasonable way of understanding the claim that necessarily a rational being wills all of his capacities be developed and hence his own perfection as a person. In short, (i) a rational being must will that *some* of every *kind* of human capacity (more or less as Kant defines this) be developed in himself, some more than others depending on his ends and circumstances, in himself; (ii) he also must will that everyone else ultimately develop a virtually limitless range of other human capacities sufficiently so that he can achieve his own ends; (iii) the inevitable outcome of this is that all human capacities will be developed fully, each of which is in some sense contained as a potential in each person's own humanity, in the fullness of time; (iv) and each person's own self-development will represent a part (however small) of this full development of the totality of human capacities.

First, regarding (i), it is easy enough to see that some capacities from *all three categories* rationally should be developed as means to the ends that any human being in fact will adopt. Insofar as we are rational agents, we will the necessary and available means to our ends. Rationally willing any end at all requires willing to possess and use the abilities that are necessary to achieve that end. Hence, I rationally will to play Mozart's Piano Sonata in B-Flat only if I will to develop the ability to play that piece. But I will to develop that ability only if in turn I will to develop the ability to play piano at all. And any higher-level abilities such as playing the piano will at some point be composed of lower abilities in several of Kant's categories. So it is at least clear that necessarily, insofar as we are instrumentally rational we will that all of the *kinds* of human capacities be developed.

Second, Kant shows that he thinks of the duty of self-development as a duty to "broaden" ourselves as much as to perfect some particular ability. Given the limitations on one's time, energy, and circumstances, complete human development is better thought of as each person being more or less "well-rounded." Developing the capacity to play piano requires rudimentary abilities from each category, but those abilities would clearly be stunted if only developed to the degree required to play piano—at whatever level of accomplishment. So a freakish obsession to develop a particular capacity as far as one can would leave one "one-sided."

Third, regarding (ii), insofar as we are instrumentally rational, we must will to develop fully some set of capacities of different kinds. But we also require others to develop capacities for which we have neither the time nor ability to develop, but also which we require in pursuit of the ends we adopt. I cannot adopt as my end playing Mozart's piano sonatas if Mozart had not composed them, if no one had invented the piano, if no one had built pianos, and so on. Indeed, apart from what is required for pursuit of our own ends, it is undeniable that human life would be a pathetic thing if no one developed herself. Each person's life is more rewarding not only for the talents she develops in herself, but for the talents that others have developed. Indeed, for a given individual to develop virtually any capacity in himself at all requires as a necessary means that others have developed capacities in themselves. Hence, each, insofar as he is rational, must will to take advantage of the developed human capacities of others.

Finally, regarding (iii) & (iv), I admit that this does not establish that all human capacities must be fully developed by humanity as a whole, since no matter how broad the range of one's own ends, not *every* human capacity is required to realize them. However, the known novelty and diversity of current and past human ends, as well as the human talents developed to realize these ends, it is reasonable to suppose that, given that there is enough time and that nothing untoward happens to the human race, eventually anything a human being can have as an end he will have as an end and this will lead to every human capacity being developed as far as it can be developed.

In any case, I submit that this is the most plausible way of understanding the notion of "complete human development" for Kant. One crucial point to remember from this, however, is that however one interprets Kant here, it is clear that, as he is thinking of it, our duty requires more than fanatical devotion to a particular skill or endeavor in ourselves. Genuine self-development, as self-perfection, requires giving thought to more than merely one side of oneself.

6. Kant uses a number of different terms in his discussion of self-development: talents [*Talents*], powers [*Kräfte*], natural predispositions [*Naturanlagen*] and capacities [*Vermögen*]. Whatever differences exist among the items in this list, the important common features are the following:

First, unlike the capacities of our sense organs, as Aristotle was first to point out, talents and abilities (or at least those Kant regards as relevant to our duty of self-development) require development in order to be used.[36] Thus, our natural perfection will consist "in what can result from [our] deeds, not in mere *gifts* for which [we] must be indebted to nature."[37] Kant is thinking primarily of gifted individuals who are so in some sense "by nature." But one cannot deliberate about capacities one simply has or doesn't have, whether they are artistic capacities or simply capacities to see, hear and so on. What one can do, however, is size up one's current endowments, however fortunate, and make reasonable judgments about what sorts of education, training and cultivation could produce a level of proficiency that would make sense in the context of some pursuit or activity.

Second, these capacities are all to be thought of as "means to all sorts of possible ends."[38] Instrumental rationality, of course, enjoins us to take the necessary and available ends to whatever ends we make for ourselves, on Kant's view.[39] Thus it would be irrational not to will to develop those talents we know to be necessary to achieve all of the ends that we will for ourselves. Kant is thinking of not only our own capacities, but those of our fellow human beings. Our duty is "to be a useful member of the world,"[40] and Kant's thoughts on the collective fate of humanity also make this plain. Thus, although it is natural to think that we ought to develop our talents as means to ends that we ourselves have, and so to think that there is some sort of prudential justification for self-development, Kant's view is that, even if this is a duty to ourselves regarding our own capacities, these capacities are valuable to other rational wills as well. That we owe it to ourselves to be a useful member of the world means that proper respect for one's own humanity requires being able to see that it is of value, not merely to oneself, but to others, and to the collective task of humanity.

Third, that these capacities and so on are useful as *means* need not exclude the possibility that their full development apart from this usefulness could be present among our ends. If my end is that I speak a language, that end includes within itself the idea of a developed linguistic capacity. Developing an ability to speak French would thus be achieving my end, even if this is of no real use to me in pursuing other ends I may have.

Fourth, that they are means both to our own ends and those of others does not, however, covertly introduce a consequentialist justification of self-development. It is not because adopting the maxim of self-development best furthers our own good or the overall good that we are required to adopt it. Each, Kant thinks, "could be satisfied with the innate scope of his capacities."[41] Indeed, Rousseau's vision of humanity happier in a natural state might well be right in Kant's view.[42] Yet however much or little a person's natural capacities contribute to overall well-being, they belong "to the worth of humanity in his own person, which he ought not to degrade."[43] Developing these capacities and abilities is thus an obligation, not because it contributes to our own or general welfare, but because it is, again, demanded by respect for our own humanity.

Fifth, although some range of levels of mastery will constitute having "developed" such capacities (being "competent," "fluent" and so on), as even the world's finest musicians and artists know, there is no end to the degree to which one can "perfect" a capacity or talent. This is true, not only of a single capacity, but of the complete development of a human being taking into account the development of a variety of such capacities.

Finally, Kant probably thought that there is some collection of uniquely human capacities and so on which set human nature apart from other animals, and that these were of particular importance in fulfilling our duty of self-development. But even if human beings have striking intellectual, emotional and physical capacities, it is unlikely that these mark an *essential* difference between ourselves and the rest of nature. Other animals—higher primates, whales, dolphins, and so on—probably have rudimentary versions of human capacities. Even so, Kant's position also provides us with other less controversial ways of circumscribing the range of capacities on which we should focus, in terms of human interests and social usefulness, available professions and realistic human ways of life. It goes without saying that learning to use twigs to fetch grub worms out of rotting logs won't count as self-development.

7. Kant was quite conscious of the fact that talents do not exist in a social vacuum: "Man is destined by his reason to live in a society of other people, and in this society he has to cultivate himself, civilize himself, and apply himself to a moral purpose by the arts and sciences."[44] Thus, he describes the duty of self-perfection as a duty to "make ourselves worthy of humanity by culture in general."[45] Indeed, part of what makes this duty imperfect is that when a person chooses talents to develop, he chooses them in the context of "the occupation for which he should cultivate" those talents.[46] Although the development of *which* capacity is left to each to decide for him or herself in the context of deliberations

about what sort of life he or she wishes to lead, that is mainly because the choice of pursuits for which that capacity can be used is itself left up to each to decide. Such pursuits—Kant mentions "trade, commerce, or a learned profession"[47]— are a part of the culture with a history and tradition of use, and so developing a talent involves taking part in that history and tradition. Therefore, when Kant speaks of the "ends set forth by reason" that the development of our capacities serves, he is thinking of these ends as nevertheless existing in a historical and social setting substantial enough to have such trades, professions and so on.

8. Readers of the *Groundwork* are first given a picture of a person who fails in his duty to develop talents as lounging on a South Pacific beach living on co-conuts and mangoes—that is, someone who is *so* lazy he fails to develop *any* capacities whatever. But this is surely a caricature. For one thing, most people must develop *some* rudimentary skills such as clothing themselves, talking, read-ing and so on. These are typically skills that we develop through parental or other adult guidance. Yet once one has developed such basic abilities as one has, one is in a position to fail in one's obligation to continue that development. For another, as is implied by the broadness of Kant's idea of human perfection, even those who have developed some capacity to a very high degree might later vio-late their duty by being idle and refusing to do anything further to broaden them-selves.

In any case, this example is not intended to be typical. Its point is to illus-trate how the duty can be derived from the Categorical Imperative. Moreover, since perfection represents a limit, it is evidently always possible to re-evaluate one's development and carry it a step further. Like lying or refusing ever to help others in need, the failure to develop talents could be a moral failing of anyone, and everyone can think of someone who actually does have this failing. So when we think about Kant's point here, we should think of it as addressed to *us*, that is, people who either have considered or might well in the future consider not developing any capacities any further.

9. To summarize, we have a duty to adopt a policy of developing at least some of a vast collection of unactualized or minimally actualized (mostly) hu-man capacities (mental, spiritual, physical), in the direction of the "limit" of per-fection. All will have leeway to choose which to develop, taking into considera-tion whatever natural predispositions they may have; the ends they and those around them have and that would be served by developing some of their capaci-ties; their material circumstances, including time, access to education, a trade or profession and so on; and the context of their cultural traditions and practices. One's obligation is, in sum, to develop some capacities to some degree, based on rational reflection on one's circumstances, broadly construed in the above ways.

Models of Failure to Develop Oneself

Based on the above summary of Kant's views, I want now to sketch five models of the *failure* to conform to this duty of self-development. I set aside various ways in which a person may fail, as I mentioned above, by pursuing self-development when doing so would violate some perfect duty (e.g., lying to get into an exclusive training program, stealing money to pay for it, and so on). I see the following as mainly models of failings where failure at other duties is not in question, allowing a variety of details to fill them out.

1. The first model of a failure to develop oneself is of one who fails to develop *any* human capacity to *any* degree, such as Kant's own *Groundwork* example illustrates: call such a person the Ne'er-Do-Well. In this category belong not just a fantasy life on an exotic tropical island, but also the "idle rich" who rely entirely on the developed talents of others, and the "slacker" who has no interest in pursuing ends lying outside the reach of his endowments as he finds them. It is important here to remember that virtually every normal human being has developed human capacities, since virtually every normal human being has parents, and has had some education. It is only once the responsibility of others to develop your capacities ends that the possibility of failing this duty begins. Thus, a complete failure to develop oneself does not imply, absurdly, that you would lack completely any skills or abilities. No doubt, a Ne'er-Do-Well's capacities, such as they are, may well be almost useless to himself and others. And, in the case of the idle rich, his possessions and money may yet be quite useful to others. But, be that as it may, he refuses to *make himself* useful. When opportunities arise for developing a talent or ability that might be useful, the Ne'er-Do-Well chooses instead not to make any effort, not to take away time and energy from enjoying what fate has thrown his way. He refuses to take part in an occupation, activity or a culture as an active member, so to speak, by developing capacities that might be of value within these pursuits.

2. The Self-Sacrificer displays a different failure: He is unlike the Ne'er-Do-Well in spending time and energy developing human talents, but like him in never developing his own. The Self-Sacrificer focuses instead entirely on the capacities of his children, friends, even people off the street, offering to provide money, help with menial or boring tasks, help in finding studio space, playing fields, coaches, teachers, and so on, going well beyond what is required by any obligations he has toward these people. The Self-Sacrificer, to be sure, has to have or develop the capacities required for focusing on the capacities of others. The moral fault is not that he lacks developed capacities, but that he does not adopt as his end the development of these or any other of his capacities. He thus treats himself—his human capacities—as *mere means* to the development of others. A Self-Sacrificer *might* be self-deprecating, thinking "I'm no good at anything. It's a waste to spend time on my pathetic 'abilities.'" But he need not be. He may simply tell himself, in a sense selflessly, "I'll never be a Mozart or an Einstein, but one of these people could be." The Self-Sacrificer refuses to make *himself* and his *own* capacities of use to himself or others, even if for apparently noble reasons.

Notice that if the justification for the development of talents appealed solely to their social value, there would be no grounds to think there is anything morally wrong with the Self-Sacrificer. One might, naturally, argue that the social goals that the development of human capacities achieve or realize would be best realized if each person developed her own capacities. But this argument would provide no basis for the claim that there is something we owe ourselves here. Indeed, it presumes that we owe the development of our talents to others, not to ourselves—as means to achieving various social goals.

3. Another model of failure to conform to the duty of self-development is the One-Dimensional person: She only aims to develop a capacity absolutely necessary to succeed at a single narrowly construed undertaking. Perhaps she ignores intellectual or emotional development in search of perfecting some athletic ability. She may refuse even the most rudimentary upkeep of her physical or emotional condition in favor of honing some intellectual skill. She would thus avoid being a Ne'er-Do-Well, since she does well in one respect. She avoids being a Self-Sacrificer, because she does not aim to sacrifice her own development for the development of others. Moreover, she will be useful to others, at least insofar as she contributes her one share. Some would take the One-Dimensional person to be boring, lacking depth, and so on. But the moral failing here would be that she is tedious, but that she utterly disregards or actively avoids tending to the range of human capacities that she possesses in service of only one. When the opportunity arises to expand her horizons, so to speak, the One-Dimensional person instead uses the time to make incremental progress on her one skill. Since she refuses to adopt full self-development as her end, but rather only pursues this in a very narrowly circumscribed way, the One-Dimensional person's fault is that she does not take to heart the idea that her obligation is to perfect *all* of herself as a person.

This may well strike many as taking well-roundedness too far.[48] For instance, what about a code-breaker in WWII, someone whose valuable abilities could only have been developed to the necessary degree by being One-Dimensional? And think of the sacrifices achieving greatness requires. Reason shouldn't pass judgment on artistic genius, it might be thought. But—and this is important—Kant's position does not condemn *being* one-dimensional—nor the mere lack of developed capacities. It only forbids failing to adopt full and complete development as your end. The fault in the One-Dimensional person is thus not that she is in fact one dimensional, but that her One-Dimensionality is principled. On the basis of adopting one-dimensionality as her end, she refuses to give any consideration *at all* to other sides of herself. Someone whose overall development as a person is waylaid by considerations of perfect duties, or by pressing considerations of the good of others, for instance, is not at moral fault.

Further, adopting full and complete development as one's end should normally be possible without sacrificing greatness as one's end. We are, again, to develop our talents "some among them more than others, insofar as people have different ends."[49] It is possible, however, for there to be a choice someone faces: Achieve greatness or adopt full development as your end. And, as I have portrayed it, the Kantian position will have to view significant human achievements as immoral because of the sacrifices to broader self-development that are required. It is thus possible on this view for artistic genius to require immorality. But other moral theories allow this possibility as well, and it seems to me that they should, or at least I see no reason why great achievement must always be morally possible. What is unique about the Kantian view is that there can be cases in which it is not possible, not because you are like Bernard Williams' Gauguin, who must wrong others to pursue an artistic vision, but because you must wrong yourself to do this.

This does not, however, imply that it is morally better to be mediocre than achieve One-Dimensional greatness. Indeed, deliberate mediocrity will also be a fault on Kant's view, as depicted in the next model.

4. This fourth model, the Mediocre Man, will not fail entirely to develop some, or not some of each kind, of capacities in himself (and so is neither a Ne'er-Do-Well nor a Self-Sacrificer), nor will he develop only one narrow capacity leaving all others utterly undeveloped (as does the One Dimensional Person). Still, those abilities he develops, the Mediocre Man develops only in a deliberately half-hearted way, never taking them seriously or putting effort or energy into their development. He commits himself to a bare minimum of development or proficiency, and opts at every opportunity to give himself over to loafing rather than to put any energy into self-development. The Mediocre Man doesn't take to heart, we might say, that his obligation is to *perfect* himself, not merely to make a feeble gesture in the direction of self-improvement.

5. The final model is the Fool. He may develop a range of capacities, and to a considerable extent, but there is a serious defect in the purposes that they serve or the way that they fit into his natural or social context. They are a mere hodge-podge or collection of capacities which are each individually and together useless for, or incompatible with, any minimally coherent plan of life. The Fool is in some ways like the Ne'er-Do-Well, since he is, for any coherent purposes, useless to himself and others. Yet this is not because the Fool does not develop his capacities; rather, he gives no thought to how the capacities he develops serve a coherent life plan for himself or fit into any possible socially defined niche. He develops capacities as the urge strikes him. He may develop randomly this or that peculiar capacity (say, medieval bloodletting or fetching grubs out of rotting logs). What is important is not the capacities in themselves, but that the Fool has given no thought to how they might serve some culturally embedded rational life plan. Thus, he develops capacities, perhaps fully and in a sense broadly, but always does so at great cost to a plan of life, or at odds with the capacities that could conceivably contribute to his culture. When opportunities to develop abilities that would serve some way of life present themselves, he invariably opts instead to hone some new bizarre trick in isolation.

These models have several intuitive features worth noting. First, each fails to do something it seems she owes to herself, by failing to develop talents, abilities or capacities. Each lets herself down by failing to develop herself. Second, this is not an obligation that it seems plausible that each of these sorts of people would owe to others, that is, they need not be thought of as letting anyone else down by failing to develop capacities in herself. In each case, the person is letting *herself* down. Third, it morally significant *whose* capacities are left undeveloped in these cases, and in particular that it is *his or her own* capacities that each ought to be tending to, not the capacities or talents of others. We need not look around for a parent or mentor as having failed the person in each of these cases. Fourth, it makes a moral difference *how far* each develops his or her capacities; some effort at *perfecting* oneself is lacking in them. Finally, it is not just *any* of their capacities that they should pay attention to, but a more or less coherent set of capacities that would serve some, if even only very sketchy, life plan they have adopted that makes sense, especially within their cultural settings.

Conclusion

The above lays out features present in Kant's account of this obligation as I have described it. I think they also reflect important features of ordinary thoughts we have about what we owe to ourselves in terms of self-development. However, it may strike many as confirming Wolff's charge of moralism. Do we really want to condemn those who conform to the models I've described above?

The answer is, No. We do not want to condemn these people. The issue is whether there is a moral failing in the character of the people who conform to these models. One can imagine, if one were a close friend or family member of someone fitting these models, thinking and saying that each of these people are letting themselves down and so owe it to themselves to develop or put more effort into developing capacities useful to themselves and others, to make something, or something more, of themselves. Indeed, one can imagine thinking or saying this in each case even if the person is not wronging anyone else by failing to develop him- or herself.

Notes

Thanks to Arnie Zweig, Thomas E. Hill Jr., Valerie Tiberius, Jon Kvanvig and Peter Vallentyne for fruitful discussions on these topics.

1. MM 6:444. Paginations refer to the volume and page numbers from the Prussian Academy edition of Kant's works. References to the first *Critique* are to the pages of the A and B editions. The following are the translations I use:

A *Anthropology from a Pragmatic Point of View*, tr. V. L. Dowdell, rev. H.H. Rudnick (Carbondale & Edwardsville, IL: S. Illinois U. P., 1978).

G *Groundwork of the Metaphysics of Morals*, tr. A. Zweig and T. Hill, (Oxford: Oxford University Press, 2003).

CPR *Critique of Pure Reason*, tr. P. Guyer and A. Wood (New York: Cambridge University Press, 1998).

CPrR *Critique of Practical Reason*, tr. M. Gregor (New York: Cambridge University Press, 1996).

MM *The Metaphysics of Morals*, tr. M. Gregor (New York: Cambridge University Press, 1991).

R *Religion within the Limits of Reason Alone*, tr. A. Wood and G. Di Giovanni (New York: Cambridge University Press 1998).

2. In Chs. 4 and 5 of my *Reason and Virtue: Kant's Conception of Moral Character*, mss.

3. Robert Paul Wolff, *The Autonomy of Reason: A Commentary on Kant's Groundwork of the Metaphysic of Morals* (New York: Harper & Row, 1973), 169.

4. MM 6:693.

5. See, for instance, the well-known exchange between Daniel Kading, Marcus Singer, and Warner Wick. Daniel Kading, "Are there Really No Duties to Oneself?" *Ethics*, 70 (1960): 155-57. Marcus G. Singer, *Generalization in Ethics* (New York: Knopf, 1961), 311-18; "Duties and Duties to Oneself," *Ethics* 73 (1963): 133-42. Warner Wick, "More about Duties to Oneself," *Ethics*, 70 (1960): 158-63; "Still More about Duties to Oneself," *Ethics*, 71 (1961): 213-17.

6. Kant's discussion of this "paradox" is at MM 6: 417-18. Others who discuss this aspect of Kant's views are Thomas E. Hill, Jr., "Servility and Self-Respect," reprinted in his *Autonomy and Self-Respect* (New York: Cambridge U. P., 1991), Andrews Reath, "Self-Legislation and Duties to Oneself," in *Kant's Metaphysics of Morals: Interpretative Essays*, ed. M. Timmons (New York: Oxford University Press, 2002), 349-70, and Lara Denis, *Moral Self-Regard: Duties to Oneself in Kant's Moral Theory* (New York: Garland, 2001), 85-123.

7. Bruce Aune argues that the only plausible construal of Kant's arguments for this duty requires that nature contains purposes and teleological laws. See his *Kant's Theory of Morals* (Princeton, NJ: Princeton University Press, 1979), 120-30, 178-79.

8. See, for instance, Kant's reference to the Parable of the Ten Talents (*Luke* 19:12-16) in *Religion* 6:51-2; also 6:6. He also says that *because* they are "given to him for all sorts of possible purposes" (G 4:423), insofar as he is fully rational, a person wills to develop all of his natural capacities. H. J. Paton, for one, emphasizes Kant's teleological views in general, and in particular regarding this duty. See *The Categorical Imperative* (New York: Harper & Row, 1963), 155.

9. An excellent discussion of some of these problems can be found in Amy Gutmann, "What's the Use of going to School?" in *Utilitarianism and Beyond*, ed. A. Sen and B. Williams (Cambridge: Cambridge University Press, 1982), 261-77.

10. Kant himself claims that it is a friend's duty to point out one's faults.

11. G 4:421-23; MM 6:445-46.

12. MM 6:446.

13. G 4:426, 431, 436-37; MM 6:389.

14. G 4:423; see also MM 6:389-91.

15. Some may react to this as overly moralistic, but Kant's interest is not in passing judgment on cultural history. It is in answering deliberative questions about what one may and may not do in the pursuit of certain ends, no matter how noble they may be. Cf. Bernard Williams, "Moral Luck," in *Moral Luck* (New York: Cambridge University Press, 1981), 20-39.

16. G 4:423.

17. There is some controversy over how much Kant requires in the pursuit of obligatory ends. See, for example, David Cummiskey, *Kantian Consequentialism* (New York:

Oxford University Press, 1996) esp. 111 and 116; and Thomas E. Hill, Jr., "Meeting Needs and Doing Favors" in his *Human Welfare and Moral Worth* (New York: Oxford University Press, 2003), 201-43.

18. MM 6:446-47.

19. R 6:29.

20. MM 6:392.

21. MM 6:393.

22. G 4:423.

23. MM 6:445.

24. G 4:430; also see MM 6:644.

25. G 4:423.

26. A 7:324; *Anthropology from a Pragmatic Standpoint*, tr. V. L. Dowdell (Carbondale: Southern Illinois University Press, 1978).

27. See Wood, p. 212.

28. He goes into more concrete detail in other works, most notably, in *Anthropology*.

29. MM 6:399-403.

30. MM 6:445. See also *Vigilantius* 27:608. Baumgarten's divisions are found in his *Philosophica Ethica*, reprinted in *Kant's Gesammelte Schriften* vol. 27 (Berlin: Walter de Gruyter, 1975).

31. G 4:423.

32. CPrR 5:122-24.

33. MM 6:445.

34. 4:422-23.

35. Cf. Aune, *Kant's Theory of Morals*, p. 56.

36. Aristotle, *Nicomachean Ethics*, 1103a15-1103b25.

37. MM 6:386-7.

38. MM 6:446.

39. G 4:414-17.

40. MM 6:446.

41. MM 6:445.

42. MM 6:444-45; also see A 7:326-30. However, in "Speculative Beginning of Human History" Kant seems to imply that we can't really be happy without developing ourselves. Thanks to Tom Hill for this reference.

43. MM 6:446.

44. A 7:324.

45. MM 6:392.

46. MM 6:392.

47. MM 6:445.

48. Thanks to Jon Kvanvig for pressing me on this.

49. MM 6:445.

Bibliography

Allison, Henry E. *Kant's Theory of Freedom*. Cambridge: Cambridge University Press, 1990.

Aristotle. *The Complete Works of Aristotle*. Edited by Jonathan Barnes. Princeton, NJ: Princeton University Press, 1984.

———. *Nicomachean Ethics*. Translated by Terence Irwin. Indianapolis: Hackett Publishing Company, 1992.

———. *Poetics*. Translated by Malcolm Heath. London: Penguin Books, 1996.

Athanassoulis, Nafsika. "A Response to Harman: Virtue Ethics and Character Traits." *Proceedings of the Aristotelian Society* 100 (2000): 215-21.

Audi, Robert. "Moral Judgment and Reasons for Action." Pp. 125-59 in *Ethics and Practical Reason*, edited by G. Cullity and B. Gaut. New York: Oxford University Press, 1997.

Aune, Bruce. *Kant's Theory of Morals*. Princeton, NJ: Princeton University Press, 1979.

Baier, Annette. *A Progress of Sentiments*. Cambridge, MA: Harvard University Press, 1991.

Baron, Marcia W. *Kantian Ethics Almost Without Apology*. Ithaca, NY: Cornell University Press, 1995.

Baumgarten, Alexander. *Philosophica Ethica*. In *Kant's Gesammelte Schriften* vol. 27. Berlin: Walter de Gruyter, 1975.

Blum, Lawrence. "Moral Perception and Particularity." *Ethics* 101 (1991): 701-25.

Bol, Peter K. *This Culture of Ours*. Stanford, CA: Stanford University Press, 1992.

Boyarin, Daniel. *Carnal Israel: Reading Sex in Talmudic Culture*. Berkeley: University of California Press, 1993.

———. *Dying for God*. Stanford, CA: Stanford University Press, 1999.

———. *Unheroic Conduct: The Rise of Heterosexuality and the Invention on the Jewish Man*. Berkeley: University of California Press, 1997.

Braithwaite, R. B. "An Empiricist Looks at Religious Beliefs." Pp. 72-91 in *The Philosophy of Religion*, edited by Basil Mitchell. London: Oxford University Press, 1971.

Burnyeat, Myles. "Aristotle on Learning to Be Good." Pp. 69-92 in *Essays on Aristotle's Ethics*, edited by Amélie Oksenberg Rorty. Berkeley: University of California Press, 1980.

Cahill, James F. "Confucian Elements in the Theory of Painting." Pp. 115-40 in *The Confucian Persuasion*, edited by Arthur F. Wright. Stanford, CA: Stanford University Press, 1960.

Carr, Karen L. and Philip J. Ivanhoe. *The Sense of Antirationalism: The Religious Thought of Zhuangzi and Kierkegaard*. New York: Seven Bridges Press, 2000.

Carroll, Noël. *Beyond Aesthetics: Philosophical Essays*. Cambridge: Cambridge University Press, 2001.

Chan, Hok-lam. *Li Chih (1527-1602) in Contemporary Historiography*. New York: M. E. Sharpe, 1980.

Chan, Wing-tsit, ed. *Chu Hsi and Neo-Confucianism*. Honolulu: University of Hawai'i Press, 1986.

Cheng, Pei-kai. "Continuities in Chinese Political Culture: Interpretations of Li Zhi, Past and Present." *Chinese Studies in History* 17, no. 2 (1983-1984).

Confucius (Kongzi). *The Analects*. Translated by Arthur Waley. New York: Vintage Books, 1938.

———. "The Analects." Translated by Edward Gilman Slingerland. Pp. 1-54 in *Readings in Classical Chinese Philosophy*, edited by Philip J. Ivanhoe and Bryan W. Van Norden. New York: Seven Bridges Press, 2001.

Cua, Antonio S. *Dimensions of Moral Creativity: Paradigms, Principles, and Ideals*. University Park: Pennsylvania State University Press, 1978.

Cummiskey, David. *Kantian Consequentialism*. New York: Oxford University Press, 1996.

Danto, Arthur. "Philosophy as/and/of Literature," *Proceedings and Addresses of the American Philosophical Society* 58 (1984).

Darley, J. M. and C. D. Batson. "'From Jerusalem to Jericho': A Study of Situational and Dispositional Variable in Helping Behavior." *Journal of Personality and Social Psychology* 27 (1993): 100-108.

Darwall, Stephen. "Empathy, Sympathy, Care." *Philosophical Studies*, 89 (1998): 261-82.

de Bary, William Theodore. *Self and Society in Ming Thought*. New York: Columbia University Press, 1970.

Denis, Lara. *Moral Self-Regard: Duties to Oneself in Kant's Moral Theory*. New York: Garland, 2001.

Descartes, René. *The Passions of the Soul*. Translated by Stephen Voss. Indianapolis: Hackett Publishing Company, 1989.

DeSousa, Ronald. *The Rationality of Emotion*. Cambridge, MA: The MIT Press, 1990.

Doris, John. *Lack of Character*. Cambridge: Cambridge University Press, 2002.
———. "Persons, Situations, and Virtue Ethics." *Nous* 32, no. 4 (1998): 504-30.
Ekman, Paul. *The Face of Man*. New York: Garland Press, 1980.
Ellison, Ralph. *Invisible Man*. New York: Random House, 1952.
Falk, W. D. "'Ought' and Motivation." *Proceedings of the Aristotelian Society* 48 (1947-1948): 492-510.
Ferrari, G. R. F. "Platonic Love." Pp. 248-76 in *The Cambridge Companion to Plato*, edited by Richard Kraut. Cambridge: Cambridge University Press, 1992.
Findlay, J. N. *Axiological Ethics*. London: Macmillan, 1970.
Finkelstein, Louis, ed. *Sifre on Deuteronomy*. New York: The Jewish Theological Seminary of America, 1993.
Fishbane, Michael. *The Kiss of God*. Seattle: The University of Washington Press, 1994.
Fonrobert, Charlotte. *Menstrual Purity: Rabbinic and Christian Reconstructions of Biblical Gender*. Stanford, CA: Stanford University Press, 2000.
Foot, Philippa. "Virtues and Vices." Pp. 1-18 in *Virtues and Vices and Other Essays in Moral Philosophy*. Berkeley: University of California Press, 1978.
Franklin, Benjamin. *The Autobiography of Benjamin Franklin & Selections from His Other Writings*. Introduction by Stacy Schiff. New York: The Modern Library, 2001.
Funder, David C. *Personality Judgment: A Realistic Approach to Person Perception*. San Diego: Academic Press, 1999.
Gardner, Daniel K. *Learning to Be a Sage: Selections from the Conversations of Master Chu, Arranged Topically*. Berkeley: University of California Press, 1990.
———. "Principle and Pedagogy: Chu Hsi and the Four Books." *Harvard Journal of Asiatic Studies* 44, no. 1 (June, 1984): 57-81.
———. "Transmitting the Way: Chu Hsi and His Program of Learning." *Harvard Journal of Asiatic Studies* 49, no. 2 (June, 1989): 141-72.
Graham, Angus C. *Two Chinese Philosophers*, reprint. La Salle, IL: Open Court Press, 1992.
Griffin, James. *Well-Being*. Oxford: Clarendon Press, 1986.
Gutmann, Amy. "What's the Use of Going to School?" Pp. 261-77 in *Utilitarianism and Beyond*, edited by Amartya Sen and Bernard Williams. Cambridge: Cambridge University Press, 1982.
Hadot, Pierre. *Philosophy as a Way of Life*, reprint. Oxford: Blackwell Publishers, 1998.
Hampshire, Stuart. *Innocence and Experience*. Cambridge, MA: Harvard University Press, 1989.
———. *Morality and Conflict*. Cambridge, MA: Harvard University Press, 1983.
Harman, Gilbert. "Moral Psychology Meets Social Psychology." *Proceedings of the Aristotelian Society* 99 (1999): 315-31.

————. *The Nature of Morality*. Oxford: Oxford University Press, 1977.

————. "No Character or Personality." *Business Ethics Quarterly* 13 (January 2003): 87-94.

Hezser, Catherine. "Rabbis and Other Friends." Pp. 189-254 in *The Talmud Yerushalmi and Graeco-Roman Culture*, Vol. 2, edited by Peter Schäfer and Catherine Heszer. Tübingen, Germany: Mohr Siebeck, 2000.

————. *The Social Structure of the Rabbinic Movement in Roman Palestine*. Tübingen, Germany: Mohr Siebeck, 1997.

Hill, Thomas E., Jr. *Autonomy and Self-Respect*. New York: Cambridge University Press, 1991.

————. *Human Welfare and Moral Worth*. New York: Oxford University Press, 2003.

Hume, David. *Enquiries Concerning Human Understanding and Concerning the Principles of Morals*, 3rd edition. Edited by L. A. Selby-Bigge. Revised by P. H. Nidditch. Oxford: Oxford University Press, 1975.

————. *Essays: Moral, Political, and Literary*. Edited by Eugene Miller. Indianapolis: Liberty Classics, 1985.

————. *A Treatise of Human Nature*, 2nd edition. Edited by L. A. Selby-Bigge. Revised by P. H. Nidditch. Oxford: Oxford University Press, 1978.

————. *A Treatise of Human Nature*. Edited by David Fate Norton and Mary Norton. Oxford: Oxford University Press, 2000.

Hursthouse, Rosalind. *On Virtue Ethics*. Oxford: Oxford University Press, 1999.

Hutton, Eric L. "Virtue and Reason in Xunzi." Ph.D. diss., Stanford University, 2001.

Ilan, Tal. *Mine and Yours are Hers: Retrieving Women's History from Rabbinic Literature*. New York: Brill, 1997.

Isen, A. M. and H. Levin. "Effect of Feeling Good on Helping: Cookies and Kindness." *Journal of Personality and Social Psychology* 21 (1972): 384-88.

Ivanhoe, Philip J. *Confucian Moral Self Cultivation*. New York: Peter Lang, 1993.

————. "Filial Piety as a Virtue." In *Working Virtue: Virtue Ethics and Contemporary Moral Problems*, edited by Rebecca Walker and Philip J. Ivanhoe. New York: Oxford University Press, 2007.

————. "History: Chinese Theories of." Pp. 446-52 in *The Routledge Encyclopedia of Philosophy*, Vol. 4. London: Routledge, 1998.

————. "Intellectual Property and Traditional Chinese Culture." *Topics in Contemporary Philosophy, Volume 3, Law and Social Justice*. Edited by Joseph Keim Campbell, Michael O'Rourke, and David Shier. Cambridge, MA: MIT Press, 2004.

Ivanhoe, Philip J. and Bryan Van Norden, eds. *Readings in Classical Chinese Philosophy*. New York: Seven Bridges Press, 2001.

James, William. "What Is an Emotion?" *Mind* 19 (1884): 19-34.

Jiang Jin. "Heresy and Persecution on Late Ming Society—Reinterpreting the Case of Li Zhi." *Late Imperial China* 22, no. 2 (December 2001): 1-34.

Kading, Daniel. "Are There Really No Duties to Oneself?" *Ethics* 70 (1960): 155-7.

Kagen, Z. "Divergent Tendencies and Their Literary Moulding in the Aggadah." Pp. 151-70 in *Studies in Aggadah and Folk Literature. Scripta Hierosolymitana*, Vol. 22, edited by J. Heinemann and Dov Noy. Jerusalem: Magnes Press, 1971.

Kamm, Frances. "The Doctrine of Triple Effect." *Supplementary Proceedings of the Aristotelian Society* 74 (2000): 41-57.

Kant, Immanuel. *Anthropology from a Pragmatic Point of View*. Translated by Mary J. Gregor. The Hague: Nijoff, 1974.

———. *Anthropology from a Pragmatic Point of View*. Translated by V. L. Dowdell. Revised by H. H. Rudnick. Carbondale & Edwardsville: Southern Illinois University Press, 1978.

———. *Critique of Practical Reason*. Translated by Mary Gregor. New York: Cambridge University Press, 1991.

———. *Critique of Pure Reason*. Translated by Paul Guyer and Allen Wood. New York: Cambridge University Press, 1998.

———. *Grounding for the Metaphysics of Morals*. Translated by James W. Ellington. Indianapolis: Hackett Books, 1993.

———. *Groundwork of the Metaphysics of Morals*. Translated by H. J. Paton. New York: Harper & Row, 1964.

———. *Groundwork of the Metaphysics of Morals*. Translated by A. Zweig and T. Hill. Oxford: Oxford University Press, 2003.

———. *Kant's gesammelte Schriften*. Edited by the Royal Prussian Academy of Sciences. Berlin: Georg Reimer, 1900.

———. *The Metaphysics of Morals*. Translated by Mary Gregor. Cambridge: Cambridge University Press, 1996.

———. *Religion within the Limits of Reason Alone*, translated by Allen Wood and George Di Giovanni. New York: Cambridge University Press, 1998.

Kister, Menahem. *Studies in Abot de-Rabbi Nathan: Text, Redaction, and Interpretation*. Jerusalem: The Hebrew University Department of Talmud, 1998.

Kline, T. C. "Ethics and Tradition in the Xunzi." Ph.D. diss., Stanford University, 1998.

Korsgaard, Christine. "Skepticism About Practical Reasons." *The Journal of Philosophy* 83 (January 1986): 5-25.

Kupperman, Joel. *Character*. New York: Oxford University Press, 1991.

———. "The Indispensability of Character." *Philosophy* 76 (2001): 239-51.

———. "Tradition and Community in the Formation of Character and Self." Pp. 103-123 in *Confucian Ethics: A Comparative Study of Self, Autonomy, and Community*, edited by Kwong-loi Shun and David Wong. Cambridge: Cambridge University Press, 2004.

———. *Value . . . And What Follows*. New York: Oxford University Press, 1999.

Lapin, Hayim. "Rabbis and Cities: Some Aspects of the Rabbinic Movement in its Graeco-Roman Environment." Pp. 58-80 in *The Talmud Yerushalmi and*

Graeco-Roman Culture, Vol. 2, edited by Peter Schäfer and Catherine Heszer. Tübingen, Germany: Mohr Siebeck, 2000.

Lee, Pauline Chen. "Li Zhi (1527-1602): A Feminist Literatus in Late Ming China." Ph.D. diss., Stanford University, 2002.

Lerner, M. B. "The Tractate Avot." Pp. 263-81 in *The Literature of the Sages*, edited by Shmuel Safrai. Philadelphia: Fortress Press, 1987.

Li, Chen-yang. "The Confucian Concept of Jen and the Feminist Ethics of Care: A Comparative Study." *Hypatia* 9, no. 1 (1994).

———, ed. *The Sage and the Second Sex*. La Salle, IL: Open Court, 2000.

Lieberman, Saul. "The Disciple of the So-Called Dead Sea Manual of Discipline." *Journal of Biblical Literature* 71 (1953): 199-206.

Lynn, Richard John. "Chu Hsi as a Literary Theorist and Critic." Pp. 337-54 in *Chu Hsi and Neo-Confucianism*, edited by Wing-tsit Chan. Honolulu: University of Hawai'i Press, 1986

MacIntyre, Alasdair. *After Virtue*, 2nd edition. Notre Dame: University of Notre Dame Press, 1984.

———. *Three Rival Versions of Moral Inquiry*. Notre Dame: University of Notre Dame Press, 1990.

March, Andrew. "Self and Landscape in Su Shih." *Journal of the American Oriental Society* 86, no. 4 (October-December 1966): 377-96.

Marcus, Ivan. *Rituals of Childhood*. New Haven, CT: Yale University Press, 1986.

McCarty, Richard. "The Maxims Problem." *The Journal of Philosophy* XCIV (January 2002): 29-44.

McDowell, John. "Virtue and Reason." Pp. 141-162 in *Virtue Ethics*, edited by Roger Crisp and Michael Slote. Oxford: Oxford University Press, 1997.

McNair, Amy. *The Upright Brush: Yen Zhenqing's Calligraphy and Song Literati Politics*. Honolulu: University of Hawai'i Press, 1998.

Mencius (Mengzi). *Mencius*. Translated by D. C. Lau. London: Penguin Books, 1970.

———. "Mengzi." Translated by Bryan Van Norden. Pp. 111-156 in *Readings in Classical Chinese Philosophy*, edited by Philip J. Ivanhoe and Bryan W. Van Norden. New York: Seven Bridges Press, 2001.

Meyer, Leonard. *Emotion and Meaning in Music*. Chicago: University of Chicago Press, 1956.

Milgram, Stanley. *Obedience to Authority*. New York: Harper and Row, 1974.

Mill, John Stuart. *On Liberty*. Edited by Elizabeth Rapaport. Indianapolis: Hackett Books, 1978.

Montmarquet, James. "Moral Character and Social Science Research." *Philosophy* 78 (July 2003): 355-68.

Murdoch, Iris. *Metaphysics as a Guide to Morals*. New York: Penguin Press, 1992.

Nathan, Rabbi. *Aboth de Rabbi Nathan, Solomon Schechter Edition*. Edited by Solomon Schechter and Menahem Kister. New York: Jewish Theological Seminary of America, 1997.

————. *The Fathers According to Rabbi Nathan (Abot de Rabbi Nathan).* Translated by Anthony Saldarini. Leiden, The Netherlands: E. J. Brill, 1975.

————. *The Fathers According to Rabbi Nathan.* Translated by Judah Goldin. New Haven, CT: Yale University Press, 1983.

Neu, Jerome. "Jealous Thoughts." Pp. 425-63 in *Explaining Emotions,* edited by Amélie Oksenberg Rorty. Berkeley: University of California Press, 1980.

Neusner, Jacob. *Judaism and Story.* Chicago: University of Chicago Press, 1992.

Nivison, David S. *The Life and Thought of Chang Hsüeh-ch'eng (1738-1801).* Stanford, CA: Stanford University Press, 1966.

Nussbaum, Martha. *Love's Knowledge: Essays on Philosophy and Literature.* New York: Oxford University Press, 1990.

————. *Sex and Social Justice.* New York: Oxford University Press, 1999.

O'Neill, Onora. *Constructions of Reason.* Cambridge: Cambridge University Press, 1989.

Paton, H. J. *The Categorical Imperative.* New York: Harper & Row, 1963.

Peterson, Willard. "Confucian Learning in Late Ming Thought." Pp. 708-788 in *The Cambridge History of China,* Volume 8, edited by Frederick W. Mote and Denis Twitchett. Cambridge: Cambridge University Press, 1998.

Plato. *Laws,* reprint. Translated by Thomas Pangle. Chicago: University of Chicago Press, 1988.

————. *Protagoras.* Translated by C. C. W. Taylor. Oxford: Clarendon Press, 1976.

————. *Republic.* Translated by G. M. A. Grube, revised by C. D. C. Reeve. Indianapolis: Hackett Publishing Company, 1992.

Reath, Andrew. "Self-Legislation and Duties to Oneself." Pp. 349-370 in *Kant's Metaphysics of Morals: Interpretive Essays,* edited by M. Timmons. New York: Oxford University Press, 2002.

Roberts, Robert C. "Will Power and the Virtues." *The Philosophical Review* 93 (1984): 227-47.

Rorty, Amélie Oksenberg, ed. *Essays on Aristotle's Ethics.* Berkeley: University of California Press, 1980.

————, ed. *Explaining Emotions.* Berkeley, CA: University of California Press, 1980.

Rosen, Charles. *The Classical Style.* New York: Norton, 1972.

Ross, Lee and Richard Nisbett. *The Person and the Situation: Perspectives of Social Psychology.* New York: McGraw Hill, 1991.

Saldarini, Anthony. *Scholastic Rabbinism: A Literary Study of the Fathers According to Rabbi Nathan.* Chico, CA: Scholars Press, 1982.

Schäfer, Peter and Catherine Heszer, eds. *The Talmud Yerushalmi and Graeco-Roman Culture.* Tübingen, Germany: Mohr Siebeck, 2000.

Schofer, Jonathan W. *The Making of a Sage: A Study in Rabbinic Ethics.* Madison: University of Wisconsin Press, 2005.

Schwartz, Seth. "Gamaliel in Aphrodite's Bath: Palestinian Judaism and Urban Culture in the Third and Fourth Centuries." Pp. 203-17 in The *Talmud Yerushalmi and Graeco-Roman Culture*, Vol. 1, edited by Peter Schäfer and Catherine Heszer. Tübingen, Germany: Mohr Siebeck, 2000.

———. *Imperialism and Jewish Society, 200 BCE to 640 BCE.* Princeton, NJ: Princeton University Press, 2001.

Sherman, Nancy. *Making a Necessity of Virtue.* Cambridge: Cambridge University Press, 1997.

Singer, Marcus G. "Duties and Duties to Oneself." Ethics 73 (1963): 133-42.

———. *Generalization in Ethics.* New York: Knopf, 1961.

Solomon, Robert. "Victims of Circumstances? A Defense of Virtue Ethics in Business." *Business Ethics Quarterly* 13 (January 2003): 355-68.

Sorce, James F., Robert N. Emde, Joseph J. Campos, and Mary Klinnert. "Maternal Emotional Signaling: Its Effect on the Visual Cliff Behavior of 1-Year-Olds." Pp. 183-89 in *Contemporary Readings in Child Psychology*, edited by E. M. Hetherington and R. D. Parke. New York: McGraw-Hill, 1988.

Smart, J. J. C. "Benevolence as an Over-Riding Attitude." *Australasian Journal of Philosophy* 55, no. 2 (1977): 127-35.

Smith, Jonathan Z. *Map is Not Territory: Studies in the History of Religions.* Chicago: University of Chicago Press, 1978.

Srinivasan, Gopal. "Errors about Errors: Virtue Theory and Trait Attribution." *Mind* 111 (January 2002): 47-68.

Stern, Daniel, Lynne Hofer, Wendy Haft, and John Dore. "Affect Attunement: The sharing of feeling states between mother and infant by means of intermodal fluency." Pp. 251-68 in *Social Perception in Infants*, edited by T. Field and N. Cox. Norwood, NJ: Ablex Publishing Company, 1985.

Sturgeon, Nicholas. "Moral Explanations." Pp. 49-78 in *Morality, Reason and Truth: New Essays on the Foundation of Ethics*, edited by David Copp and David Zimmerman. Totowa, NJ: Rowman and Allanheld, 1984.

Swain, Kathleen M. *Pilgrim's Progress, Puritan Progress: Discourses and Contexts.* Chicago: University of Chicago Press, 1993.

Taylor, Charles. *Sources of the Self: The Making of the Modern Identity.* Cambridge, MA: Harvard University Press, 1989.

Thomson, Judith Jarvis. "The Trolley Problem." In *Rights, Restitution, and Risk*, edited by William Parent. Cambridge, MA: Harvard University Press, 1986.

Velleman, J. David. "Well-being and Time." *Pacific Philosophical Quarterly* 72 (1991): 48-77.

Watson, Burton. *Ssu-ma Ch'ien: Grand Historian of China.* New York: Columbia University Press, 1958.

Watts, Edward. "The Student Self in Late Antiquity." In *Self-Revelations: Religion and the Self in Antiquity*, edited by David Brakke, Michael Satlow, and Steve Weitzman. Bloomington: Indiana University Press, 2005.

Wick, Warner. "More about Duties to Oneself." *Ethics* 70 (1960): 158-63.

———. "Still More about Duties to Oneself." *Ethics* 71 (1961): 213-17.

Wiggins, David. "Truth, Invention and the Meaning of Life." Pp. 87-137 in *Needs, Values, Truth: Essays in the Philosophy of Value*, 3rd edition. Oxford: Clarendon Press, 1988.

Williams, Bernard. *Ethics and the Limits of Philosophy*. Cambridge, MA: Harvard University Press, 1985.

———. *Moral Luck*. New York: Cambridge University Press, 1981.

Wolff, Robert Paul. *The Autonomy of Reason: A Commentary on Kant's Groundwork of the Metaphysic of Morals*. New York: Harper & Row, 1973.

Wong, David. "On Flourishing and Finding One's Identity in a Community." Pp. 324-41 in *Midwest Studies in Philosophy, Volume XIII. Ethical Theory: Character and Virtue*, edited by Peter A. French, Theodore E. Uehling Jr., and Howard K. Wettstein. Notre Dame, IN: University of Notre Dame Press, 1988.

Xunzi. "Xunzi." Translated by Eric L. Hutton. Pp. 247-94 in *Readings in Classical Chinese Philosophy*, edited by Philip J. Ivanhoe and Bryan W. Van Norden. New York: Seven Bridges Press, 2001.

Yearley, Lee. *Mencius and Aquinas*. Albany: SUNY Press, 1990.

Yü Ying-shih. "Morality and Knowledge in Chu Hsi's Philosophical System." Pp. 228-54 in *Chu Hsi and Neo-Confucianism*, edited by Wing-tsit Chan. Honolulu: University of Hawai'i Press, 1986.

Zhuzi. *Zhuzi yülei*. Beijing: Zhonghua shu ju, 1986.

Index

Alcibiades, 55, 63-65
Allison, Henry, 122n2
Aristotle, 2, 4, 25-26, 37, 50, 53-
    54, 56-64, 71, 73-75, 77, 80,
    107, 114-17, 119, 138
Athanassoulis, Nafsika, 124n34
Audi, Robert, 123n4
Aune, Bruce, 145n7

Baier, Annette, 23
Baron, Marcia, 122n2
Batson, C. D., 124n27
Baumgarten, Alexander, 146n30
ben Parahyah, Yehoshua, 93
ben Yoezer, Yose, 88, 92
Billy Budd: A Sailor, 32
Blum, Lawrence, 59-60
Book of Songs, 24, 26
Boyarin, Daniel, 98n14, 99n23
Braithwaite, R. B., 42n3
Broad, C. D., 17
Buddhism, 34-35; Chan tradition
    of, 375
Bunyan, John, 42n3
Burnyeat, Miles, 45n22

Camus, Albert, 22
Carroll, Noël, 44n12
casuistry, 19
Categorical Imperative, 131, 140
Cheng Yi, 44n20, 45n21

A Christmas Carol, 31
Confucians and Confucianism, 1, 5,
    8-9, 11n11, 22, 30, 32-41
Confucius. *See* Kongzi
Cua, Antonio, 25

Danto, Arthur, 30
dao, 34-35, 37, 39
Daoism, 34-35
Darley, J. M., 124n27
Descartes, René, 79
desire-belief model of human
    action, 10, 77-78
DeSousa, Ronald, 79
dharma, 34
Dickens, Charles, 31, 39-40
Doris, John, 101, 114-20
dufa, 33, 41

Ekman, Paul, 81
Eliot, George, 22
Ellison, Ralph, 43n8
Epictetus, 52
Epicureanism, 10, 51
eudaimonia, 49, 53
Eudoxus, 63-64

feminism, 22
Ferrari, Giovanni, 64
Fonrobert, Charlotte, 98n15
Foot, Philippa, 54-55, 60

Franklin, Benjamin, 5, 104-7, 112,
    116
Funder, David, 28n9

Hadot, Pierre, 31, 51
Hampshire, Stuart, 99n28
Harman, Gilbert, 101, 115-21
Hersey, John, 60
Heszer, Catherine, 97n4, 99n19,
    99n23
Hsün Tzu. *See* Xunzi
Hume, David, 7, 71, 79, 102, 107-
    12, 114, 116, 120
Humean naturalism, 2, 9-10, 102-4,
    111-14
Hutton, Eric, 47n36
Hyrcanus, 91-92

imperfect duties, 22, 128-30
intellectualism, 8, 10, 50-51
internalism, 103

James, Henry, 31, 40
James, William, 80

Kant, Immanuel, 8-11, 17, 19, 23,
    37, 51-54, 101-3, 125-44
Kongzi, 1, 4, 13, 20-27, 29, 42n2
Kupperman, Joel, 124n37

liberalism, 15-16
literature, 5-6, 8, 31-41, 64-65
Li Zhi, 35-37
Lynn, Richard, 45n21

MacIntyre, Alasdair, 15, 43n12,
    83n11, 88
McDowell, John, 59
Mencius. *See* Mengzi
Mengzi, 22, 47n40, 47n42, 71
Meyer, Leonard, 25
Milgram experiments, 115, 117,
    121, 124n38
Mill, John Stuart, 15-16, 23
Mishnah, 86, 94

Moore, G. E., 21
Murdoch, Iris, 39

Nietzsche, Friedrich, 21, 26-27
Nussbaum, Martha, 31, 39-41

Odysseus, 39
O'Neill, Onora, 122n2
Ostwald, Martin, 58

perfect duties, 128
Plato, 22-23, 25-26, 37, 49, 55, 61,
    64, 66, 71
Plutarch, 46n35, 65

Rabban Yohanan ben Zakkai, 87,
    91-92
Rabbi Akiva, 87-90, 92, 96
Rabbi Eliezer, 87-89, 91-92, 96
Rabbi Joshua, 94
Rabbi Nathan, 86
Rabbi Nathan, 86-96
Rabbinic tradition, 2, 85-96
Rabbi Yehoshua, 89, 92
Rachel, 90
ritual, 5, 24-25
Roberts, Robert, 80
Rosen, Charles, 25

Saldarini, Anthony, 99n20
salience, 18, 59-61
sangha, 34
Schwartz, Seth, 97n4
Sherman, Nancy, 46n28
situationist psychology, 116-21
Smart, J. J. C., 17
Smith, Jonathan, 97n9
Socrates, 7, 25, 49, 55, 63-65
stoicism, 51, 55
Su Shi, 33-35
Swain, Kathleen, 42n3
sympathy, 10, 108

Taylor, Charles, 43n12
Thomson, Judith Jarvis, 14

Thucydides, 65
Tocqueville, Alexis de, 15
Torah, 86-93, 95-96
trolley example, 13-14

Universal Law of Nature, 131
utilitarianism, 17, 23, 51

Wang Anshi, 33-34
Watson, Burton, 46n35
Wiggins, David, 14

Williams, Bernard, 15, 99n29
Wittgenstein, Ludwig, 13, 59
Wolff, Robert Paul, 125-26, 144
Wong, David, 85

Xunzi, 24, 33

Yearley, Lee, 97n9

Zhang Xuecheng, 39-40
Zhu Xi, 33-35, 39

About the Contributors

Philip J. Ivanhoe is professor of philosophy at the City University of Hong Kong. Ivanhoe has written widely on Chinese philosophy and ethics, including books such as *Confucian Moral Self Cultivation* and *Ethics in the Confucian Tradition: The Thought of Mengzi and Wang Yangming*.

Robert N. Johnson is associate professor of philosophy at the University of Missouri at Columbia. Johnson is the author of numerous articles in moral philosophy, focusing in particular on Kant.

Joel J. Kupperman is professor of philosophy at the University of Connecticut. He has written extensively in ethics, aesthetics, metaphysics, and Chinese philosophy. Two of his many books are *Six Myths About the Good Life* and *Character*.

William J. Prior is professor of philosophy at Santa Clara University. Prior works in the fields of Ancient Greek philosophy and ethics. Two of his books are *Virtue and Knowledge* and *Unity and Development in Plato's Metaphysics*.

Elizabeth S. Radcliffe is professor of philosophy at Santa Clara University. Her research interests include Hume, ethics, and early modern philosophy. She is the author of *On Hume* and was the co-editor of *Hume Studies* from 2000 to 2005.

Jonathan W. Schofer is assistant professor of comparative ethics at Harvard Divinity School. His main interest is classical rabbinic literature and thought, and he is the author of *The Making of a Sage: A Study in Rabbinic Ethics*.

Brad K. Wilburn is assistant professor at Chadron State College. His scholarly interests are in the area of virtue ethics, particularly issues having to do with the development of character.